Sorting Shapes, Show Me, and Many Other Activities for Toddlers

Creative Resources Infant and Toddler Series

Dedication

THIS BOOK IS DEDICATED TO:

My grandchildren, Jeffrey and Eva Herr.

J. H.

My son, Randy, and my nieces and nephews.

T. S.

Join us on the web at
EarlyChildEd.delmar.com

Sorting Shapes, Show Me, and Many Other Activities for Toddlers

Creative Resources Infant and Toddler Series

by

Judy Herr **Terri Swim**

PHYSICAL

COGNITIVE

EMOTIONAL

LANGUAGE & COMMUNICATION

SOCIAL

DELMAR
CENGAGE Learning

Australia • Brazil • Japan • Korea • Mexico • Singapore • Spain • United Kingdom • United States

Susan L. Simpfenderfer

Acquisitions Editor: Erin O'Connor

Editorial Assistant: Ivy Ip

Executive Production Manager:
Wendy A. Troeger

Production Editor: Joy Kocsis

Technology Project Manager: Joseph Saba

Executive Marketing Manager:
Donna J. Lewis

Channel Manager: Nigar Hale

Cover Design: Joseph Villanova

Composition: Stratford Publishing
Services, Inc.

For product information and technology assistance, contact us at
Cengage Learning Customer & Sales Support, 1-800-354-9706
For permission to use material from this text or product, submit all
requests online at **cengage.com/permissions**
Further permissions questions can be emailed to
permissionrequest@cengage.com

Library of Congress Control Number: 2002031234

ISBN-13: 978-1-4018-1834-0
ISBN-10: 1-4018-1834-X

Delmar
10 Davis Drive
Belmont, CA 94002-3098
USA

Cengage Learning is a leading provider of customized learning solutions with office locations around the globe, including Singapore, the United Kingdom, Australia, Mexico, Brazil, and Japan. Locate your local office at: **international.cengage.com/region**

Cengage Learning products are represented in Canada by Nelson Education, Ltd.

For your lifelong learning solutions, visit **delmar.cengage.com**

Visit our corporate website at **cengage.com**

Join us on the Web at **EarlyChildEd.delmar.cengage.com**

NOTICE TO THE READER

Publisher does not warrant or guarantee any of the products described herein or perform any independent analysis in connection with any of the product information contained herein. Publisher does not assume, and expressly disclaims, any obligation to obtain and include information other than that provided to it by the manufacturer.

The reader is expressly warned to consider and adopt all safety precautions that might be indicated by the activities herein and to avoid all potential hazards. By following the instructions contained herein, the reader willingly assumes all risks in connection with such instructions.

The Publisher makes no representation or warranties of any kind, including but not limited to, the warranties of fitness for particular purpose or merchantability, nor are any such representations implied with respect to the material set forth herein, and the publisher takes no responsibility with respect to such material. The publisher shall not be liable for any special, consequential, or exemplary damages resulting, in whole or part, from the readers' use of, or reliance upon, this material.

Printed in the United States of America
4 5 6 7 8 11 10 09 08

Contents

Responding in a warm, loving, and responsive manner to a crying infant or playing patty-cake with a young toddler both exemplify ways that caregivers and families promote healthy brain development. In fact, recent research on brain development emphasizes the importance of the environment and relationships during the child's first three years of life (Shore, 1997). With this in mind, *Sorting Shapes, Show Me, and Many Other Activities for Toddlers: 13 to 24 Months* was written for you, the caregivers and families. The ultimate goal of this book is to assist in promoting healthy development of our youngest children. Thus, it should be part of all parents' and caregivers' libraries.

The book focuses on the growth of the whole child by including norms for physical, language and communication, cognitive, social, and emotional development. To support, enhance, and promote the child's development in all of these areas, this unique book includes specially designed activities for toddlers. Note that the book has several sections. The first section includes information for understanding, assessing, and promoting development, as well as suggestions for interacting with young children. The next sections include innovative activities to promote development for toddlers. The last section includes references for the material cited in the text. The appendices are a rich resource including, but not limited to, lists of recipes, songs, finger plays, chants, and books. They also contain a list of toys and equipment, as well as criteria for making selections.

To assist you, the experiences are grouped by age ranges and developmental areas. Each of these activities is designed to illustrate the connection between a broad area of development and specific goals for children. For example, physical development may be the primary area and eye-hand coordination may be one specific goal. The materials, preparation, and nurturing strategies for the activities are designed for easy and effective implementation. Moreover, variations and additional information have been incorporated to enrich the experience for both you and the child. Highlighting Development boxes provide valuable information for fostering an understanding of young children's development. Collectively, the information and experiences provided in this book will enhance your ability to meet the developmental needs of toddlers, fostering optimal development of the whole child. Furthermore, these early experiences will create a strong foundation for children's subsequent thinking, interacting with others, and learning.

ONLINE RESOURCES™

The Online Resources™ to accompany *Sorting Shapes, Show Me, and Many Other Activities for Toddlers: 13 to 24 Months* is your link to early childhood education on the Internet. The Online Resources™ contains many features to help focus your understanding of the learning and teaching process.

- ♡ Sample Activities and Preface
- ♡ Developmental Milestones
- ♡ Books for Toddlers
- ♡ Books for Two-Year-Olds
- ♡ Criteria for Selecting Materials and Equipment for Children
- ♡ Materials and Equipment for Promoting Optimal Development
- ♡ Movement Activities for Children from Thirteen to Thirty-Six Months
- ♡ Favorite Finger Plays, Nursery Rhymes, and Chants
- ♡ Songs
- ♡ Rhythm Instruments
- ♡ Recipes
- ♡ Resources Related to Toddlers
- ♡ Developmental Checklist
- ♡ Sample Running Record
- ♡ Panel Documentation
- ♡ Lesson Plan
- ♡ Daily Communications
- ♡ A Summarized list of Web links is provided for your reference.
- ♡ On-line Early Education Survey – This survey gives you the opportunity to let us know what features you want to see improved on the Online Resources™.

The authors and Delmar Learning make every effort to ensure that all Internet resources are accurate at the time of printing. However, due to the fluid, time-sensitive nature of the Internet, we cannot guarantee that all URLs and Web site addresses will remain current for the duration of this edition.

 You can find the Online Resources™ at www.EarlyChildEd.delmar.com

Furthermore, this book would not have been possible without the inspiration of the numerous young children who have touched and influenced our lives in so many meaningful ways. The children we have met in university laboratories and child care settings and their teachers and parents have all demonstrated the importance of the early years of life.

We want to acknowledge the contributions of the numerous colleges, universities, colleagues, and students that have fostered our professional growth and development:

College of William and Mary, Norfolk, Virginia; University of Akron, Ohio; Harvard University, Cambridge, Massachusetts; Purdue University, West Lafayette, Indiana; University of Minnesota, Minneapolis, Minnesota; University of Missouri, Columbia, Missouri; University of Texas, Austin, Texas; and University of Wisconsin-Stout, Menomonie, Wisconsin.

Specifically we would like to thank Carla Ahman, Carol Armga, Michelle Batchelder, Chalandra Bryant, Mary Jane Burson-Polston, Bill Carver, Linda Conner, Kay Cutler, Sandi Dillon, Loraine Dunn, Nancy File, Nancy Hazen-Swann, Debra Hughes, Susan Jacquet, Elizabeth Johnson, Joan Jurich, Susan Kontos, Gary Ladd, Julia Lorenz, Pat Morris, Linda Norton-Smith, Barbara O'Donnel, Diana Peyton, Douglas R. Powell, Kathy Pruesse, Julie Rand, Karin Samii, Jen Shields, Cathy

vided continuous encouragement, support, and creative ideas; and Deb Hass and Vicki Weber, who typed the manuscript.

The authors and publisher would like to thank the following reviewers for their constructive suggestions and recommendations:

Davia Allen
Western Carolina University
Cullowhee, NC

Alice Beyrent
Hesser College
Manchester, NH

Billie Coffman
Pennsylvania College of Technology
Williamsport, PA

Irene Cook
Taft College Children's Center
Taft, CA

Linda Estes
St. Charles County Community College
St. Peters, MO

Jody Martin
Children's World Learning Centers
Golden, CO

Introduction

Smiling, crying, bicycling with their legs, and laughing at caregivers are all signals infants use to gain and maintain attention. Watching them is exciting. They are amazing. Each infant has an individual style; no two are alike. Differences in temperament are apparent from birth. Some infants are quiet, while others are active. Each is unique. However, all infants grow and develop in predictable patterns, even though the exact rate varies from infant to infant.

Development can be defined as change over time. According to Bentzen (2001), development refers to any "change in the structure, thought, or behavior of an individual that comes from biological and environmental influences" (p. 15). Human development occurs in two distinct patterns. First, development proceeds from the top of the body to the bottom. For example, control of the head develops before control of the torso or the legs. The second pattern is for development to proceed from the center of the body outward. To illustrate, the arm muscles develop before those of the hands or fingers.

dren develop according to their own individual timetable, regardless of environmental influences. In contrast, there are nurture-based theories that emphasize the importance of environmental factors. These theories assume that children enter the world as blank slates. According to these theories, the children's environment is instrumental in molding their abilities. A third set of theories incorporates aspects from both of these two extremes, nature and nurture. These interactional theories are based on the premise that biology and environment work in concert to account for children's development.

While reading this book, you will note that it celebrates interactional theories. Current research on brain development supports the belief that human development hinges on the dynamic interplay between nature and nurture (Shore, 1997). At birth, the development of the child's brain is unfinished. Through early experiences, the brain matures and connections are made for wiring its various parts. Repeated experiences result in the wiring becoming permanent, thereby creating the foundation for the brain's organization and functioning throughout life.

Your role is critical because early experiences significantly affect how each child's brain is wired. The child's relationships with parents, caregivers, and significant others will all influence how the brain becomes wired. Therefore, loving encounters and positive social, emotional, language and communication, cognitive, and physical experiences all influence the development of a healthy brain.

However, this influence is far from unidirectional. Children, for example, are born with different temperaments. Research has shown that children's dispositions influence their involvement with both people and materials in their environment. To illustrate, Quincy is a quiet, slow-to-warm-up child. He initially holds back and observes. Moreover, he becomes very distressed in new situations. To prevent Quincy from feeling distressed, his caregivers and parents sometimes respond by minimizing the introduction of new experiences or situations. Consequently, his physical, language and communication, emotional, social, and cognitive development are shaped by his characteristics and his caregivers' and parents' responses to these characteristics.

patterns are called developmental norms. Norms provide evidence of when a large group of children, on average, accomplishes a given task. Because norms are averages, they must be interpreted with caution. There are differences from child to child in the timing for reaching developmental milestones within one specific domain and across different domains. For example, a child may reach all developmental milestones as expected in the cognitive domain but develop on a later timetable in the language domain. Hence, each child has a unique pattern of timing of growth and development that must be taken into account.

Notwithstanding their limitations, developmental norms are useful to caregivers and parents for three main reasons. First, they allow for judgments and evaluations of the relative normalcy of a child's developmental progression. If a child is lagging behind in one developmental task, generally there should be little concern. But if a child is behind on numerous tasks, human development specialists should be consulted for further evaluations.

Second, developmental norms are useful in making broad generalizations about the timing of particular skills and behaviors. Understanding the child's current level of development in relation to the norms allows predictions about upcoming tasks. For example, a child who can easily find a toy that is partially hidden is ready to begin searching for a toy that is completely out of view.

This knowledge of future development ties into the third reason why developmental norms are helpful. Developmental norms allow caregivers and parents to create and implement experiences that support and enhance the child's current level of development. Following the example just given, an adult playing a hide-and-seek game could begin by partially hiding a toy with a towel and then add the challenge of completely covering the toy.

The following table includes a list of developmental norms for infants and toddlers, highlighting significant tasks. Norms are grouped by areas of development, and within each area the specific tasks have been arranged sequentially. When using this table, please remember that it represents universal patterns of development. You will need to be cognizant of each child's unique patterns.

Developmental Milestones*

Birth to Three Months	Four to Six Months	Seven to Nine Months	Ten to Twelve Months	Thirteen to Eighteen Months	Nineteen to Twenty-Four Months
Acts reflexively— sucking, stepping, rooting	Holds cube in hand	Sits independently	Supports entire body weight on legs	Builds tower of two cubes	Walks up stairs independently, one step at a time
Swipes at objects in front of body, uncoordinated	Reaches for objects with one hand	Stepping reflex returns, so that child bounces when held on a surface in a standing position	Walks when hands are held	Turns the pages of a cardboard book two or three at a time	Jumps in place
Holds head erect and steady when lying on stomach	Rolls from back to side	Leans over and reaches when in a sitting position	Cruises along furniture or steady objects	Scribbles vigorously	Kicks a ball
Lifts head and shoulders	Reaches for objects in front of body, coordinated	Gets on hands and knees but may fall forward	Stands independently	Walks proficiently	Runs in a modified fashion
Rolls from side to back	Sits with support	Crawls	Walks independently	Walks while carrying or pulling a toy	Shows a decided preference for one hand
Follow moving objects with eyes	Transfers objects from hand to hand	Pulls to standing position	Crawls up stairs or steps	Walks up stairs with assistance	Completes a three-piece puzzle with knobs
	Grabs objects with either hand	Claps hands together	Voluntarily releases objects held in hands		Builds a tower of six cubes
	Sits in tripod position using arms for support	Stands with adult's assistance	Has good balance when sitting; can shift positions without falling		
		Learns pincer grasp, using thumb with forefinger to pick up objects	Takes off shoes and socks		
		Uses finger and thumb to pick up objects			
		Brings objects together with banging noises			

Developmental Milestones* (continued)

LANGUAGE AND COMMUNICATION DEVELOPMENT

Birth to Three Months	Four to Six Months	Seven to Nine Months	Ten to Twelve Months	Thirteen to Eighteen Months	Nineteen to Twenty-Four Months
Communicates with cries, grunts, and facial expressions	Babbles spontaneously	Varies babble in loudness, pitch, and rhythm	Uses preverbal gestures to influence the behavior of others	Has expressive vocabulary of 10 to 20 words	Continues using telegraphic speech
Prefers human voices	Acquires sounds of native language in babble	Adds *d, t, n,* and *w* to repertoire of babbling sounds	Demonstrates word comprehension skills	Engages in "jargon talk"	Able to combine three words
Coos	Canonical, systematic consonant-vowel pairings; babbling occurs	Produces gestures to communicate, often by pointing	Waves good-bye	Engages in telegraphic speech by combining two words together	Talks, 25 percent of words being understandable
Laughs	Participates in interactive games initiated by adults	May say *mama* or *dada* but does not connect words with parents	Speaks recognizable first word	Experiences a burst of language development	Refers to self by name
Smiles and coos to initiate and sustain interactions with caregiver	Takes turns while interacting		Initiates familiar games with adults	Comprehends approximately 50 words	Joins three or four words into a sentence
					Comprehends approximately 300 words
					Expressive language includes a vocabulary of approximately 250 words

Developmental Milestones* (continued)

COGNITIVE DEVELOPMENT

Birth to Three Months	Four to Six Months	Seven to Nine Months	Ten to Twelve Months	Thirteen to Eighteen Months	Nineteen to Twenty-Four Months
Cries for assistance	Recognizes people by their voice	Enjoys looking at books with familiar objects	Solves sensorimotor problems by deliberately using schemas, such as shaking a container to empty its contents	Explores properties of objects by acting on them in novel ways	Points to and identifies objects on request, such as when reading a book, touring, etc.
Acts reflexively	Enjoys repeating acts, such as shaking a rattle, that produce results in the external world	Distinguishes familiar from unfamiliar faces	Points to body parts upon request	Solves problems through trial and error	Sorts by shapes and colors
Prefers to look at patterned objects, bull's-eye, horizontal stripes, and the human face	Searches with eyes for source of sounds	Engages in goal-directed behavior	Drops toys intentionally and repeatedly looks in the direction of the fallen object	Experiments with cause-and-effect relationships such as turning on televisions, banging on drums, etc.	Recognizes self in photographs and mirror
Imitates adults' facial expressions	Enjoys watching hands and feet	Anticipates events	Waves good-bye	Plays body identification games	Demonstrates deferred imitation
Searches with eyes for sources of sounds	Searches for a partially hidden object	Finds objects that are totally hidden	Shows evidence of stronger memory capabilities	Imitates novel behaviors of others	Engages in functional play
Begins to recognize familiar people at a distance	Uses toys in a purposeful manner	Imitates behaviors that are slightly different than those usually performed	Follows simple, one-step directions	Identifies family members in photographs	Finds objects that have been moved while out of sight
Discovers and repeats bodily actions such as sucking, swiping, and grasping	Imitates simple actions	Begins to show interest in filling and dumping containers	Categorizes objects by appearance		Solves problems with internal representation
Discovers hands and feet as extension of self	Explores toys using existing schemas such as sucking, banging, grasping, shaking, etc.		Looks for objects hidden in a second location		Categorizes self and others by gender, race, hair color, etc.

Developmental Milestones* (continued)

SOCIAL DEVELOPMENT

Birth to Three Months	Four to Six Months	Seven to Nine Months	Ten to Twelve Months	Thirteen to Eighteen Months	Nineteen to Twenty-Four Months
Turns head toward a speaking voice	Seeks out adults for play by crying, cooing, or smiling	Becomes upset when separated from a favorite adult	Shows a decided preference for one or two caregivers	Demands personal attention	Shows enthusiasm for company of others
Recognizes primary caregiver	Responds with entire body to familiar face by looking at the person, smiling, kicking legs, and waving arms	Acts deliberately to maintain the presence of a favorite adult by clinging or crying	Plays parallel to other children	Imitates behaviors of others	Views the world only from own, egocentric perspective
Bonds to primary caregiver		Uses adults as a base for exploration, typically	Enjoys playing with siblings	Becomes increasingly aware of the self as a separate being	Plays contently alone or near adults
Finds comfort in the human face	Participates actively in interactions with others by vocalizing in response to adult speech	Looks to others who are exhibiting signs of distress	Begins asserting self	Shares affection with people other than primary caregiver	Engages in functional play
Displays a social smile	Smiles at familiar faces and stares solemnly at strangers	Enjoys observing and interacting briefly with other children	Begins developing a sense of humor	Shows ownership of possessions	Defends possessions
Is quieted by a voice	Distinguishes between familiar and unfamiliar adults and surroundings	Likes to play and responds to games such as patty-cake and peekaboo	Develops a sense of self-identity through the identification of body parts	Begins developing a view of self as autonomous when completing tasks independently	Recognizes self in photographs or mirrors
Begins to differentiate self from caregiver		Engages in solitary play	Begins distinguishing boys from girls		Refers to self with pronouns such as *I* or *me*
		Develops preferences for particular people and objects			Categorizes people by using salient characteristics such as race or hair color
		Shows distress when in the presence of a stranger			Shows less fear of strangers

Developmental Milestones *(continued)

EMOTIONAL DEVELOPMENT

Birth to Three Months	Four to Six Months	Seven to Nine Months	Ten to Twelve Months	Thirteen to Eighteen Months	Nineteen to Twenty-Four Months
Feels and expresses three basic emotions: interest, distress, and disgust	Expresses delight	Responds to social events by using the face, gaze, voice, and posture to form coherent emotional patterns	Continues to exhibit delight, happiness, discomfort, anger, and sadness	Exhibits autonomy by frequently saying "no"	Expresses affection to others spontaneously
Cries to signal a need	Responds to the emotions of caregivers	Expresses fear and anger more often	Expresses anger when goals are blocked	Labels several emotions	Acts to comfort others in distress
Quiets in response to being held, typically	Begins to distinguish familiar from unfamiliar people	Begins to regulate emotions through moving into or out of experiences	Expresses anger at the source of frustration	Connects feelings with social behaviors	Shows the emotions of pride and embarrassment
Feels and expresses enjoyment	Shows a preference for being held by a familiar person	Begins to detect the meaning of others' emotional expressions	Begins to show compliance to caregivers' requests	Begins to understand complicated patterns of behavior	Uses emotion words spontaneously in conversations or play
Shares a social smile	Begins to assist with holding a bottle	Looks to others for cues on how to react	Often objects to having playtime stopped	Demonstrates the ability to communicate needs	Begins to show sympathy to another child or adult
Reads and distinguishes adults' facial expressions	Expresses happiness selectively by laughing and smiling more with familiar people	Shows fear of strangers	Begins eating with a spoon	May say "no" to something they want	Becomes easily hurt by criticism
Begins to self-regulate emotional expressions			Assists in dressing and undressing	May lose emotional control and have temper tantrums	Experiences a temper tantrum when goals are blocked, on occasion
Laughs aloud			Acts in loving, caring ways toward dolls or stuffed animals, typically	Shows self-conscious emotions such as shame, guilt, and shyness	Associates facial expressions with simple emotional labels
Quiets self by using techniques such as sucking a thumb or pacifier			Feeds self a complete meal when served finger foods	Becomes frustrated easily	
			Claps when successfully completes a task		

Assessment is the process of observing, listening, recording, and documenting behavior in order to make decisions about a child's developmental and, thus, educational needs. This process is applicable for an individual child, a small group, or an entire group of children. Your observation skills are the main tools needed for assessing development. By observing and listening, you will discover much about children's needs, interests, and abilities.

This is a simple process. Your eyes and ears are like a video camera capturing children's behaviors, language, attitudes, and preferences. Most of the time you should be examining the children's abilities on worthy and meaningful tasks that you have created. Thus, your assessments will be directly tied to the curriculum that you have planned and implemented. For example, you do this when interacting with an infant or when assisting a toddler who is busy "working" at an experience. In other words, this is a spontaneous process that is continuously occurring. Authentic assessment requires your focused attention and some additional time for documenting your observation. To assist you in this process, a checklist has been included in Appendix K. If you are caring for more than one child, reproduce a copy for each.

Appendix L provides a sample running record. This method of assessment allows you to continuously observe and record, in narrative form, behaviors over a specific period of time. A running record provides a complete view of a particular time period or behavior.

You can also collect artifacts that represent the children's abilities. For example, collect samples of artwork, writing (scribbling), or sculptures. To record the children's performance during an activity that does not result in a product, use a camera to document behavior and abilities.

There are several reasons why caregivers and parents need to assess the development of young children. First, assessment tracks growth and development, noting progress and change over time, thereby providing evidence of learning and maturation. Each observation conducted by a parent or caregiver provides a "snapshot" of the child's development. Combining several snapshots over time provides a comprehensive composite of the changes in the child's growth and development. These changes can be in one of three directions. Typically, children's growth and development follow a predictable sequence. That is, infants coo before they babble. Likewise, they produce a social smile before they are able to wave good-bye. Children can also continue working on the same skills. For example, they may

styles, interests, and dispositions. This information is invaluable in determining the correct level of responsiveness by parents and caregivers. It is much easier to meet a child's needs when you understand, for example, that the infant has difficulty transitioning from one activity to another. Knowing this assists you in preparing the infant for the next component of your daily routine, such as eating lunch.

Third, assessment data provides you with information regarding the normalcy of children's growth and development. This information directly impacts the experiences you create for the children. You should plan a balance of activities that support, enhance, and foster all areas of development. Some activities should be repetitious and represent developmental tasks that a child has accomplished yet still shows interest in and enjoys. Other activities should be a continuation of developmental tasks that the child is currently mastering. Still other activities should stimulate the child's development by requiring a higher skill level, thereby providing a challenge. At these times, children may need more adult support and assistance for scaffolding their learning as well as building their confidence as competent learners.

Fourth, developmental data must be gathered for effectively communicating the child's development with others. For example, if you are caring for children other than your own, you could discuss their progress with their parents or guardians. Likewise, if you are a parent, you will want to share this information with your child's caregiver, your significant other, or your child's pediatrician. Then, too, you may want to compile a portfolio or scrapbook containing a developmental checklist, photographs, videotapes, artwork, and other documents representing the child's growth and development.

Finally, assessment must be conducted to ensure that data is gathered for all areas of development. People have different biases and values. As a result, they may overlook or slight one area of development because of selective attention. If all areas are not assessed, experiences, toys, and equipment provided for children may not meet their developmental needs.

To undertake effective assessment, you will want to compile the data you collect into a meaningful form. The format you choose will depend on how you intend to use the data (Helm, Beneke, & Steinheimer, 1998). For example, if you wish to communicate with others about learning that occurred during a specific activity, as a developmental checklist, anecdotal records, running records, photographs, videotapes, and artwork that represents the child's growth and development.

RESPECTING TODDLERS

Respect. Regard. Honor. Value. These words are seldom used to describe very young children. Yet, these are traits or characteristics that are desired and valued in older children and adults. How better to teach such traits than to model them to infants and toddlers from the very beginning? Respect must be demonstrated in your behaviors. More importantly, respect for infants and toddlers must be something that emanates from inside of you. You have to believe that infants and toddlers are worthy of your time and attention as individuals, because a respectful relationship is vital to all aspects of child development. For example, when infants are respected, they learn to trust that adults can be counted on to meet their needs. This foundation of trust allows them to actively explore their environment during toddlerhood. Hence, trust leads to learning about the world and the toddler's place in it.

It may seem hard to demonstrate respect to infants and toddlers because we are unaccustomed to thinking about very young children in this manner. However, it is not difficult. Respect means believing in the children's abilities to explore, solve problems, or cause events to happen in their world. It also means setting and enforcing clear boundaries for behavior. This is not always easy to do as toddlers are gaining a sense of autonomy and want to do things by themselves. We think that this is the most important time to demonstrate respect. Watch them for cues on how to help. Monitor your own behaviors to avoid doing too much or too little. Toddlers need help that is "appropriate" to support their development and learning.

Furthermore, employing positive guidance techniques promotes a sense of autonomy and self-efficacy. To illustrate, when a toddler is exploring her body in space by climbing and jumping, ensure that she has a safe place for these behaviors. If the spot she has selected is not appropriate, guide her toward a safer location by saying, "If you want to jump, jump from this step onto the mat. It is safe to jump over here." This redirection technique recognizes the child's underlying desire for activity and finds a more acceptable, safer substitution (Marion, 1999). Moreover, setting clear limits allows toddlers to make decisions within a framework of

A great deal has been written for parents/guardians and teachers about toddlerhood. Unfortunately, much of the focus is on the "terrible twos." It is easy to see how this could happen. On one hand, toddlers can be challenging to be around because they want to do so many things on their own that they actively resist help, even when help is clearly warranted. They are also continuing to learn about emotions and ways to control them. Unfortunately, they do lose control, but we all have at some point in our lives. On the other hand, a two-year-old can be an absolute delight, full of humor and self-confidence, and a remarkable source of pleasure for adults. Within a framework of respect, both "hands" of toddlerhood are valued and cherished for what they are at any given moment and for what they can be in the future. Respectful caregivers of toddlers realize that important life lessons and foundations for future life lessons are being learned now.

Take the time to look through the eyes of toddlers. From their perspective, there is so much to see and the world is absolutely fascinating. No wonder they are so enthusiastic, energetic, and inquisitive. With this mindset, you will come to share their never-ending curiosity.

COMMUNICATING WITH TODDLERS

Parents and caregivers play a vital role in helping children master communication and language skills. Listen to the infant-directed speech people use while interacting with and speaking to infants. Originally, this speech was referred to as "motherese"; now it is called "parentese." This type of speech involves speaking slowly and exaggerating changes both in intonation and pitch.

When people use parentese while speaking to an infant, the higher pitch and slower pace capture the child's attention. Then, too, the careful enunciation and simplified style and meanings make the speech easier for the child to understand. By emphasizing one word in a sentence, the adult helps to provide a focal point for the child. When speaking parentese, adults consciously reinforce the infant's role in the conversation by encouraging turn taking and responding to the child's utterances. The following example illustrates the components of parentese:

Caregiver: *"Look at the kitteeee."*
Infant responds by cooing: *"Ahhhhh."*
Caregiver: *"The kitty is black."*

Common Features of "Parentese"

Producing Sounds

♡ Exaggerates intonation and uses higher pitch

♡ Moves frequently between high and low pitches, occasionally whispers

♡ Enunciates more clearly

♡ Emphasizes one or two words in a sentence

♡ Parrots a child's pronunciation, correct or incorrect

Simplifying Meanings

♡ Substitutes simple words for more complicated ones: moo moo for cow

♡ Uses diminutives: doggy for dog

♡ Labels objects according to simplest category: bird for parrot

♡ Repeats words invented by child: baba for bottle

Modifying Grammar

♡ Simplifies sentences grammatically to use short sentences: daddy go

♡ Uses nouns in lieu of pronouns: mommy helping Jeffrey

♡ Uses plural pronouns, if spoken: We drink our bottle

Interacting with a Child

♡ Focuses on naming objects, sounds, or events in the immediate environment

♡ Asks and answers own questions

♡ Uses questions more than statements or commands

♡ Pauses to allow for turn taking

♡ Repeats own utterances

♡ Responds to the child's utterances through repeating, expanding, and recasting

(Baron, 1992; Snow, 1998; Zigler & Stevenson, 1993)

Once young children begin understanding language, they begin using it. Language comprehension occurs before production. In the beginning, new words emerge slowly, then suddenly there is a burst. Nouns are acquired more rapidly than verbs. Children's first words focus on their body parts, toys, clothing, and words for social

and communicating. Toddlers need unlimited opportunities for conversing, reading stories, engaging in finger plays, singing, and pretend play where they construct their own version of reality. Therefore, provide them with toys and household items to stimulate their language development. Then, too, it is important to talk often to help them learn that talking is communication.

Because language is learned in authentic interactions, talk to toddlers in meaningful contexts as well as in social situations. Whenever possible, get down to their level and give them your full attention to reinforce the importance of the spoken word. Nonverbal cues, voice tones, and facial expressions convey important information. While communicating, provide the children with labels for objects, feelings, and ideas. To engage them, use prompting techniques by either asking a question or creating a situation that requires a response.

Kratcoski and Katz (1998) offer some guiding principles that can be used to support the children's language growth including:

♡ Use simple sentences.

♡ Speak slowly and clearly.

♡ Vary your tone/expression to emphasize key words.

♡ Use concrete vocabulary.

♡ Build from the child's utterance/phrase.

♡ Follow the child's topic of interest.

♡ Try to "comment" more than question. (p. 31)

Likewise, you need to:

♡ Provide the child with labels for objects, feelings, ideas, colors, and shapes.

♡ Give the child an opportunity to learn vocabulary in meaningful ways, and provide new objects and experiences to expand the child's language.

♡ Expose the child to a variety of books, catchy rhymes, and music.

♡ Connect the child's actions, ideas, and emotions with words.

♡ Engage in verbal interactions focusing on the child's interest. Prompt the child either by asking questions or creating a situation that requires a response.

♡ Engage the child in problem solving.

♡ Provide toys and household items that stimulate the child to talk.

abilities. At this point, you are ready to begin searching for activities in this book that provide a balance of experiences to support, enhance, and foster all developmental areas.

When undertaking this process, you will need to narrow your selection of activities to prevent overstimulating the child(ren) in your care. This minimizes your preparation time and the amount of materials and

We hope you enjoy reading and implementing the activities in this book as much as we did developing them. We leave you with this thought:

For a baby, those early weeks and months of growth, understanding, and reasoning can never be brought back to do over again. This is not the rehearsal. This is the main show. (Irving Harris)

Promoting Optimal Development in Toddlers

THIRTEEN to EIGHTEEN MONTHS

NINETEEN to TWENTY-FOUR MONTHS

PHY

LANGUAGE & C

COG

SO

EMOT

Physical Development

♡

THIRTEEN to EIGHTEEN MONTHS

Teddy Bear Push

PHYSICAL

Child's Developmental Goals

✓ To improve balancing skills

✓ To continue developing eye-hand coordination skills

MATERIALS:

☐ 2 eight-foot pieces of wool yarn

☐ 2 teddy bears

PREPARATION:

♡ Attach the teddy bear to a sturdy structure. To do so, tie one end of each piece of yarn around an arm of one teddy bear. Wrap the opposite ends of the yarn around the structure. Secure the yarn and adjust the height of the bear so that it can be easily reached by the toddler. Lay the other teddy bear on the ground near the structure.

NURTURING STRATEGIES:

1. When a child selects the activity, observe closely.
2. If the infant is pulling rather than pushing the bear, redirect the child's attention by saying:
   "Johannes, push it like a swing."
   "Move the teddy bear back and forth. Use your hands."
3. Talk about the skills this activity requires while the infant is working. Comments include:
   "Johannes, it is hard to keep your balance."
   "You are pushing with your hands while walking forward."
   "Move back so the teddy bear won't knock you off balance."
4. Providing positive reinforcement may help the toddler develop a positive self-identity. Comments include:
   "Johannes, you worked hard to push the teddy bear."
   "You are pushing the teddy bear high."
   "You are good at keeping your balance."

5. The toddler may wish to carry the teddy bear. If so, point out the other teddy bear and suggest playing with it. Comments to say include:
   "Johannes, here is a teddy bear that you can carry around."
   "I have another teddy bear over here. You can carry this one."

☀ Highlighting Development

The fundamental motor skills infants develop during the first year of life continue to be refined during the second year. Children use their eyes to provide feedback on the use of their hands. During this process, children monitor their movement. While this occurs, their brain sends messages for making adjustments to increase accuracy. Thus, their hand-eye coordination continues to improve.

VARIATION:

♡ For nonmobile children, lower the teddy bear so it may be reached from a sitting position.

ADDITIONAL INFORMATION:

♡ This activity will prove to be great fun for the child. Depending on the number of children, you may need to set up two teddy bear pushes to prevent problems that could arise from waiting or taking turns. Young toddlers have yet to master these skills.

13 to 18 months

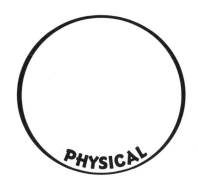

PHYSICAL

Child's Developmental Goals

✓ To refine eye-hand coordination

✓ To practice motor coordination skills

MATERIALS:

❑ Easel

❑ Large sheets of easel paper

❑ Masking tape

❑ Newspaper

❑ Smock or painting shirt

❑ Drying rack

❑ Clothespins

❑ Short, thick paintbrushes

❑ Containers of red tempera paint

PREPARATION:

♡ Select a container and fill it one-third full with paint to prevent excessive cleanup. Place the brush inside the container.

♡ Cover the easel, if available, with newspapers and secure with masking tape.

♡ Attach the paper to the easel. If an easel is unavailable, tape the paper to a wall.

♡ Cover the floor with newspaper to make cleanup easier.

NURTURING STRATEGIES:

1. When a toddler chooses the area, assist with putting on a smock or paint shirt. Explain why you would like the covering worn. Comments include:
   "Devon, it will protect your clothes from the paint."
   "This will keep your clothes clean."
   However, avoid forcing the toddler to wear a smock.

2. Observe the child experimenting with the materials.

3. Guide the child to engage in appropriate behaviors by stating limits in a positive manner. To illustrate, say:
   "Devon, paint on the paper."
   "Use the paintbrush for painting."

4. Describe the toddler's actions in creating a picture. In other words, focus on the process of painting rather than the product. While pointing to the painting, say:
   "You are making long, red lines. They go from the top to the bottom."
   "You are making tiny, red dots."

☀ Highlighting Development

The child's fine motor skills are improving. Observe. The toddler now can pick up small objects between a forefinger and a thumb. As a result, the child's ability to pick up and examine toys and other objects has improved. Additionally, the child is beginning to gain control of tools such as a spoon, paintbrush, toothbrush, etc.

VARIATIONS:

♡ Paint at a child-size table or coffee table.

♡ Paint outdoors by attaching larger pieces of paper to a fence.

ADDITIONAL INFORMATION:

♡ When talking to the toddler, focus on the process rather than the product. This strategy will prevent the child from having to explain the artwork. At this stage, the child is interested in manipulating the tools and observing the reaction.

♡ Never force a child to wear a smock. Immediately change and rinse out the clothes if paint spills or splatters.

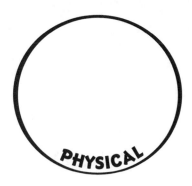
PHYSICAL

Child's Developmental Goals

✓ To refine fine motor skills

✓ To improve eye-hand coordination skills

MATERIALS:

❑ Set of foam blocks

❑ Plastic container

PREPARATION:

♡ Separate the blocks so that you have two identical sets of blocks. Remove any blocks that are round. These blocks are too difficult to work with at first.

♡ Place the set of blocks in the container. Clear a spot on the floor and place the container there.

NURTURING STRATEGIES:

1. Observe the toddler's behavior when selecting the blocks.
2. Describe what the toddler is doing with the blocks. To illustrate, say:
   "Austin, you are lining up the squares."
   "You are filling up the container with the blocks."
3. Join the toddler by sitting on the floor. Position your body so that you can continue to observe any other children you may be supervising.
4. Continue conversing with the toddler regarding the interactions with the blocks.
5. In the meantime, model building a tower with the blocks.
6. Verbally describe what you did with the blocks. To illustrate, say:
   "Austin, I made a tower. I used three blocks."
   "I stacked two blocks on top of each other."

7. Encourage the toddler to stack the blocks in the same manner. Comments include:
   "Austin, stack your blocks like I did."
   "Can you do this? Stack the blocks."
8. Provide positive reinforcement for attempts or accomplishments. For example, say:
   "Austin, you did it! You stacked two blocks."
   "Oh, they fell over. Keep trying. You can do it."

☼ Highlighting Development

Although the toddler may use one hand more than the other, the child is developing skills using both. Now the toddler is beginning to enjoy activities such as stacking blocks that require the use of both hands. Typical behaviors include stacking the blocks into towers and then knocking them down. Observe the child's facial expression during this process. Some children revel in the delight of watching the blocks tumble.

VARIATION:

♡ Use small wooden blocks or just the square ones from a set of unit blocks.

ADDITIONAL INFORMATION:

♡ You must carefully select the blocks to give the children. Select square or rectangular blocks at first because they are easier to stack. Round blocks are too difficult to stack and should be added later. Therefore, removing the round blocks may prevent some frustration and promote a successful learning experience for toddlers.

13 to 18 months

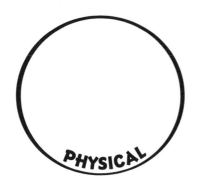

PHYSICAL

Child's Developmental Goals

✔ To refine balancing skills

✔ To improve eye-foot coordination skills

MATERIALS:

❑ Ladder that can be laid flat

❑ Tunnel

PREPARATION:

♡ Select a flat, grassy area that can be constantly supervised. Clear this area of any movable equipment or debris. Place the tunnel and ladder in this area. Make sure that each piece of equipment is lying flat on the ground.

NURTURING STRATEGIES:

1. While preparing the child to go outside, talk about the new activity. To illustrate, say:
   "Zalika, you can crawl through a tunnel. Then, walk on a ladder."
   Use your voice as a tool for communicating enthusiasm.
2. Once outdoors, observe the toddler's behaviors with the equipment.
3. For safety reasons, only one child should be in the tunnel at a time. The number of children on the ladder will vary depending on its size. Clearly state and reinforce these limits as needed. Comments include:
   "One person at a time. The tunnel is made for one person."
   "Zalika, you can go next. Two people are already on the ladder."

4. If necessary, you may need to model walking between the rungs of the ladder. While modeling the behavior, reinforce your actions with words by saying, for example:
   "I'm walking on the grass between the ladder parts. This is tricky."
   "Walking between the ladder parts takes lots of balance."
5. Reinforce the toddler's attempts and accomplishments. Comments to make include:
   "You crawled through the tunnel."
   "What balance! You walked on the ladder."

☀ Highlighting Development

Children change physically as they grow. In the first 12 months of life, an infant increases in size by approximately 50 percent. To illustrate, a child who was 22 inches long at birth will be approximately 33 inches at one year. With increasing activity, toddlers' muscles are also becoming more developed. After walking for a few months, their stance changes. Their feet will begin pointing forward rather than being positioned outwardly to the sides of the body. However, even after beginning to walk, children may revert back to creeping when they need to get someplace quickly. Creeping is often faster for them.

VARIATION:

♡ If a tunnel is unavailable, drape a blanket over an object to create a tentlike structure.

 For safety purposes, carefully observe toddlers to make sure they walk on the grass between the rungs of the ladder. Walking directly on the ladder can cause toddlers to lose their balance or twist an ankle.

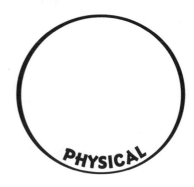

PHYSICAL

Child's Developmental Goals

✓ To reinforce the pincer grasp

✓ To continue developing fine muscle skills

MATERIALS:

❑ 2 wooden puzzles with knobs, if available

❑ Child-size table or coffee table

PREPARATION:

♡ Clean a child-size or coffee table and display the puzzles on it. Remove one piece from each puzzle and lay it on the table.

NURTURING STRATEGIES:

1. When a toddler is looking for an activity, direct the child to the table with the puzzles. Say, for example:
   "Paul, look at what is on the table. You can do a puzzle."

2. Show the toddler how to take out the pieces one by one. Discuss the puzzle pieces as the child removes them.

3. Replace the pieces and then encourage the child to repeat your actions. Use comments such as:
   "You are removing a piece of the puzzle."
   "Now you have taken out two pieces."

4. Verbally encourage the child when he is replacing the puzzle pieces. Comments include:
   "Paul, keep turning. That's where the piece goes."
   "That piece is round. Find the round place on the puzzle."

5. Providing positive reinforcement may help maintain the toddler's attention and may result in him spending more time with this activity. For example, comment:
   "Paul, that's it! Only one more piece. You are good at putting together puzzles."
   "All done! You are quick. Are you going to put together another puzzle?"

☼ Highlighting Development

As toddlers' hand-eye coordination skills improve, they are able to construct puzzles. In addition to promoting physical skills, puzzles can be used to promote language skills and concepts. For example, colors can be introduced and reviewed. In addition, spatial concepts such as above, below, in, and on can be taught.

VARIATIONS:

♡ Place the puzzles on the floor out of traffic paths.

♡ Introduce new puzzles for variety.

ADDITIONAL INFORMATION:

♡ Young toddlers need very simple puzzles that have knobs. They lack the fine muscle coordination skills to pick up puzzle pieces without knobs. In addition, children at this stage of development are most successful with three to five puzzle pieces. When children acquire the fine muscle skills, you can challenge them by providing puzzles with smaller knobs and more pieces.

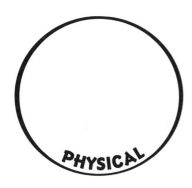

PHYSICAL

Going Shopping

Child's Developmental Goals

✓ To refine balancing skills
✓ To improve coordination skills

MATERIALS:

❑ A child-size shopping cart, if available
❑ Multiethnic baby doll
❑ Construction paper
❑ Felt-tip marker

PREPARATION:

♡ Place a baby doll in the shopping cart. If introducing this activity in a center rather than a home setting, make a "cart return" sign.
♡ Hang the cart return sign on the wall and park the cart under it.

NURTURING STRATEGIES:

1. Observe the toddlers as they experiment with moving the cart.
2. You may need to set and reinforce limits specific to the use of a shopping cart. For example, you may need to remind the child to walk inside the area designated.
3. Encourage the child to take the baby shopping. Comments to make include:
   "Sasheen, your baby is crying. Do you need to buy some food?"
   "You are shopping with your baby. What are you going to buy at the toy store?"
   Note: Your comments should directly relate to the materials available in your area.

4. Reinforce the toddler's positive behaviors with the shopping carts by commenting:
   "You are slowly pushing your baby in the shopping cart."
   "Look at all you bought at the store. You've been busy."
5. When the toddler is finished with the shopping cart, encourage returning the cart to the "cart return" area. This will foster independence and respect for property. To illustrate, while pointing or moving toward that area, say:
   "The cart goes over here when you are done."
   "Help clean up the room. Put the shopping cart in the cart return area."
6. Thank the toddler for returning the cart.

☀ Highlighting Development

Activities that encourage large muscle exercise and refine whole-body coordination are of more interest to toddlers than activities that require small muscle coordination (Bukato & Daehler, 1992). Some activities of interest include pushing carts or cars; stacking or nesting large boxes; and, eventually, riding a toy or pulling a wagon.

VARIATION:

♡ Using the shopping cart outdoors will increase the challenge. Wheeled toys are difficult to push on grass, sand, or uneven surfaces.

ADDITIONAL INFORMATION:

♡ When stating limits, word them in a positive manner. In other words, highlight acceptable behaviors by saying:
   "Walk while pushing."
   "Push your cart slowly."

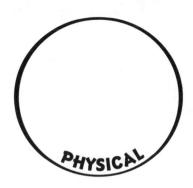

PHYSICAL

Child's Developmental Goals

✓ To refine eye-hand coordination skills

✓ To continue developing large motor skills

MATERIALS:

❏ 4 to 5 boxes of similar size

PREPARATION:

♡ To prevent possible cutting or scratching, place tape over the edges and lid of the boxes. If desired, you can decorate the boxes by covering them with colored, self-adhesive paper.

♡ Clear and place the boxes in an open area where they will attract the toddler's attention.

NURTURING STRATEGIES:

1. Observe the toddler interacting and experimenting with the blocks.

2. Describe the toddler's actions. To illustrate, say:
   "Ismail, you are lining up the blocks."
   "You have stacked two blocks."

3. Encourage the toddler to build a tower. Suggestions include:
   "Can you put the blocks on top of each other?"
   "How tall can you build?"

4. Reinforcing your words with actions may be necessary. If so, while touching the block, say:
   "Ismail, put this block on top of this one."

5. Encourage the child to work with you to stack the blocks. Comment, for example:
   "Ismail, I can help. The box is heavy. Let's work together to move it."

6. Reinforce the toddler's efforts at building a tower and working with you. Comments to make include:
   "Ismail, you worked hard to build a tower! You used three boxes."
   "Your tower is three boxes high."

☀ Highlighting Development

Toddlers' bodies are top-heavy. As a result, they walk with their toes pointed outward and waddle from side to side. At the beginning of the process, they are slow in moving. Often they tumble over. However, balance improves as their bodies become less top-heavy. With maturity, their pace also increases.

VARIATION:

♡ Choose boxes of different sizes and shapes.

ADDITIONAL INFORMATION:

♡ Toddlers love to build and move things around. Providing lightweight boxes or containers may encourage such behaviors. Boxes from typing or copier paper are particularly effective for children this age because they are lightweight and sturdy. In addition, this activity fosters social skills by encouraging the child to interact with others.

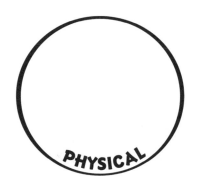

PHYSICAL

MATERIALS:

❑ Liquid soap
❑ Disposable towels
❑ Poster with steps and pictures, if available or desired
❑ Sink

PREPARATION:

♡ If desired, make a poster with all of the steps for washing hands sequenced in the correct order. Include as many pictures or graphics as possible.

♡ Hang this poster at the toddler's eye level beside the sink.

♡ If you have more than one sink, make a poster for each.

♡ Review the handwashing steps:

1. Turn on water to a comfortable temperature.
2. Wet hands.
3. Apply liquid soap.
4. Vigorously rub hands together for at least 10 seconds.
5. Rinse the soap off the hands from the wrist to fingertips.
6. Dry hands.
7. Turn off water.

NURTURING STRATEGIES:

1. Take the toddler to the sink or bathroom.
2. Using the poster as a tool, verbally and physically guide the toddler through the steps. In other words, at each step, tell the toddler what to do. Begin by turning on the water. Reinforcing your words with actions may be necessary. If so, physically guide the toddler through the motion while verbally describing the action.

3. During the step of rubbing the hands together vigorously, sing the following song. Doing this may increase the time spent rubbing the hands together and, therefore, remove more germs.

♫ Wash, wash, wash your hands
♫ Wash them all day long
♫ Wash, wash, wash your hands
♫ While we sing this song.

4. Throughout the procedure, continue providing positive reinforcement. Comments include: *"Sahara, you're really getting your hands clean."* *"What dry hands."*

☀ Highlighting Development

Children need to develop the routine of washing their hands before eating and after having a diaper changed. During this stage of development, the coordination of their hands and fingers improves. This progress helps provide them with the necessary coordination needed to begin caring for their own bodies.

VARIATION:

♡ Make up your own song that varies with what steps the toddlers are doing such as "push, push, push the soap" while pushing the liquid soap dispenser down three times.

ADDITIONAL INFORMATION:

♡ Because toddlers are more stable when standing, they can now learn the proper procedures for washing their hands at a sink.

♡ Toddlers will be unable to follow all of these steps independently for some time but starting now will foster the development of positive skills and attitudes.

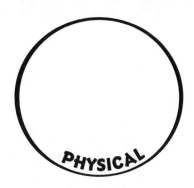

PHYSICAL

Child's Developmental Goals

✓ To practice walking up stairs

✓ To practice walking down stairs

MATERIALS:

❏ Commercially produced stairs with railing, if available

❏ Mat

PREPARATION:

♡ If a commercial staircase is available, select an area of the room that allows ease in supervision.

♡ Clear this area and spread out the mat. Place the stairs on the mat. This helps create a safe fall zone around the stairs. Without this equipment, stairs within a home can be used if carefully supervised.

NURTURING STRATEGIES:

1. When the toddler moves close to the stairs, join the child.

2. Observe the child working and provide physical assistance as necessary.

3. Provide positive reinforcement as often as possible while remaining honest about the toddler's abilities. Comments include:

   "Raj, you are holding on to the rail. That keeps you safe."

   "One foot, then the other foot. That's how you walk up stairs."

4. Set and maintain limits as necessary to protect the safety of the toddler. Say, for example:

   "Hold on to the railings. Hold on with both hands, Raj."

   If the child continues without holding on, it is time to state a logical consequence, such as:

   "No hold. No walk on stairs."

   If the child continues without holding on, physical removal from the stairs may be necessary. Enact the consequence while saying:

   "No hold. No walk on stairs."

   "No hold. No walk. You can try again later."

☀ Highlighting Development

Most children learn to walk at about one year of age. With their improved mobility, they are attracted to stairs; consequently, navigating stairs is an important skill. Note their mode of locomotion. First, children move one foot up to the step, and then they bring the second foot to the same step. Learning to walk up the stairs with alternating steps occurs later. Also, note that children learn walking up stairs before walking down.

VARIATION:

♡ Practice walking up and down real stairs having the child hold one of your hands while placing the other on the railing. This will encourage the child to use handrails. For safety purposes, provide lots of support and assistance.

ADDITIONAL INFORMATION:

♡ Due to developmental variations, some children will practice walking up the stairs while others practice creeping.

 For safety reasons, you should never leave a toddler unattended near the steps.

13 to 18 months

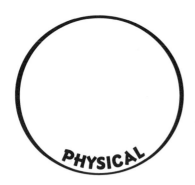

PHYSICAL

Child's Developmental Goals

✔ To continue developing fine muscle skills

✔ To learn through sensory exploration

✔ To experience cause and effect

MATERIALS:

☐ One color of nontoxic finger paint
☐ Child-size table or coffee table
☐ Spoon
☐ Paper towel
☐ Sponge
☐ Container
☐ Washable table covering, if needed
☐ Smocks, paint shirts, bibs, or aprons

PREPARATION:

♡ Clean and sanitize a child-size table or coffee table. If appropriate, place a spoonful of paint directly onto the table. Otherwise, lay down a washable table covering. Fill the container with lukewarm water and a sponge. Place the container so it is easily accessible.

NURTURING STRATEGIES:

1. Help the toddler put on a smock, paint shirt, apron, or bib. Then roll up the child's sleeves as necessary.
2. Help the toddler sit on a chair, if needed, and move it closer to the table. After this, introduce the activity by saying:
   "Chloe, you can paint on the table using your hands."
   "Move the paint around with your fingers."
3. Talk to the toddler about how the paint is being manipulated. Comments might include:
   "Chloe, you are painting."
   "You are pushing the paint with one finger."
4. To foster language development, introduce a new word that describes an action. You must know the toddler's vocabulary skills to do this. Repeat the

word several times while the child is working. For example, if the word is *squishing*, state:
"Chloe, you are squishing the paint. Squish, squish, squish. You are smiling. It must be fun to squish the paint."

5. Paint with the child. Discuss how each of you is using different and similar processes with the paint. For example, say:
   "Chloe, you are painting a picture. You are making circles while I am making lines."
   "We are friends. We are working together."
6. When the child is finished, wipe her hands with the paper towel. Then have the toddler finish washing off the paint at the sink.

☀ Highlighting Development

Finger painting is an activity that can stimulate the child's senses. It involves seeing and touching. In addition, the child experiences cause and effect. This occurs when the paint responds to movement of the fingers and hands, which work as application tools or brushes.

VARIATIONS:

♡ By placing a piece of paper over the paint on the table, you will create a reverse print. Display the toddler's work on the wall, refrigerator, or bulletin board.

♡ Place paint on the table only after child is ready to begin the activity.

♡ Substitute shaving cream for the paint.

ADDITIONAL INFORMATION:

♡ Keep a sponge handy for wiping up spills.

 Toddlers love to get messy and still place things in their mouths. Hence, close supervision is necessary to ensure that paint or shaven cream are not eaten or wiped into a child's eyes. Even if the paints are nontoxic, consuming the paint may cause an upset stomach.

Lining Up the Pins

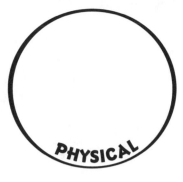

PHYSICAL

Child's Developmental Goals

✓ To continue developing fine muscle coordination skills

✓ To refine pincer grasp

MATERIALS:

❑ Cardboard shoe box

❑ 10 peg clothespins

PREPARATION:

♡ Select and clear an area for this activity.

♡ If desired, cover the shoe box with self-adhesive paper. Place all but one clothespin in the box. Place the one remaining clothespin on the rim of the box. For the toddler, this will help by modeling the purpose of the activity.

NURTURING STRATEGIES:

1. Observe the toddler's behavior while engaging in the activity.
2. Position yourself near the child, allowing the toddler to work independently.
3. If the child initiates interaction, respond promptly. Likewise, respond promptly to sounds of distress with verbal support. Using your voice as a tool, communicate warmth and support. Comments might include:
   "Omar, the clothespin fell off. Put it back on."
   "You're working hard."
4. After the child has placed the clothespin on the rim of the box, model counting them while pointing to each pin. This not only connects your actions with words but also promotes the development of the mathematical concept of one- to-one correspondence.

5. Provide positive reinforcement when the child appears to be finishing up the activity. Comments include:
   "Omar, you worked hard at this activity."
   "You used all of the clothespins."
6. Encourage the toddler to return the materials to their original location. State, for example:
   "Place the box back on the table."

☀ Highlighting Development

Children need to learn responsibility for picking up their toys. Therefore, encourage them to clean up after they are finished playing. During this process, the children may need to be assisted both verbally and physically. Then, too, provide them with positive reinforcement so they develop responsibility and autonomy for continuing this behavior.

VARIATIONS:

♡ Use a round plastic container such as a gallon ice cream pail instead of the shoe box.

♡ When a toddler is ready for a new challenge, introduce the squeeze-type clothespins.

ADDITIONAL INFORMATION:

♡ Young toddlers lack the strength and fine muscle control to successfully manipulate the squeeze-type clothespins. In six to eight months, they may be able to master this skill.

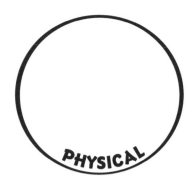

PHYSICAL

Activity Walker

Child's Developmental Goals

✓ To practice the locomotion skill of walking

✓ To continue practicing balance skills

MATERIALS:

❑ Activity walker

PREPARATION:

♡ Clear the floor of obstacles.

NURTURING STRATEGIES:

1. Observe the child's behavior with the activity walker. It may be necessary to set and maintain limits with this activity. To illustrate, say:
   "Hillary, walk while pushing the activity walker."
   "Walk around people."
2. If the activity walker gets blocked, help the toddler solve the problem. Comments include:
   "Hillary, pull the walker backward."
   "It is caught in the table. Walk backward."
3. Reinforcing your words with actions may be necessary. If so, while pulling the walker back-ward, say:
   "The walker is caught. Pulling it backward helps."
4. Provide positive reinforcement for using the toy properly. To illustrate, say:
   "Hillary, you are pushing the toy while walking."
   "Thank you for walking around the chair."

5. Encourage the toddler to return the walker to the wall when finished. For example, say:
   "Hillary, put the walker back by the wall."

☀ Highlighting Development

Shoes are unnecessary for babies who have not yet begun to walk. They can interfere with the growth of the feet and make balancing more difficult. Shoes reduce the ability of the children's toes to grip surfaces under their feet. However, children who are walking need comfortable, well-fitting shoes with nonskid soles to promote safety.

VARIATION:

♡ Use the walker in an outdoor area.

ADDITIONAL INFORMATION:

♡ This is a wonderful activity to use with children this age, who are enjoying their mobility skills. The activity provides them with confidence in their large muscle abilities and it also fosters their problem-solving skills.

"Open, Shut Them"

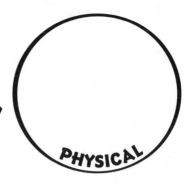

PHYSICAL

Child's Developmental Goals

✔ To coordinate hands in a clapping motion

✔ To imitate the adult's movements

MATERIALS:

❑ Poster board

❑ Felt-tip marker

PREPARATION:

♡ If you have the finger play memorized, no materials are needed. If you do not have the finger play memorized and are working with a group of children, make a poster with the words. This can serve as an effective teaching tool that adults can use for reinforcing this activity.

NURTURING STRATEGIES:

1. Slowly introduce the motions to "Open, Shut Them" two times. Notice who is imitating your motions.

   Open, shut them
   Open, shut them
   Open, shut them
   Give a little clap.

   Open, shut them
   Open, shut them
   Open, shut them
   Put them in your lap.

2. Introduce the finger play by saying:
   "Let's put some words to these actions."
3. Slowly recite the finger play. Share your enthusiasm by smiles, gestures, and the intonation of your voice.
4. Providing positive reinforcement may increase the toddler's desire to perform the actions. Comments include:
   "What a wonderful job! You learned a new finger play. I heard you clap!"
5. Repeat the finger play if the child seems interested.

☀ Highlighting Development

Clapping is a difficult skill for young children to master. Even though they may have been working on this skill for several months, they may be less than proficient. This skill requires not only eye-hand and bilateral coordination but also timing of movements.

VARIATION:

♡ As the children develop these motions, increase the number of verses. Refer to Appendix F for the entire finger play.

ADDITIONAL INFORMATION:

♡ If other children or siblings are present, encourage them to participate in the finger play activity.

♡ Observe the child to identify favorite finger plays and songs. Frequently repeat these.

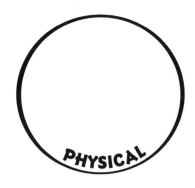

PHYSICAL

Scooping Sand

MATERIALS:
- ❑ Plastic quilt box
- ❑ Clean sand
- ❑ Metal spoons
- ❑ 1-cup measuring cup
- ❑ ½-cup measuring cup
- ❑ Broom and dustpan or vacuum cleaner

PREPARATION:
- ♡ Place 1½ to 2 inches of sand in the quilt box. Place the spoons and measuring cups on the sand.
- ♡ Select an area that can be constantly supervised. Clear this space and lay out the vinyl tablecloth. Place the sandbox on the cloth.
- ♡ Keep a broom, dustpan, and vacuum cleaner in a convenient location.

NURTURING STRATEGIES:
1. When the child approaches the activity, state the basic limits. For example, say:
   "Jaron, the sand stays in the container."
   "Sand is for scooping."
2. Observe the toddler's handling of the tools.
3. If necessary, encourage the toddler to use the tools or handle them differently. Comments include:
   "Jaron, use the spoon to fill the cup.
   "Hold the cup by the handle. Use your thumb."

4. To promote both sensory awareness and language development, ask questions about how the sand feels. To illustrate, ask:
   "How does the sand feel?"
5. Continue the conversation by responding to the toddler's vocalizations and gestures. Use comments such as:
   "Jaron, that's right! The sand is rough."
   "The sand is bumpy."
6. Provide positive reinforcement to encourage the continuation of desirable behaviors. Comments include:
   "Jaron, you filled both cups. You used the spoon."
   "You are working hard. You've filled both cups."

☀ Highlighting Development

Young children find pleasure in sensory experiences such as sand or water play. These experiences encourage relaxation by the release of tension.

VARIATION:
- ♡ If the children are tall enough, place the container of sand on the top of a small table.

ADDITIONAL INFORMATION:
- ♡ Add a small amount of water to the sand. This makes the sand easier to handle and provides a new form of tactile stimulation.

Language and Communication Development

THIRTEEN to EIGHTEEN MONTHS

Shoulders

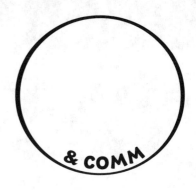

& COMM

Child's Developmental Goals

✓ To increase receptive language skills

✓ To promote self-expression through spoken language

MATERIALS:

❑ Felt-tip marker

❑ Index card

PREPARATION:

♡ If needed, write the words to the action song on an index card and place it in your pocket.

NURTURING STRATEGIES:

1. Repeat this song spontaneously whenever a toddler appears to need a new experience.

2. Introduce the action song to the child by saying:
   "Jee-Eun, let's play a game. Show me where your head is."
   Pause. *"Great! Now show me where your knees are."*
   Help the toddler identify all the body parts in the song.

3. Begin singing the action song and modeling the actions. Touch each body part as you sing it:

   ♪ Head, shoulders, knees, and toes
   ♪ Knees and toes
   ♪ Eyes and ears and mouth and nose
   ♪ Head, shoulders, knees, and toes
   ♪ Knees and toes.

4. Encourage the child to join you in singing the action song. Comments include:
   "Jee-Eun, do it with me."
   "Let's do it together."

5. Provide positive reinforcement when the child verbally and physically joins you by participating in the song. To illustrate, say:
   "Jee-Eun, you were singing along! I heard you say the word 'toes'!"
   "You did all of the actions!"
   "Good for you."

6. Repeat the action song if the toddler seems interested.

☀ Highlighting Development

Most children start linking words to meaning by their first birthday. At this point, they build their vocabulary slowly. When they are about 18 months of age, the rate of acquiring words explodes (Cowley & Foote, 1997).

VARIATION:

♡ Repeat the action song, including other children or family members.

ADDITIONAL INFORMATION:

♡ When singing the song and modeling the actions, go very slowly, allowing the toddler to successfully participate.

♡ Increase the pace when the toddler is ready.

& COMM

Child's Developmental Goals

✓ To associate sounds with the objects that make them

✓ To increase expressive language skills

MATERIALS:

❏ Tape recorder-player and blank cassette
❏ Photographs of objects that made sounds

PREPARATION:

♡ Record four or five communication sounds in the child's immediate environment such as the sound of a microwave buzzer. While recording, leave space between the sounds to allow time for the children to identify them. Then take photographs of the taped objects.

♡ If desired, mount the photographs on tagboard and cover with clear, self-adhesive paper to provide support and protection.

♡ Select an area for this activity that has a table and chairs. There also should be an electrical outlet nearby.

♡ To promote independent use of this center, label the play button with a green dot and the stop button with a red dot.

♡ Place the tape player and photographs on the table.

NURTURING STRATEGIES:

1. When a child appears interested in the activity, introduce it by saying, for example:
   "Akbar, we are going to play a game. Listen to the sounds. You can match the sound with the object in the photograph."

2. Assist the toddler in turning on the tape by saying:
   "Green means go. Press the green button."

3. Reinforcing your words with actions may be necessary. If so, press the green button while saying:
   "The tape is playing now."

4. After the first sound plays, ask the child:
   "Akbar, listen. What was that?"
   Direct the child's attention to the pictures on the table. To illustrate, say:
   "Which of these objects made the sound?"

5. If the next sound begins before the first sound is identified, stop the tape. Verbalize your actions. Comments include:
   "Akbar, I'm going to push the red button. That means stop. The tape will stop while you look for the source of the sound."

6. Assist the child by verbally labeling and describing the photographs. To illustrate, say:
   "This is the microwave. It heats our bottles. When it's done, it says 'beep, beep, beep.'"

7. Provide positive reinforcement if the toddler chooses the photograph that matches the sound on the tape. Use comments such as:
   "Akbar, you did it!"
   "Yes. The vacuum cleaner makes that noise!"

8. If the child does not identify the object, you need to continue with the game. To do this, suggest that the toddler turn on the tape.

☀ Highlighting Development

Children at this stage of development enjoy cause-and-effect relationships. Watch them. They enjoy turning the television or radio on and off. They also enjoy banging on objects to create sounds and splashing water. Therefore, the children may delight in identifying these taped sounds.

VARIATIONS:

♡ Repeat this activity with a small group of children.
♡ Increase the difficulty of the sounds when the child has identified the ones recorded on the first tape.

ADDITIONAL INFORMATION:

♡ Move out of the child's immediate environment by recording sounds such as a dog barking, a car horn, a train whistle, etc.

Child's Developmental Goals

✓ To verbally identify family members

✓ To communicate excitement when identifying oneself in a photograph

MATERIALS:

❑ Family photographs
❑ Colored paper
❑ Yarn
❑ Marker

PREPARATION:

♡ Collect photographs of family members.
♡ Mount each photograph on a piece of colored paper. Write a caption for each photograph, being sure to include the names of all the people in the pictures. If desired, prepare a book of the pages by punching holes in the left-hand side of the paper and lacing with yarn or placing in a three-ring binder.
♡ Place the book in a convenient location for the child.

NURTURING STRATEGIES:

1. When a toddler selects the book, observe the child's behavior.
2. Ask the toddler questions about the pictures. Questions to ask include:
   "Sadie, who is in that picture?"
   "Porter is your brother. What is he doing in this photograph?"
3. Encourage the toddler to verbally respond to the questions rather than just using gestures. To illustrate, say:
   "Who is this?"
   "Sadie, what is your dog's name?"
4. Providing positive reinforcement may result in the toddler talking more about all of the photographs. Say, for example:
   "You've told me a lot by using your words."
   "Yes! That is your mama."
5. Describe the toddler's reaction to the book. Comments to make include:
   "Sadie, you were excited when you saw yourself in the photograph."
   "You are smiling. You must like this book."
6. Read the book again if the toddler desires.

☀ Highlighting Development

Although speech begins slowly, by 18 months of age most children's speaking ability begins to explode. Studies show the size of a toddler's vocabulary is dependent on how many times the child hears different words. Therefore, it is important that you provide language-rich experiences that are meaningful to the child.

VARIATIONS:

♡ Prepare similar books using magazine pictures of animals, foods, clothing, etc.
♡ Allow the toddler to read the book independently after you've read it together two or three times.

ADDITIONAL INFORMATION:

♡ Toddlers love to identify family members in photographs. Activities such as this one can be used not only for stimulating language development but also for emotional development. For example, if the child is experiencing separation anxiety, you can direct attention to the photograph.
♡ Toddlers at this stage of development understand more words than they can say. That is, they have better receptive than expressive language skills.

13 to 18 months

& COMM

Child's Developmental Goals

✓ To expand expressive language skills

✓ To practice engaging in telegraphic speech

MATERIALS:

None

PREPARATION:

♡ To understand what the child is saying, observe for behavior cues.

NURTURING STRATEGIES:

1. Whenever working with a toddler, engage the child in conversation. During routine care times such as snack, this activity works especially well.

2. While he is eating snack, ask the child about activities in the recent past. For example, ask:
   "Jacques, what did you do outside?"
   "Did you have fun with the ball?"

3. Depending on the child's developmental level, the response will vary. Some children will engage in "jargon" talk. When this happens, you will probably be able to understand one word. Use that word to continue the conversation with the child. To illustrate:
   If the child says, "xyzgrstuv ball crput yrusd," respond by saying:
   "Yes, I remember you playing with the ball. You rolled it down the hill. Did you kick the ball?"
   If the child engages in telegraphic speech, you will want to use expansion. This involves expanding the toddler's telegraphic sentence into a more complete sentence. For example:
   If the toddler says, "Wash baby," respond by saying:
   "You washed a baby. Was that fun?"

4. If more than one toddler is present, encourage another child to join in the conversation. Begin by focusing on things the children did that were similar or that they did together. To follow one of the previous examples, say:
   "Marnie, I saw you rolling the ball down the hill also. Did you kick the ball?"
   You will need to connect the children's answers and then continue. To illustrate, state:
   "Neither of you kicked the balls. How did you get the balls to move?"

5. Continue engaging in the conversation as long as possible. When you sense that the topic is exhausted, move on to another.

☀ Highlighting Development

At about 15 months, toddlers become increasingly interested in learning language. They may want you to read to them more often, and they may even watch your mouth while you are talking. Therefore, this is a prime time to focus on language development. Provide the toddlers with pictures; books; tapes; puppets; and, most important, your own voice.

VARIATION:

♡ Describe the toddler's behavior while engaging in experiences. This provides language skills to use in later conversations.

ADDITIONAL INFORMATION:

♡ As an adult, you will need to frequently ask questions. However, you will often need to answer them yourself.

♡ More complex sentences can be introduced. Studies show that children who hear complex sentences are more inclined to use them.

"Where Is My. . .?"

& COMM

Child's Developmental Goals

✔ To practice asking questions

✔ To use expressive language to receive desired object

MATERIALS:

None

PREPARATION:

♡ Observe the toddler's desire for interaction.

NURTURING STRATEGIES:

1. Respond to the toddler's cues for interaction. Such cues might include touching your body or repeating a word/phrase. If the toddler, for example, is saying the word "blankie," expand this by asking a question about the blanket such as:
   "Edo, where is your blanket?"
   "Have you lost your blanket?"

2. Help the child solve the problem. Ask, for example:
   "Where is your blanket?"
   "Did you leave it in your crib?"
   Verbally answer your own question. If the toddler doesn't respond, for example, say:
   "I saw you with your blanket in your crib. Let's look there."
   Then, move to look for the lost item.

3. Verbally describe what you are doing. To illustrate, say:
   "I'm looking for your blanket. I don't see it. Let's look somewhere else."

4. Provide positive reinforcement to the toddler when solving the problem. Comments to make include:
   "Edo, thank you for helping me locate your blanket."
   "I am happy we found it."

☀ Highlighting Development

Between 12 and 18 months, toddlers learn how to ask questions. They use intonations rather than words such as *where, why,* and *what* to indicate a question. Therefore, you must pay close attention to how things are being said to understand the child's meaning.

VARIATION:

♡ Repeat the activity, capitalizing on other words the child uses.

ADDITIONAL INFORMATION:

♡ Remember, using a higher-pitched voice when talking to infants and toddlers typically captures a child's attention.

♡ Parentese is useful when talking to toddlers. The simplified utterances and repetition serve to maintain their attention and foster language development.

& COMM

Child's Developmental Goals

✓ To continue developing receptive language skills

✓ To verbally identify animals

MATERIALS:

❑ Book with animals such as *Moo, Baa, La La La!* by Sandra Boynton

PREPARATION:

♡ Place the book in an area that will attract the child's attention.

NURTURING STRATEGIES:

1. When a toddler selects the book, observe the child's behavior.
2. Ask the toddler if you can read the book together. Carefully observe the toddler's nonverbal cues to know what to do next. For example, if the toddler shakes her head "no" or doesn't make eye contact, say:
   "Maybe you would like to look at the book alone."
   On the other hand, if the child smiles at you or hands you the book, ask:
   "Jenisa, would you like to sit on my lap?"
3. Read the title of the story. Ask the toddler:
   "What do you think the story is about?"
   Always pause and provide the child time to think or respond.
4. Begin reading the story.
5. To promote language skills, make this experience interactive by asking questions. To illustrate, ask:
   "Jenisa, what sound does a cat make?"
   "What animal is this?" (while pointing to a picture).

6. Provide positive reinforcement for vocalizations or gestures. Comments might include:
   "Jenisa, you're pointing to the pig."
   "That's right. Cats say 'meow.'"
7. Read the story again if the toddler seems interested.

☀ Highlighting Development

Repeating children's utterances is an important technique for promoting language development. When you repeat an utterance, you are assuring them that they are understood. To illustrate, if the child says "car," recast this word into a full sentence. For example, you might say, "That's right! This is a car. This is a red car."

VARIATION:

♡ Create a book by cutting out pictures of animals, objects, or people from magazines.

ADDITIONAL INFORMATION:

♡ Children will grasp grammar more readily when short sentences are spoken to them. However, do not completely avoid complex sentences.

♡ Toddlers are slowly developing a sense of humor. This book may be particularly interesting because it mixes up the sounds a pig might say. Those who know the correct sound will find this humorous.

& COMM

Child's Developmental Goals

✓ To continue developing expressive language skills

✓ To connect verbal labels to objects

MATERIALS:

None

PREPARATION:

♡ Have the child wash hands prior to coming to snack.

NURTURING STRATEGIES:

1. Engage the child in conversation about snack. To illustrate, say:
   "Raul, what are we eating for snack today?"
   "Where do bananas come from?"
2. While passing out snack, discuss any limits for the snack time. To illustrate, say:
   "Sit at the table while eating."
   "You can have three pieces of banana and two glasses of milk."
3. Encourage the toddler to verbally express desires. For example, when a toddler points to the milk container, say:
   "Raul, what do you want?"
4. Expand upon the child's responses to your question. For example, if a child says "more," respond:
   "Do you want more milk?"
   Extend your hand and say:
   "Please hand me your cup and I'll pour you more milk."

5. Provide positive reinforcement for verbal expressions. Comments include:
   "You used words to tell me what you needed."
   "Thank you for using words."

☀ Highlighting Development

Some letters are difficult for toddlers to pronounce such as *t* and *b*. For most children, these sounds will be added in time. Therefore, there is no need to push children to pronounce words correctly. For example, accept "wawa" for water and "nana" for banana while continuing to model the correct pronunciation.

VARIATION:

♡ Language interactions should occur continuously throughout the day.

ADDITIONAL INFORMATION:

♡ Communicate often throughout the day about real-life experiences. Repeating the children's utterances is important because it reassures them that they have been heard and that language is important.

& COMM

Objects

MATERIALS:

❑ 1 flashlight for each child

❑ Clear, heavy adhesive tape

PREPARATION:

♡ Tape the opening of each flashlight to prevent the batteries from being removed.

NURTURING STRATEGIES:

1. During free play exploration, introduce flashlights. To illustrate, you might say:
   "These are flashlights. Have you seen one before?" Pause to allow response. *"Flashlights give light. Watch me. I can turn the flashlight on. Then I'm going to place this rattle in the light. Now it is your turn. What can you put in the light?"*

2. Observe the children interacting with the lights.

3. Converse with the children about the focus in their "spotlight." To guide your behavior, use your knowledge of each of the toddlers. For example, if you know the toddler has a particular vocabulary word, encourage verbal labeling by asking:
   "Hannah, what is that?"
   "Tell me. What do you have your light on?"
   On the other hand, if you know the toddler is lacking a vocabulary word, say:
   "Hannah, you have your light on the doorknob."

4. After labeling an item, reinforce your words with actions while physically touching the object:
   "This is a doorknob."

5. When the toddler is familiar with the flashlight, begin to discuss ways to increase the brightness of the flashlights. One way to do this is to turn off the room lights.

6. Reinforce the toddler when objects are correctly labeled. Comments include:
   "Yes, that is a puppet."
   "What a tough word! It is a banana."

7. Continue this activity as long as the toddler remains interested.

☀ Highlighting Development

Social interaction is viewed as an important factor in language development. Adults are the main models of language for young children. Therefore, language-rich environments and interactions promote the development of both expressive and receptive language skills.

VARIATIONS:

♡ For an adult-directed activity, use the flashlight to spotlight unfamiliar objects to foster the development of expressive language skills.

♡ To reinforce the toddler's expressive language skills, use the flashlight to spotlight familiar objects.

ADDITIONAL INFORMATION:

♡ When you turn off the lights, keep the blinds or drapes open. This will permit some light into the room, thus reducing the possibility of fear of the dark.

🚫 To promote safety, the batteries should not be handled by the toddler.

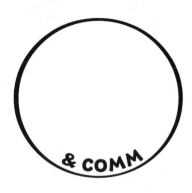

& COMM

Developmental Goals

✓ To continue developing expressive language skills

✓ To associate a label with a sensory experience

MATERIALS:

❑ 3-by-3-inch squares of different textures of fabric such as satin, fur, flannel, or corduroy

❑ A 4-by-6-inch index card for each piece of fabric and 2 additional cards

❑ Hole punch

❑ Key ring

❑ Rubber cement

❑ Felt-tip marker

PREPARATION:

♡ Punch a hole in the top left corner of each index card.

♡ Attach each square of fabric to an index card using the rubber cement. Promote durability by securely adhering the corners of the fabric to the index card.

♡ Use the marker to write a title, such as "Our Feely Book," on one index card and write "The End" on another card.

♡ When everything is dry, stack the index cards in order from title card to end card. Secure the cards together by inserting the key ring through the hole in the top left corner of each index card.

NURTURING STRATEGIES:

1. When a toddler selects the book, observe the child's reaction to each fabric texture. Notice if there is a preference for one type of fabric over another.

2. Talk to the toddler about the book. Comments include:
   "Todd, this is very soft. Feel it. It reminds me of your blanket."
   "Feel the fabric. It feels bumpy."

3. Engage the child in conversation by asking questions such as:
   "How does this feel on your fingers?"
   "What else feels like this?"

4. Providing positive reinforcement may encourage the toddler to practice expressive language skills even more. To illustrate, say:
   "Yes, that is smooth."
   "It feels like my shirt."

☀ Highlighting Development

Toddlers learn words that are relevant to them. Consequently, introducing words that are out of context or not part of their environment will be meaningless, making the words difficult for them to remember. Therefore, focus on introducing and reinforcing words associated with their immediate environment.

VARIATION:

♡ Use real objects instead of pieces of fabric. For example, glue sand, pebbles, or sandpaper to the index cards. For safety reasons, spray each card with a light coat of clear varnish or cover with clear self-adhesive paper.

ADDITIONAL INFORMATION:

♡ Introduce or reinforce one descriptive word for each type of fabric. This will assist the toddler in associating the physical sensation with the verbal label. Use terms such as *rough, smooth, bumpy, furry* depending on the fabric samples you have.

& COMM

Child's Developmental Goals

✓ To continue developing expressive language skills

✓ To verbally apply labels to objects

MATERIALS:

None

PREPARATION:

♡ Observe. When a toddler appears to need attention, pick up the child and begin this activity.

NURTURING STRATEGIES:

1. Walk around the room touching items. Encourage the toddler to verbally label the item you are touching by asking questions such as:
   "Meena, what is this?"
   "What am I touching?"

2. Pausing after asking a question may prompt the toddler to respond. If the child fails to respond, use your knowledge of the toddler to decide the next strategy to introduce. For example, if the toddler fails to identify the object, provide a verbal label while touching it. To illustrate, say:
   "This is the microwave. This heats your bottle."

3. Foster conversational skills by asking additional questions about familiar objects. For example, ask:
   "What do we do with a ball?"
   "Show me how to sort these shapes."

4. Providing positive reinforcement for responses may encourage the toddler to continue talking. Comments might include:
   "Tell me more about the ball."
   "Excellent, Meena! The block fits in the hole."

☼ Highlighting Development

Soon after their first birthday, young children begin producing two-word sentences. These sentences focus on meaning and express needs or ideas. Children make their wants known through speech. Examples include "me milk," "mama bye-bye," or "all done."

VARIATION:

♡ Repeat a similar tour of objects outdoors.

ADDITIONAL INFORMATION:

♡ Focus on common items within the toddler's environment.

Board

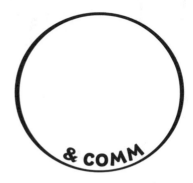

& COMM

Child's Developmental Goals

✓ To create markings on a piece of paper

✓ To communicate through art

MATERIALS:

❑ 1 large sheet of heavy tagboard
❑ 1 plastic container
❑ 1 damp sponge
❑ Transparent lamination or clear self-adhesive paper
❑ 1 set of washable, nontoxic felt-tip markers
❑ Smock

PREPARATION:

♡ Laminate the tagboard sheet to create a write-and-wipe board. Hang one write-and-wipe board on an easel, wall, or refrigerator.

♡ Place the markers in the container and set it next to the tagboard. Lay the damp sponge beside the markers.

♡ Hang or display the smock so the toddler knows your expectations for the experience.

NURTURING STRATEGIES:

1. When a toddler chooses the activity, observe the child's behavior.

2. If necessary, introduce the activity. Most likely, you will need to explain the use of the sponge. To illustrate, while marking a little mark and then erasing it, say:
   "Write with the markers on this special paper. Then erase it with the sponge."

3. As the child works, describe what you see. For example, say:
   "Tyrone, you're making a red circle."
   "Here are long green lines."
   "These go up and down. Up and down."

4. Encourage the child to discuss the work by asking open-ended questions or making statements such as:
   "Tyrone, would you like to tell me about your work?"
   "Tell me about your picture."

5. Discuss the cause or effect of the damp sponge on the markings. Comments to make include:
   "Tyrone, you erased that green mark."
   "Look. The red circle is all gone."

6. Elaborate on the emotional expressions of the toddler. Say, for example:
   "You're smiling. You like to write and then erase."
   "What a sad face. Did you erase too much? Use the markers again."

☀ Highlighting Development

During the second year of life, a child's vocabulary begins expanding rather quickly. Language development is promoted by the child's increasing mobility and experiences. Typically, the number of people, events, and objects in his life is increasing. As a result, growth is rapid. At 12 months, the child generally has a vocabulary of 3 words. By 15 months, the child's vocabulary has increased to 22 words. Around 18 months, the child's vocabulary usually increases to approximately 100 words (Snow, 1998).

VARIATIONS:

♡ Use finger paints instead of felt-tip markers on the tagboard sheet.

♡ Use chalk rather than markers.

ADDITIONAL INFORMATION:

♡ This activity promotes not only development of written communication skills but also emotional development. It gives toddlers a sense of self-efficacy because they can erase what they've written.

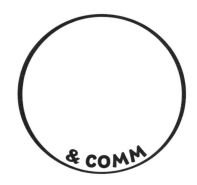

& COMM

after Snack

Child's Developmental Goals

✓ To follow simple directions

✓ To continue developing receptive language skills

MATERIALS:

❑ Serving tray

PREPARATION:

♡ Prepare and serve snack as usual. Place the tray for dirty snack dishes in the center of the table.

NURTURING STRATEGIES:

1. While you are eating snack with a toddler, discuss the tray in the center of the table. Foster divergent thinking by asking open-ended questions such as:
   "What is this tray for?"
   "Why is that tray there?"

2. Accept and discuss the toddler's answers. For example, if the child says "paint," you may respond:
   "We carry paint on trays? Do you see any paint?"

3. Whenever you are able, guide the conversation back to the relationship between snack and the tray. For example, ask:
   "How could we use the tray for snack?"

4. Responding to the toddler's comments may encourage continuation of the conversation.

5. As the toddler finishes with snack, explain the purpose of the tray. To illustrate, say:
   "This tray is for dirty dishes. Put your cup, bowl, and spoon on the tray when you are finished eating."

6. Remind the child to assist with cleaning after snack. Say, for example:
   "Rosario, put your cup on the tray. Then you need to wash your hands."

7. Reinforcing your words with actions may be necessary. If so, gently guide the toddler through each step while repeating the directions. For example, while helping the toddler put the cup on the tray, say:
   "Rosario, put the cup on the tray."

8. Providing positive reinforcement may encourage the toddler to complete the tasks independently. Comments include:
   "Rosario, you did a great job of cleaning up after snack."
   "What a good helper. All of the snack items are cleaned up."

☼ Highlighting Development

Listen to toddlers. Many of their words are overgeneralized. They may identify any four-legged animal, such as a cow or horse, as a being a dog. Initially, toddlers begin by having only one or two meanings for a word. Gradually, over a period of years, children add new meanings to words. Eventually, their definitions will correspond to an adult's definition.

VARIATION:

♡ Perform similar "following directions" activities throughout the day. These activities can be introduced during routine activities such as washing hands, picking up toys, or getting dressed for outdoor play.

ADDITIONAL INFORMATION:

♡ Young toddlers should be able to follow two to three simple directions given at the same time. However, if a toddler has difficulty doing this, provide only one instruction at a time. Slowly build up to two or three directions at once.

♡ Keep your commands as simple and direct as possible.

in a Basket

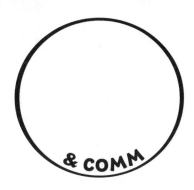

& COMM

Child's Developmental Goals

✓ To understand the meaning of the words *full* and *empty*

✓ To continue developing expressive language skills

MATERIALS:

❑ 5 or 6 plastic colored eggs
❑ 2 baskets for holding the eggs

PREPARATION:

♡ Place the eggs in one of the baskets; then set both baskets in an accessible location.

NURTURING STRATEGIES:

1. Observe the child's behavior with the eggs and basket.
2. If the toddler doesn't seem to know what to do, introduce the activity. To illustrate, say:
   "Kano, empty the basket . Dump out the eggs. Then fill it up again."
3. You may need to model emptying and filling by using the second basket.
4. Reinforce your actions with words by describing what you or the child is doing. Comments include:
   "Kano, your basket is full of eggs."
   "Show me how to dump it."
5. Check the child's understanding of the terms *full* and *empty* by asking the toddler questions. For example, say:
   "Can you empty your basket?"
   "How can you make your basket full?"
   "Is your basket full or empty?"
6. Providing positive reinforcement may increase the time spent at the activity. Comments include:
   "Kano, you did it! Your basket is now full."

Highlighting Development

Listen to the child's speech. The first words are generally nouns referring to things that are familiar or of interest. Among them typically are *cat, dog, no, go, ball,* and *car.* First words tend to end with "ie" such as *birdie, blankie,* and *doggie.* Moreover, new vocabulary words are likely to appear one at a time. Later the child will begin acquiring verbs, adjectives, adverbs, and prepositions (Snow, 1998).

VARIATIONS:

♡ Substitute favorite toys such as balls, blocks, or cars for the eggs.
♡ Use six plastic eggs and an egg carton instead of a basket.

ADDITIONAL INFORMATION:

♡ Toddlers love to fill and spill. Providing them with these types of activities reduces the occurrence of random dumping of other containers. Through these activities, they are learning the interrelationship of the size of objects.
♡ As the toddler becomes older and more experienced with this activity, add a new element. For example, count the number of objects in the basket or label the color of each object.

& COMM

Hot"

Child's Developmental Goals

✓ To develop a sense of rhythm

✓ To continue developing expressive language skills

MATERIALS:

❑ A large sheet of heavy tagboard

❑ Washable, felt-tip markers

❑ Transparent lamination or clear, self-adhesive paper

PREPARATION:

♡ Create a teaching aid by writing the nursery rhyme on the tagboard sheet:

Peas, porridge hot
Peas, porridge cold
Peas, porridge in the pot nine days old.
Some like it hot
Some like it cold
Some like it in the pot nine days old.

♡ Laminate or cover the tagboard with the transparent self-adhesive paper.

♡ Hang the poster in a convenient location.

NURTURING STRATEGIES:

1. Hold the toddler in your lap or sit in a position to visually connect with the child.
2. If necessary, position yourself to allow a view of the teaching aid.
3. Slowly recite the nursery rhyme while clapping to the rhythm.

4. Encourage the toddler to clap along with you. Say, for example:
   "Katelyn, clap when I do."
5. Provide positive reinforcement for attempts and accomplishments. Comments include:
   "Katelyn, we're clapping together."
   "What a big smile. You must enjoy clapping to the rhyme."
   "You're saying the words with me."
6. Continue to recite the nursery rhyme as long as the toddler seems interested.

☀ Highlighting Development

When toddlers can join two words to create a sentence, they are demonstrating their knowledge of language syntax. This important milestone is called telegraphic speech—like a telegram, only key words are included in the sentence. These words occur in an order that reflects an adult's language.

VARIATION:

♡ Recite and clap to the rhythm of other favorite nursery rhymes. See Appendix F for a list of other nursery rhymes.

ADDITIONAL INFORMATION:

♡ Favorite nursery rhymes should be repeated over and over. This repetition fosters the development of expressive language skills. The more times the toddler hears a word, the more likely it will be repeated.

Cognitive Development

♡

THIRTEEN to
EIGHTEEN MONTHS

Is It In?

COGNITIV

Child's Developmental Goals

✓ To search for a hidden object

✓ To engage in problem solving using trial and error

MATERIALS:

❑ Toy that is small enough to fit inside your hand

PREPARATION:

♡ If the child appears to need a new activity, tell the toddler you have a game.

NURTURING STRATEGIES:

1. Introduce this game by saying:
    "Yuri, I'm going to hide this toy. See if you can find it."
    At the same time you are speaking, show the child the toy.
2. Put your hands behind your back. Shuffle the toy between your hands. Using your voice as a tool to communicate enthusiasm, ask:
    "Where do you think it is?"
3. Put the toy in one hand and make a fist to surround it. Show the toddler both fists and ask:
    "Yuri, where is the car? Point to the hand where you think it is hiding."
4. When a toddler points, verbally describe the actions. Comments include:
    "You think it is in my right hand."
    "You pointed to my left hand."

5. Open the hand that the toddler picked. If it was the correct choice, respond with enthusiasm and positive reinforcement. To illustrate, say:
    "Yuri, you found the car!"
    "You're good at this game."
    If the toddler chooses the empty hand, respond with disappointment while saying:
    "No, that is the empty hand. Try again."
6. Repeat the game as many times as the toddler desires.

☀ Highlighting Development

During this period, children recognize that a hidden object is somewhere. They will continue searching for an object long after it is out of sight. Moreover, they will gradually begin to remember where hidden objects are housed after leaving their sight. To illustrate, if you remove a toy and place it in your purse, toddlers usually will remember it. Moreover, they probably will begin searching for it.

VARIATION:

♡ Let the child hide the toy in a hand and you search for it.

Never leave the child unattended with the toy for this activity. If the toy easily hides in your hand, it can be a choking hazard for young toddlers. As a result, remove the toy from the area or from the toddler's reach as soon as you are finished with the game.

13 to 18 months

Separating Blocks

Child's Developmental Goals

✓ To focus on one dimension or shape

✓ To categorize objects by shape

MATERIALS:

❑ 10 round and 10 square blocks

❑ A round and a square unbreakable container

❑ Child-size table or coffee table

PREPARATION:

♡ Clear an area on a child-size or coffee table. Place the blocks and containers on the table.

NURTURING STRATEGIES:

1. When a toddler selects the activity, carefully observe the child's behavior. Ask yourself, "What is the child's response to the blocks?"

2. If the blocks are being used for building, encourage this behavior. Say, for example:
   "Esme, you've stacked three blocks. What a tall tower!"
   When the child is finished building, introduce the activity.

3. Discuss the shapes of the blocks. To illustrate, while pointing to the shapes, say:
   "There are two shapes here, a square and a circle."

4. Encourage the toddler to sort the blocks by shapes. Say, for example:
   "Let's put the square blocks in a pile."

5. Provide positive reinforcement while the toddler is sorting the blocks. Comments include:
   "Esme, look at this big pile of square blocks."
   "You've put all of the circles in one pile."

6. If the toddler has not discovered the round and square containers, show the child the containers and ask:
   "What could we do with these?"

7. While the child is putting the blocks into the containers, count the number of square and round blocks.

8. Continue the interaction as long as the toddler seems interested.

☀ Highlighting Development

Children need challenging materials and experiences. Therefore, making the match of appropriate play experiences and developmental abilities is important. When presented with materials and equipment that they were interested in at an earlier period, the toddlers may reject them. Likewise, if the materials are too advanced, chances are the children will not show an interest.

VARIATIONS:

♡ Introduce circle and square blocks that are different colors.

♡ To increase the challenge, use square and rectangular blocks.

ADDITIONAL INFORMATION:

♡ Toddlers often move from one activity to another quickly. However, their ability to attend to one activity for longer periods of time is increasing. When interested, toddlers can spend 5 to 10 minutes at one activity. Your presence will often increase their participation.

Goop

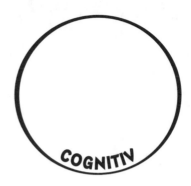

COGNITIV

Child's Developmental Goals

✓ To explore materials through the senses

✓ To add information and modify existing cognitive structures

MATERIALS:

❑ Box of cornstarch
❑ Water
❑ ½-cup measuring cup
❑ Sensory table or plastic dishpan
❑ Smock

PREPARATION:

♡ Empty the box of cornstarch into the sensory table or plastic dishpan. Add small amounts of water and mix with a spoon or with fingers. The mixture will be the right consistency when it feels hard to the touch and molds in your hand.

♡ Place a smock close to the sensory table as a visual reminder.

NURTURING STRATEGIES:

1. When a toddler chooses the sensory activity, help the child put on a smock if necessary.

2. Discuss the material in the sensory table, including how it feels. You might say:
   "Wolf, we have goop to play with today. It feels funny! Sometimes it is hard and sometimes it is runny."

3. If the child seems hesitant, provide ample time for exploring the medium.

4. If the child remains hesitant, modeling ways to explore the goop may be helpful. For example, scoop some goop into your hand and let it run between your fingers. Then verbally describe the child's and your actions. To illustrate, say:
   "Look. I'm poking the goop with my fingers."
   "It feels hard."

5. If the toddler seems worried about getting dirty, demonstrate how easily the goop washes away with soap and water.

6. Providing positive reinforcement may result in extended exploration by the toddler. Use comments such as:
   "Wolf, you are really working hard."
   "Squish. Squish. You're squishing the goop in your hand."

☀ Highlighting Development

During this period, there are subtle changes in the children's ability to use their hands and fingers. Gradually, more control is developed. As a result, the children will engage in manipulating and exploring materials as well as objects. By using a multisensory approach, the children will gain cognitive information about the media: how it looks, feels, moves, responds, etc.

VARIATIONS:

♡ Have the child assist in preparing the goop by mixing the cornstarch and water together with his hands. What a unique sensory experience that is!

♡ Introduce other sensory materials such as sand or shaving cream.

ADDITIONAL INFORMATION:

♡ Goop can be kept for up to one week if covered and refrigerated when not in use. However, you may need to add a slight amount of water before using it again.

♡ If a child seems particularly hesitant to play in the goop, provide gloves or tools to use instead of just bare hands.

 This experience requires constant supervision to ensure that the shaving cream is not accidentally wiped into the children's eyes or ingested.

13 to 18 months

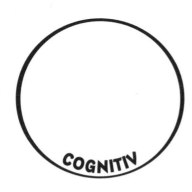

COGNITIV

Sorting Shapes

Child's Developmental Goals

✓ To differentiate objects by shape
✓ To match individual shapes to forms and the sorter

MATERIALS:

❑ Shape sorter containing three different shapes
❑ Child-size table or coffee table

PREPARATION:

♡ Clear an area on a child-size or coffee table. Remove the shapes from the sorter. Then place them next to it.

NURTURING STRATEGIES:

1. When a toddler chooses the activity, observe the child's behavior.
2. Describe the shapes as the child picks them up. Comment, for example:
   "Tilda, you are holding a triangle. It has three sides."
   "This is a circle. It is round."
3. Verbally encourage the child to put the object into the shape sorter. Comments include:
   "Find the circle on the sorter. Put it through the circle form."
   "Match the triangles."
4. It may be necessary to reinforce your words with actions while modeling putting the triangle in the sorter. Say:
   "Match up the triangles."

5. Providing positive reinforcement may encourage the toddler to continue the activity for a longer period of time. To illustrate, say:
   "Tilda, you've matched up all the circles!"
   "You did it! You matched all of the shapes."
6. If the toddler demonstrates interest, allow the child to work independently with the shape sorter.

☀ Highlighting Development

At this stage of development, children may begin understanding positions in space. To promote this development, introduce words such as *up, down, in,* and *out* while the child is constructing puzzles, playing with shape sorters, or placing round pegs in holes.

VARIATIONS:

♡ When the child is ready, introduce a shape sorter with more than three shapes.
♡ Provide the child with simple puzzles containing knobs.

ADDITIONAL INFORMATION:

♡ Encourage the child by introducing and using words referring to spatial relationships. Refer to the Highlighting Development box for this activity.

the Bag?

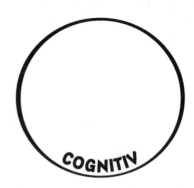

COGNITIV

Child's Developmental Goals

✓ To use an existing scheme to solve a problem

✓ To identify sounds

MATERIALS:

❑ Cloth bag such as a pillowcase

❑ Several rattles

PREPARATION:

♡ Place the rattles in a cloth bag. Then place the bag in a safe and easily accessible location.

NURTURING STRATEGIES:

1. When a toddler appears to be searching for a new activity, retrieve the cloth bag. Then introduce the activity. While shaking the bag to gain the toddler's attention, say:
   "Alfredo, what could be in the bag?"
2. Encourage the child to use expressive language skills by saying:
   "Guess. What could be in the bag?"
3. Provide positive reinforcement for vocalizations and gestures. Say, for example:
   "Alfredo, what a good guess."
4. Encourage the child to explore the contents of the bag by using the hands and fingers. To illustrate, say:
   "Let's use our hands to explore."
   "Can you guess what is in the bag?"
5. Again, provide positive reinforcement for vocalizations and gestures:
   "Alfredo, that's it! We'll take turns. We will take something from the bag with our hands."
6. Call the child by name and say:
   "Alfredo, choose something from the bag. Pull something from the bag with your hand."
7. Ask the child:
   "Alfredo, what did you find?"
8. If the child doesn't respond, label the item. Say, for example:
   "You found a red rattle."
9. If another child is present, encourage participation in the game by asking:
   "Did you find the same thing in the bag?"
10. Respond to whatever the child communicates.

☀ Highlighting Development

Children at this stage particularly enjoy hiding games. They also will begin communicating the role they expect you to play. To illustrate, a child may hand you a shaker. Then, looking directly at you, the child may pick one up and begin shaking it. With these actions, the toddler is trying to engage and direct your involvement in the play.

VARIATION:

♡ Put different types of objects in the bag such as balls, blocks, cars, etc.

ADDITIONAL INFORMATION:

♡ Toddlers may be better at labeling the objects taken from the bag than guessing what could be in the bag. This is due to their expressive language skills. Therefore, don't spend too long in the guessing part. As children become more skillful in speaking, the guessing part will naturally begin to take up more time.

13 to 18 months

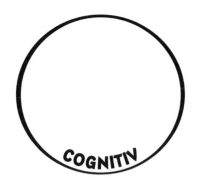

COGNITIV

Child's Developmental Goals

✓ To observe a transformation

✓ To follow simple directions

MATERIALS:

❑ Recipe card including pictures and words

❑ Mixing bowl

❑ Eggbeater

❑ Small bowls

❑ Measuring cups

❑ Milk

❑ Instant pudding

❑ Individual and serving spoons

PREPARATION:

♡ If interested, prepare a recipe card.

♡ Gather all of the supplies and place them on a tray. Carry the tray to the table when you are ready to begin the activity.

♡ If working in a child care center, you may want to place a Hand Washing sign on a table. This serves as a visual reminder to encourage hand washing before the beginning of the activity.

NURTURING STRATEGIES:

1. Remind the child that hand washing is needed prior to preparing the pudding. Say, for example:
   "We need to wash our hands before cooking."
   "Keisha, please go into the bathroom. Wash your hands. Then we will make our pudding."

2. Introduce the activity by saying:
   "Today we are going to make pudding."

3. Respond to the child's comments. Discuss how pudding tastes and feels.

4. If prepared, introduce the recipe card. Explain that the card shows how to make the pudding. Read the recipe card to the child.

5. Assist the child in completing the tasks. Provide more verbal assistance than physical assistance whenever possible. For example, say:
   "Keisha, hold the measuring cup with both hands. There you go. You are doing it! You didn't spill a drop!"

6. Refer back to the recipe card often for guidance. Say:
   "Let's look at the recipe card to see what to do next."

7. Ask open-ended questions throughout the activity to spark a conversation with the toddler. For example, ask:
   "Keisha, what happened to the dry mix that we put in the bowl first?"
   "How can we get rid of the bumps in the pudding?"
   "What is your favorite flavor of pudding?"

8. Once the preparation of the pudding is completed, thank the child for assisting. Then have the child wash her hands.

9. Divide the pudding into the smaller bowls and place them in the refrigerator until snack time.

☀ Highlighting Development

Engaging children in cooking experiences teaches important development skills. Included are basic concepts such as color, shape, size, and number. Critical thinking skills are learned by exploring similarities and differences. In addition, children learn about transformations when observing the outcome of mixing dry and liquid ingredients.

VARIATION:

♡ Add bananas to vanilla or chocolate pudding.

ADDITIONAL INFORMATION:

♡ Toddlers are developing independence. You can foster this trait by introducing simple cooking activities. Preparing snack also seems to be a successful technique for encouraging picky eaters to sample different foods.

Feely Bag

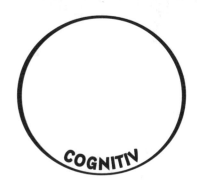

COGNITIV

Child's Developmental Goals

✓ To distinguish common objects through touching
✓ To associate a verbal label with an object

MATERIALS:

❑ Decorated paper gift bag
❑ 6 common objects such as balls, blocks, cars, etc.

PREPARATION:

♡ Place all six objects in the decorated bag. Then set the bag so that it is easily accessible for the child.

NURTURING STRATEGIES:

1. When a toddler selects the activity, observe the child's behavior.
2. Encourage the toddler to feel the objects without looking into the bag. Say, for example:
   "Waylon, put your hand in the bag. What do you feel?"
   "Use your fingers. Touch the objects."
3. Encourage guessing about what the toddler is touching before actually looking at the object. Comments include:
   "What object do you have in your hand? What does it feel like?"
   "Guess before you look."
4. Encourage the toddler to look at the object to verify the verbal label.
5. Provide positive reinforcement for attempts and accomplishments. To illustrate, say:
   "Waylon, it was a ball! You were right!"
   "It is fuzzy like a bear, but that is a duck."

6. If a toddler is having difficulty, change the game slightly by asking the child to "find the ball." As before, encourage the toddler to explore the objects by touching with fingers and hands.
7. Continue the game as long as the toddler seems interested.

☀ Highlighting Development

Cognitive and language development overlap. Learning labels for objects is one example of this overlap. Cognitively the child is developing and refining memory and classification skills. As for language, the child is learning to match labels with objects and communicate through expressive language skills.

VARIATION:

♡ Suggest that the toddler find objects to put inside a decorated bag.

ADDITIONAL INFORMATION:

♡ Encourage the child to slowly explore the object before labeling it.
♡ Carefully choose the items to place in the bag. At first, select only familiar objects. As the child becomes skilled at the game, try introducing one or two new items each time you play the game.

13 to 18 months

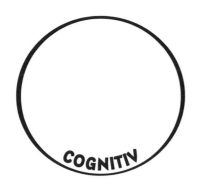

COGNITIV

MATERIALS:

- ❑ 5 to 6 pictures of toys from magazines or catalogs
- ❑ Toys to match the pictures
- ❑ 2 baskets
- ❑ Glue
- ❑ Tagboard sheet
- ❑ Transparent self-adhesive paper
- ❑ Child-size table or coffee table

PREPARATION:

♡ Cut the tagboard sheet into pieces of equal size so that the largest pictures will fit on it. Mount each picture on a piece of tagboard. If desired, cover the pictures with transparent self-adhesive paper.

♡ Place the pictures in one of the baskets and the matching items in the other.

♡ Sit both baskets on a child-size table. Match one picture and item as an example.

NURTURING STRATEGIES:

1. When a toddler selects the activity, observe the child's behavior.
2. If necessary, introduce the activity to the toddler. To illustrate, say:
   "Debbie, this is a matching game. Find the toy that is in the picture. Watch me. See how these two match? They are both cars."

3. If necessary, help the toddler find a match. To connect your words with actions, verbally describe your actions. To illustrate, say:
   "Here is a picture of a ball. I'm going to look in the basket for a ball. Here it is! The ball was hidden! Now I have two balls."
4. Encourage the toddler to play the game. Say, for example:
   "Debbie, it is your turn. You find a match."
5. As the child is working, provide assistance to promote visual discrimination skills by pointing out the similarities and differences between two items. For example, say:
   "They are both green, but only one is a frog. Which one hops?"

☼ Highlighting Development

To promote the child's development, a technique called scaffolding can be used. This technique is used when the child is about to give up. It involves providing tutoring or prompting to assist the child in learning.

VARIATION:

♡ Match two identical magazine or catalog pictures.

ADDITIONAL INFORMATION:

♡ You will need to carefully select pictures for this matching game. The pictures need to be of familiar objects. At first, items should be fairly distinct such as a ball and rattle. After the child is familiar with the game, promote cognitive development by providing categories of items such as animals, transportation vehicles, foods, clothing, etc.

Comparing Apples

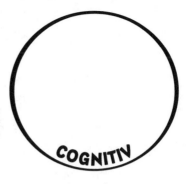

COGNITIV

Child's Developmental Goals

✓ To identify similarities between objects

✓ To identify differences between objects

MATERIALS:

- ❑ 3 different colors of apples: green, red, and yellow
- ❑ Crackers
- ❑ Knife to slice apples
- ❑ Bowl
- ❑ Water
- ❑ Cup
- ❑ Napkins
- ❑ Tray

PREPARATION:

- ♡ Wash the apples.
- ♡ Fill a pitcher with water and place the crackers in the bowl.
- ♡ Put the first seven materials listed above on a tray for ease in transporting to a table for snack.

NURTURING STRATEGIES:

1. Sanitize the table for snacking.
2. Assist the toddler with hand washing and finding a seat at the snack table. Wash your own hands.
3. Carry the tray containing the snack to the table.

4. Show the child the apples. Then ask: *"What are these?"* Pause. *"Are these all the same color?"* *"Do you think they all taste the same?"*
5. Cut the apples into slices. Provide one color at a time for the child to taste.
6. Discuss how each type of apple tastes. Introduce words such as *sweet* or *tart*.
7. Ask the toddler if one type of apples is preferable. Discuss how some people like the same apples and some like different ones.
8. Provide crackers and water to balance the snack. Continue conversing about the apples throughout the remainder of the snack.

☀ Highlighting Development

The ability to perceive, store, recall, and use information is a key element in cognitive development. Observe the toddlers. At this stage of development, they concentrate on everything they do. If activities are developmentally appropriate, the toddlers will be interested. However, if handed a toy from an earlier period, they may be bored and move away.

VARIATION:

♡ To increase the challenge, introduce a variety of different fruits for the child to taste.

 Extreme caution must be taken to keep the knife out of the reach of children.

Stop Me From . . .

COGNITIV

Child's Developmental Goals

✓ To identify body parts

✓ To associate body parts with function

MATERIALS:

None

PREPARATION:

♡ Observe the child's desire for interaction.

NURTURING STRATEGIES:

1. Share this activity with one child at a time. Position your body so that you can visually connect with the toddler and still supervise the other children, if present.
2. Introduce the experience to the toddler by saying:
   "Christopher, what do we talk with?" Pause. *"What do we see with?"* Pause.
   "In this game, I want you to gently use your hands to stop me from doing something."
3. Begin the game by asking the toddler to:
   "Stop me from seeing."
   "Stop me from talking."
   "Stop me from hearing."
   Continue the activity using other examples such as smiling, eating, walking, touching, kissing, hugging, and tickling.

4. Throughout the game, provide positive reinforcement to the child for gently covering the correct body part. Comments include:
   "Christopher, you covered my eyes! Now I can't see."
   "That's right. I can't smell with my nose covered."
   "You are playing so gently."
5. When necessary, give the toddler clues for locating the correct body part. For example, if the toddler is having difficulty with touching, you can say:
   "Christopher, I also use this part to eat a snack."
6. Continue this game as long as the toddler seems interested.

☀ Highlighting Development

Children are gathering information about themselves at this stage of development. Knowing the proper labels for body parts adds important information to their cognitive structures, including sense of themselves.

VARIATION:

♡ Reverse roles in the activity by having the toddler direct you to cover body parts.

ADDITIONAL INFORMATION:

♡ When older children are present, they may want to play the game with the toddler.

Disappearing Toy

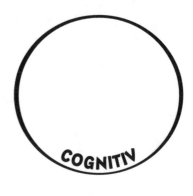

COGNITIV

Child's Developmental Goals

✓ To refine the understanding of object permanence

✓ To find a hidden toy

MATERIALS:

❏ Tube from paper toweling

❏ 20-inch piece of string

❏ Toy that will fit inside the paper towel tube

PREPARATION:

♡ Thread a piece of strong string through a paper towel tube. Then tie both ends of the string to one of the toys, creating a loop. Test your knots by tugging on them to ensure the toy is secure.

NURTURING STRATEGIES:

1. When the toddler selects the toy, observe the child's interaction with the toy.
2. As the toy disappears into the tube, ask in an excited voice:
   "Sheila, where did the duck go? It was just here and now I don't see it! Where is it?"
3. Encourage the toddler to look for the toy. Say, for example:
   "Look for it. Where could it be?"
4. If the child seems confused, suggest a way to find the toy. You might suggest:
   "Pull the string. Pull it and see what happens."

5. Share in the toddler's excitement when the toy is found by providing positive reinforcement. Comments to say, while clapping, include:
   "Sheila, you did it! You found the duck."
   "Yes, you found it."
6. Allow the toddler to work independently with the toy. However, if the child seeks interaction, be a willing participant.

☀ Highlighting Development

There is a developmental progression to laughter. During the first year of life, infants laugh in response to loud sounds or from physical stimulation such as tickling. Now you will observe that children's laughter is based more on cognition. At this stage, they are beginning to laugh at things while participating. In this game, they burst into laughter when the toy emerges after pulling the string.

VARIATIONS:

♡ Hide a toy behind another object and see if the toddler can find it.

♡ Increase the challenge by hiding an object in another location.

ADDITIONAL INFORMATION:

♡ Typically, finding a disappearing toy is an easy task for children at this developmental level; however, an important part of learning is repetition.

13 to 18 months

COGNITIV

Blocks

Child's Developmental Goals

✔ To stack blocks either horizontally or vertically

✔ To sort blocks by size

MATERIALS:

❏ 10 blocks of similar shapes but of 2 different sizes

❏ Child-size shelf

PREPARATION:

♡ Place the blocks on a shelf, grouping by size.

NURTURING STRATEGIES:

1. When beginning to build, allow the child to work independently while you observe.
2. Describe the toddler's actions with the blocks. Comments might include:
   "Gabriel, you are carrying three blocks."
   "You've stacked four rectangle blocks in a row."
3. Model stacking the blocks vertically and horizontally. Comment on your behavior as well.
4. Encourage the toddler to use the blocks in a new way. For example, if the child is carrying the blocks, ask:
   "Gabriel, can you lay the blocks in a row?"
   "Can you help me build my tower?"
5. When it is time to clean up, focus on the size of the blocks by asking:
   "Which size are you going to pick up?"
6. Identify the size of the block by stating:
   "Gabriel, you're picking up the small blocks. Then I'll pick up the larger blocks."

7. Discuss where the blocks are to be placed on the shelf. To illustrate, say:
   "I'm putting the larger blocks together. See, they are all the same size."
8. Thank the toddler for cleaning up the area. Use comments such as:
   "Gabriel, thanks for your help with the blocks."
   "What a big helper. Now the blocks are ready for playing with later."

☀ Highlighting Development

Toddlers learn block building, like other skills, through imitation and practice. Therefore, you can assist them by demonstrating new ways to use their hands and materials. Observing, you will note that children enjoy manipulating objects at this stage of development. At 18 months, typically they are able to build a tower of four blocks. By 24 months of age, their skills will increase and they can build a tower of seven blocks.

VARIATION:

♡ Provide cars and trucks as accessories when stacking the blocks horizontally.

ADDITIONAL INFORMATION:

♡ The very first stage of block building is carrying the blocks to learn about things such as length and weight. Stacking blocks horizontally and vertically develops next.

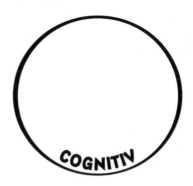

COGNITIV

Child's Developmental Goals

✓ To use a variety of schemas to solve a problem

✓ To increase the understanding of object permanence

MATERIALS:

☐ Object for hiding such as a rattle
☐ 3 hand towels
☐ 20-inch piece of wool yarn

PREPARATION:

♡ Tie the wool yarn to the rattle. Lay three towels down on the table. Place the rattle under one towel, leaving the wool yarn exposed.

NURTURING STRATEGIES:

1. When the activity is selected, observe the toddler's behavior.
2. Ask questions or make statements to expand the toddler's level of play with the materials. For example, if the toddler reveals the rattle by lifting up the towel, while pointing to the string, ask:
   "Keren, what could this string be used for?"
   This may encourage the toddler to use a different scheme for locating the hidden toy.
3. Providing encouragement may result in the toddler extending the search for the hidden toy. Comments to make include:
   "Keren, keep looking. You'll find it."
   "You're looking so hard."
   "I know you'll find it."

4. Provide positive reinforcement when the toddler finds the hidden toy. Use comments such as:
   "Keren, you did it!"
   "You found the rattle."
5. Encourage the toddler to play independently by observing and commenting from 3 to 4 feet away.

☀ Highlighting Development

According to Piaget (1952, 1977), cognitive structures, or schemes, are created to organize or interpret our experiences. Cognitive structures, then, develop through the interaction of individuals with the environment. This perspective has come to be called constructivism because children actively create knowledge of the world or "construct reality" from their experiences.

VARIATION:

♡ Minimize the challenge of the game by partially hiding the toy.

ADDITIONAL INFORMATION:

♡ Toddlers enjoy repeating successful activities. Therefore, the same activity may be frequently repeated during a day, week, or even month.

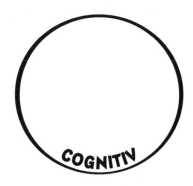

COGNITIV

MATERIALS:

❑ Small stuffed bear

❑ 3 hand towels

PREPARATION:

♡ Spread out the three hand towels on the table and place the bear under one of them.

NURTURING STRATEGIES:

1. If a toddler fails to choose the activity, extend an invitation for joining you in play.
2. Briefly introduce the activity. To illustrate, say:
   "Luther, I put down a bear. Now I can't find it. Could you help me find it?"
3. Provide positive reinforcement when the toddler finds the bear. Say, for example:
   "Luther, you found the bear!"
   "Way to go!"
4. Increase the challenge of the game for the toddler. Begin by hiding the toy in one place and then moving it to a second location. Make sure the toddler watches you move the bear to the second location.
5. Again, invite the toddler to find the bear.
6. Provide support and encouragement for finding the bear. Comments include:
   "Luther, you can do it."
   "Take your time. Think about where you last saw the bear."
   "Keep looking. I know you'll find it."

7. React with enthusiasm when the toddler finds the bear. You could, for example, smile, clap, and say: *"You did it, Luther. You found the bear."*
8. Continue the game as long as the toddler seems interested.

☀ Highlighting Development

The technique of matching the amount of assistance to the developmental needs of the child is called scaffolding. When first introducing a task, you may have to provide the child with more direct instruction. As the child begins to learn through practice, the amount of assistance you provide should be reduced. When this occurs, the child begins taking more responsibility for the task.

VARIATION:

♡ Hide the bear and another stuffed animal. Instruct the toddler to find a particular animal.

ADDITIONAL INFORMATION:

♡ Vary the activity depending upon the abilities of the child. Avoid creating excessive frustration. Some frustration leads to learning, but too much may decrease the child's desire to participate or show interest in the activity.

Social Development

THIRTEEN to
EIGHTEEN MONTHS

SOCIAL

Child's Developmental Goals

✓ To participate in a joint activity
✓ To work with others to make music

MATERIALS:

❑ 1 set of rhythm sticks for each child and adult
❑ Container to hold rhythm sticks

PREPARATION:

♡ Place the rhythm sticks in the container.
♡ Introduce this activity with the child in a sitting position.

NURTURING STRATEGIES:

1. Show the child the rhythm sticks. Then verbally describe how to use the sticks. To illustrate, you might say:
    "Morgan, these are called rhythm sticks."
    "Watch me hit the sticks together to make music. Listen to the sounds I make when I hit the sticks together."
2. Before you give the child a set of rhythm sticks, it will be necessary to set some limits. For example, state:
    "Rhythm sticks are only for hitting together."
3. Pass out one set of rhythm sticks to each child if more than one child is in your care.
4. While she is still sitting, encourage the child to make music. Comments include:
    "Morgan, let's make music together."
    "You can play your instruments now."
5. Provide positive reinforcement for the behaviors you want continued. To illustrate, you might say:
    "We are working together to make music."
    "What beautiful music we are making."

6. When the toddler is familiar with using the rhythm sticks, ask the child to stand up and follow you while parading around the room. To gain the child's attention, say:
    "Morgan, let's have a parade! Stand up and follow me. Don't forget to make music."
7. Walk around the room making music. Continue as long as the toddler seems interested.
8. Stop the parade by walking toward the container and depositing your rhythm sticks. Likewise, encourage the toddler to repeat your behavior.
9. Conclude the activity by saying, for example:
    "Morgan, we worked hard together. We made beautiful music."

☀ Highlighting Development

Toddlers at this age love audiences and are in the process of distinguishing between themselves and others. They enjoy your applause when they are attempting to master new skills.

VARIATION:

♡ Use sand blocks or wrist bells instead of rhythm sticks.

ADDITIONAL INFORMATION:

♡ Rhythm sticks are one of the first musical instruments to use with toddlers because they are easy to use and very difficult to break. Young toddlers are typically unable to produce a consistent rhythm but practicing will assist with advancing this type of development.

SOCIAL

Child's Developmental Goals

✓ To contribute to a group activity
✓ To engage in parallel play

MATERIALS:
❑ Wooden rocking boat
❑ Mat that is larger than the boat

PREPARATION:
♡ Select an area that can be constantly supervised. Clear this area for the mat. Then place the boat on top of the mat.

NURTURING STRATEGIES:
1. When a child selects the activity, position yourself in the area.
2. Help the child get into the boat. Typically, your role may focus on steadying the boat to prevent it from rocking while the child is stepping into it.
3. State any limits at this time. For example, say:
   "Thayer, rock gently."
   "Sit down while rocking the boat."
   "Hold on with both hands."
4. If the child is alone in the boat, suggest that a friend join the activity, if available. To illustrate, say:
   "Shaline, Thayer needs someone to rock with him. Would you like to rock in the boat?"
5. If a second child joins the activity, repeat steps 2 and 3.

6. While the children are rocking, comment on their behavior. To illustrate, say:
   "Shaline and Thayer are working together. You are rocking the boat together."
   "What fun it must be to rock with a friend. You are both smiling."
7. To foster language development, engage the toddlers in conversation while they are rocking. They may enjoy talking about fishing or riding in a real boat.

☀ Highlighting Development

During this developmental stage, toddlers are beginning to demonstrate an interest in others. Their increased mobility skills bring them in close proximity to other children. Watch them. You will notice they will share the space and materials. However, their preference is for interacting with you or other adults rather than each other.

VARIATION:
♡ Sing songs such as "Row, Row, Row Your Boat" while the children are rocking in the boat.

ADDITIONAL INFORMATION:
♡ At this age, toddlers more than likely will be engaging in parallel play rather than associative play.

 To prevent injuries, young children need to be constantly supervised while in or around the boat.

the Rosie"

SOCIAL

Child's Developmental Goals

✓ To interact with an adult

✓ To participate in a small-group activity

MATERIALS:

None

PREPARATION:

♡ Memorize words to the song "Ring around the Rosie."

♡ Select either a soft, grassy outdoor or carpeted indoor area for conducting this activity.

NURTURING STRATEGIES:

1. Observe. When you see a toddler wandering around and appearing to have difficulty choosing an activity, invite the child to play a game with you. Comments to make include:
   "Tira, let's play 'Ring around the Rosie.' Do you know that game?"

2. Explain the activity if the toddler indicates the game is new. To illustrate, say:
   "We'll sing a song while walking in a circle. When the song says, we all fall down."

3. Sing the song while walking in a circle. Hold the toddler's hand while walking. Fall down when the song indicates while smiling and giggling. The words to the song are:

   ♫ Ring around the rosie
   ♫ Pocket full of posie
   ♫ Ashes, ashes
   ♫ We all fall down!

4. If other children are available, invite them to join in the game.

5. Provide positive reinforcement when the children interact with each other. Say, for example:
   "There are four of us playing this game."
   "Tira and Sidney are holding hands."

6. Continue this game as long as the children show signs of being interested.

☀ Highlighting Development

During the second year of life, toddlers are becoming interested in interacting with others around them. With your assistance, they can engage in brief interactions. To provide a positive experience with others, keep the number of people to a minimum.

VARIATION:

♡ Using a compact disc or cassette player, play music and instruct the child to fall down when the music stops.

ADDITIONAL INFORMATION:

♡ Children love this game! Eventually, the children will initiate the game with you instead of vice versa.

13 to 18 months

SOCIAL

Child's Developmental Goals

✔ To engage in parallel play

✔ To take ownership of toys

MATERIALS:

❑ 2 plastic quilt boxes

❑ Water

❑ 4 identical unbreakable cups

❑ 2 water wheels

❑ Smock

❑ Vinyl tablecloth

❑ Towel

PREPARATION:

♡ Spread out a vinyl tablecloth to protect the flooring and prevent slipping.

♡ Fill the quilt boxes with 1 or 2 inches of lukewarm water. Place two unbreakable cups and a water wheel in each quilt box. Place the quilt boxes on the tablecloth.

♡ Lay the smock adjacent to the box.

NURTURING STRATEGIES:

1. When a child chooses the area, help the toddler put on the smock. Explain to the toddler why the smock is needed:
   "Milos, wear a smock so your clothes stay dry."

2. Observe the child interacting with the materials. Suggest new ways to use the tools. To illustrate, say:
   "Milos, you can use the water to move the wheel."
   "Fill the cup with water."

3. If another toddler is available, extend an invitation to use the other wheel by saying:
   "Tanner, would you like to play with the water wheel?"
   Repeat steps 1 and 2 with this child.

4. Comment on how the children are working with the same types of materials by saying:
   "Milos and Tanner are both moving the water wheels."
   "Milos is using his hands to scoop the water. Tanner is using the cup."
   "Everyone is scooping the water with the cups."

5. If a child takes another's materials, discuss how their tools are identical by reinforcing who the tools "belong to." To illustrate, say:
   "This blue cup is Milos's. It was in his tub."
   "Tanner, this blue cup is yours. You both have blue cups to work with."

☀ Highlighting Development

Engaging in parallel play fosters identity as well as social development. Toddlers need to learn ownership—what is theirs as well as what belongs to others. They must learn this before they are able to engage in prosocial behaviors.

VARIATION:

♡ Use sand or dirt with the water wheels.

ADDITIONAL INFORMATION:

♡ Toddlers, in their quest for independence, begin to identify what materials belong to them. Sharing skills, you will note, are not developed. Therefore, it is very important that you provide identical materials so that more than one child can use the desired object.

♡ Toddlers can focus on only one aspect of an object such as color or shape.

SOCIAL

Child's Developmental Goals

✓ To engage in parallel play

✓ To contribute to a group project

MATERIALS:

❑ 2 plastic containers to hold felt-tip markers

❑ 2 sets of nontoxic, washable felt-tip markers

❑ Large cardboard box

❑ White butcher paper to cover box

❑ Transparent tape

PREPARATION:

♡ Clear an area that can be constantly supervised.

♡ Cover the box by taping white butcher paper on it. Place the box in the cleared area.

♡ Check each felt-tip marker to make sure it contains fluid. Divide the markers so that one set is in each plastic container.

♡ Place the plastic containers on opposite corners of the cardboard box.

NURTURING STRATEGIES:

1. Invite a child to color the box by saying:
   "This box is for coloring. Look at all the markers you can use to decorate the box."

2. If necessary, help the toddler remove and replace the caps on the markers.

3. Observe the toddler's behavior with the markers.

4. Set limits as necessary. For example, to prevent the markers from leaving the area, say:
   "The markers go in the container when you're finished with them."

5. Describe the work being done by the toddler. Comments to say, while pointing, include:
   "Baraka, you're using red. You're making red circles."
   "You're making lines. Long lines and short lines."

6. Discuss how the child is working independently or with another child, when applicable. To illustrate, say:
   "Baraka and David are working at the same time. You both are coloring the box."
   "Baraka, you are working all by yourself."

7. As the child finishes coloring, print her name in the area next to her marks on the box. This will provide recognition of the toddler's contribution to the project.

8. Close the activity for each child or group of children by focusing on how everyone worked together to color the box. Say, for example:
   "You worked hard today. Everyone helped to color the box."
   "We did this together."

☀ Highlighting Development

During the second year of life, children begin showing a possessiveness of their toys and belongings. To illustrate, if another child picks up one of their marking tools or toys, there will be a reaction. The child may grab it out of the hand of the other child. When this occurs, remind the child who took the object that it is another's property. Tell the child, "You have David's toy. Give it back to him. Here is a blue crayon just like his. You can mark with it."

VARIATIONS:

♡ Prepare smaller paper-covered boxes for children to decorate individually.

♡ Decorate using crayons or washable tempera paint instead of markers.

♡ Crawl inside the box and decorate it with crayons or markers.

ADDITIONAL INFORMATION:

♡ When talking to toddlers about their art, be descriptive. Discuss what you see. Talk about color, shape, size, and the use of space. In other words, focus on the process rather than the product being made.

13 to 18 months

SOCIAL

Child's Developmental Goals

✓ To engage in a game with an adult

✓ To participate in a verbal conversation

MATERIALS:

❑ Adult-size sock

❑ Common items to hide such as a block, spoon, ball, and toy car

❑ Child-size table

PREPARATION:

♡ Place one item inside the sock and lay it on a child-size table. Place the other items beside the sock.

NURTURING STRATEGIES:

1. When a child chooses the activity, ask:
   "What's in the sock?"
2. Encourage the toddler to guess what is in the sock before looking.
3. Suggest that the toddler shake or feel the sock if he is having trouble guessing. In addition, you could provide the toddler with some verbal clues such as:
   "You can roll this, Dion"
   "It has wheels."

4. After the toddler guesses, either remove the item from the sock or encourage the toddler to do the task. During the process, provide positive reinforcement for attempts and accomplishments. Comments include:
   "Dion, you guessed it!"
   "Oh, it rolls like a ball but it is a car."
5. Continue the game by asking the toddler to look away while you are adding a new toy to the sock.

☼ Highlighting Development

Children at this stage of development love an audience. They enjoy repeating performances. They also enjoy sociability. Therefore, they continue enjoying hide-and-seek games and receiving applause from adults for their attempts as well as accomplishments.

VARIATION:

♡ Encourage the toddler to put an item in the sock for you to guess.

ADDITIONAL INFORMATION:

♡ Toddlers love guessing games. These types of games advance not only social development but also cognitive skills such as object permanence and language/communication skills.

SOCIAL

Child's Developmental Goals

✓ To imitate an adult's behavior

✓ To experience participating in a small group activity

MATERIALS:

None

PREPARATION:

None

NURTURING STRATEGIES:

1. When a toddler needs something to do, introduce this activity. To illustrate, say:
   "Do what I do. Follow my lead."
2. Engage in the following types of behavior: clap hands, pat head, rub tummy, and tap toes. Go slowly so that the toddler has time to observe and repeat the behavior.
3. Provide positive reinforcement for attempts or accomplishments. Comments to make include:
   "Wow! You are skilled at patting your head."
   "What a loud clap."
4. If another toddler is present but hasn't voluntarily joined in the activity, invite the child to play. Say, for example:
   "Peta, would you like to play a game with Elle and me?"
   "Indira, Donah would like to play with you."

5. Discuss how the children are playing a game together by saying:
   "Peta and Elle are both tapping their toes."
   "Indira and Donah are imitating me."
   "You are both clapping your hands."
6. Continue this activity as long as the child remains interested.

☀ Highlighting Development

From the moment of birth, a child is a social being. Through social interaction with other people, the child is learning about human relationships and the values of the society. Consequently, as a caregiver, your behavior will either help or inhibit the child's social development (Kostelnik, et al., 2002).

VARIATION:

♡ Reverse roles by having the toddler provide the leadership, with you following her lead.

ADDITIONAL INFORMATION:

♡ Carefully select the behaviors to model. Begin by introducing actions that you have observed the toddlers doing independently. Then introduce new behaviors.

13 to 18 months

SOCIAL

Child's Developmental Goals

✔ To improve self-awareness

✔ To interact with an adult

MATERIALS:
❑ Unbreakable mirror for viewing the entire body
❑ Felt-tip marker
❑ Index card

PREPARATION:
♡ Place a mirror in the room so that there is space for you to work with child in front of it.
♡ Write words to "I'll Touch" on note card, if desired:

I'll touch my nose
My head, my lips.
I'll touch my toes.
And then my hips.
I'll touch my chin.
And I'll touch my knees.
Then you have seen most of me.

Refer to card as needed throughout the activity.

NURTURING STRATEGIES:
1. When a toddler is seeking an activity, tell the child you have a new rhyme. Then direct the child to the mirror.
2. Ask the toddler to point to the different body parts in the rhyme. Say, for example:
   "Mareo, where is your hair?"
   Encourage the toddler to view the behavior in the mirror.

3. Provide positive reinforcement for correctly identifying the parts. Comments include:
   "Correct."
   "Great job. I can see in the mirror that you are pointing to your hair."
   "You are good at this, Mareo."
4. Begin saying the rhyme, repeating it slowly to allow the toddler to follow along.
5. Increase the pace of the song as the toddler gains familiarity.
6. Continue singing the song as long as the toddler seems interested.

☀ Highlighting Development

Touch is important for building and maintaining relationships. It can also be an effective tool for guiding young children. When children need guidance, use a caring approach. To illustrate, position yourself so you are at the child's eye level. Then communicate your interest in the child by leaning forward and maintaining a relaxed posture. To gain the child's attention, gently touch the child on the arm. Then provide the appropriate guidance.

VARIATION:
♡ Repeat just the movements of the song without saying the words. Observe to see if the child imitates your movements.

ADDITIONAL INFORMATION:
♡ Observe carefully while saying the rhyme. Alter your speed to allow time for the toddler to touch the identified body part.

Friendship Tree

SOCIAL

Child's Developmental Goals

✓ To contribute to a group project

✓ To interact with an adult

MATERIALS:

☐ Green butcher paper cut slightly larger than table

☐ Brown butcher paper cut in shape of tree trunk

☐ Damp sponge or towel

☐ Transparent tape

☐ 2 plastic containers

☐ Red tempera paint

☐ Liquid hand soap

☐ Smocks

☐ Child-size table

PREPARATION:

♡ Remove chairs from around a child-size table.

♡ Cover the table with green butcher paper and secure with tape.

♡ Mix the paint and liquid hand soap to desired thickness and divide into the plastic containers. Place one container on each side of the table.

♡ Lay smocks near the activity so the toddler knows to wear one.

♡ Tape the tree trunk to a wall.

NURTURING STRATEGIES:

1. When a toddler shows interest in the activity, assist the child with rolling up shirt sleeves and putting on a smock.

2. Introduce the activity to the toddler as needed. To illustrate, say:
   "We are making a friendship tree. Everyone will paint on this paper. You can paint with your hands. I'll hang the painting on the wall when we are done."

3. Observe while the toddler is working.

4. Comment on how the toddler is painting using the fingers or hands as tools. Comments include:
   "Rachael, you're spreading the paint with both hands."
   "You made two handprints."

5. Converse with the toddler about the friendship tree, being sure to point out that everyone is working together to make one picture.

6. Have a damp sponge or towel nearby to immediately clean up drips or spills.

7. When the toddler is finished, help wash the paint off her hands.

8. When everyone is finished or it is time to stop, lay the painting in a safe place to dry.

9. When the paint is dry, cut the paper into a treetop and tape it to the wall on top of the tree trunk.

☀ Highlighting Development

The beginnings of self-awareness continue during this stage of development. Children begin to distinguish between themselves and others. Often they may use the words *me* or *mine* when referring to tools, toys and materials. In fact, they may even claim other's belongings by hugging them and saying "mine." This behavior will continue because sharing toys is a difficult skill to learn. By 2½ to 3 years of age, children begin sharing their toys more. Meanwhile, adult support and supervision are vital.

VARIATION:

♡ Cut sponges into apple shapes as tools for applying the paint. Otherwise, purchase apple sponges from a craft store or early childhood catalog.

ADDITIONAL INFORMATION:

♡ This activity requires constant supervision to help minimize the spread of paint. However, the fact that it is messy is the real attraction for toddlers. They are exploring with the senses.

♡ Depending on the interest and the number of children you are working with, it may be necessary to limit the number of children at the activity. Likewise, the amount of time may have to be limited to allow everyone an opportunity to participate.

13 to 18 months

SOCIAL

Child's Developmental Goals

✓ To participate in an activity with at least one other child

✓ To engage in parallel play

MATERIALS:

❑ Cassette tape or a compact disc of dancing music

❑ Tape or compact disc player

PREPARATION:

♡ Plug in the tape or compact disc player and place it out of the reach of children. Place the tape or compact disc in the player. Then select a song for dancing.

♡ Select and clear a large area for this activity.

NURTURING STRATEGIES:

1. Gather at least two children in the area you cleared. Introduce the activity by saying:
   "I have some special dancing music. We will listen to the music. Then we will dance."

2. Turn on the music and begin dancing.

3. Suggest different ways to dance. These may include squatting while bouncing to the beat, lying down while wiggling to the beat, sitting while clapping or bouncing the upper body to the beat, crawling to the beat, and walking while bouncing to the beat.

4. It may be necessary to connect your words with actions. If that is the case, state the behavior while modeling it at the same time.

5. Describe how the toddlers are moving to the beat.

6. Comment on how the children are dancing at the same time by saying:
   "Yancey and Lydia are dancing together."
   "There are four children dancing to the music."

7. If the children seem interested, dance to a second or third song.

☀ Highlighting Development

Moving to rhythm is a lifelong skill. Music is important for children this age. It is noted for promoting listening, language, and coordination skills. Observe. Children love hearing the same music over and over again. While you may become bored, the children gain a sense of comfort.

Make music experiences pleasurable by choosing developmentally appropriate music. If the tempo is too fast for moving, children at this stage of development will be unable to rhythmically move their bodies.

VARIATION:

♡ Repeat this activity when you observe toddlers dancing spontaneously to music.

ADDITIONAL INFORMATION:

♡ Dancing is an important skill for toddlers to practice because it exercises both sides of the brain simultaneously. Encourage the toddlers to dance often and experiment with various movements.

Round"

SOCIAL

Child's Developmental Goals

✓ To interact with another person

✓ To participate in singing an action song

MATERIALS:

None

PREPARATION:

None

NURTURING STRATEGIES:

1. If you see a toddler turning in circles or needing something to do, invite the child to play with you.
2. Sing the song while walking in a circle. The song is as follows:

   ♫ Here we go round the mulberry bush
   ♫ The mulberry bush, the mulberry bush
   ♫ Here we go round the mulberry bush
   ♫ On a cold and frosty morning.

3. Encourage other children, if present, to join in singing the song. Comments include:
   "April, Clayton needs a partner. Come sing with us."
   "Marcos, would you like to sing with us?"
4. As soon as possible, remove yourself from the interaction by saying:
   "I'm tired. I'll sing while you three play."
5. Provide positive reinforcement for playing together. Make comments such as:
   "April and Clayton are playing together."
   "I see three friends playing a game together."

☀ Highlighting Development

Brain development continues as young toddlers create pathways. These pathways develop through sensory motor experiences: seeing, hearing, touching, and experiencing body movements. Examples include singing, dancing, and acting out songs. These teach young children spatial relationships, cause and effect, and body awareness. Therefore, surrounding the children with these types of experiences advances their development.

VARIATION:

♡ Introduce other action songs. See Appendix G for a list.

♡ Bring in a mulberry bush for the children to look at, touch, and dance around, if available. This may help them to understand the song.

ADDITIONAL INFORMATION:

♡ After the introduction, usually you can physically withdraw while providing verbal assistance when necessary. For example, you may need to extend an invitation for a child to join the activity. If the child joins, comment to show you are aware of the child's developing abilities.

SOCIAL

a Musician

MATERIALS:

None

PREPARATION:

♡ Invite a musician to visit during a time the child or group of children is dry, fed, and well rested. Ask the musician to play an instrument while the toddlers sing. Provide the musician with a list of the children's favorite songs.

NURTURING STRATEGIES:

1. When the musician arrives, provide an introduction such as:
   "This is Yusuf. He is my friend. He wanted to visit today. Yusuf is going to play his instrument. Would you like to sing with Yusuf?"
2. Sing along with the music.
3. Provide positive reinforcement between songs. Comments to make include:
   "What a good singer. I heard your voice."
   "You were singing."
4. If time permits and the child is interested, ask for suggestions of songs to sing.

5. Thank the guest for playing the instrument.
6. Write a formal thank-you letter and encourage the child to decorate it.
7. Take a walk and mail the letter.

☼ Highlighting Development

Like separation anxiety, stranger anxiety represents social progress. Stranger anxiety is evident during this stage of development for most children. Observe and you will notice that there are differences. Not all strangers evoke the same reaction. For some children, female strangers tend to elicit less anxiety than those who are male. Then, too, strangers who are children tend to elicit less anxiety than adults.

VARIATION:

♡ Invite a friend who plays a different musical instrument or wants to read to the child to visit.

ADDITIONAL INFORMATION:

♡ Pay close attention to the child's reactions to the visitor. If a child appears to be upset, move closer and offer a hug or words for calming the child.

♡ Children pay close attention to our reactions to other people. Therefore, calm, relaxed interactions model that the individual is friendly.

SOCIAL

Child's Developmental Goals

✓ To participate in a group project

✓ To share supplies with another child

MATERIALS:

❑ White butcher paper cut slightly larger than the child-size or coffee table

❑ Transparent tape

❑ Plastic container

❑ 1 set of oil pastels

❑ Smock, if desired

PREPARATION:

♡ Cover the table with the butcher paper and secure the edges with the tape.

♡ Select the bright colors from the set of oil pastels and place them in the container.

NURTURING STRATEGIES:

1. Observe the toddler using the oil pastels.
2. Describe the toddler's behavior. Say, for example:
   "Winona, you are making dark, red lines."
   "Look at all the colors you've used. I see red, blue, green, and orange."
3. If available and possible, encourage another child to join the experience. Then comment on how the children are working together to create a picture by saying:
   "Winona and Dylan are working on the picture at the same time."
4. Encourage the children to help each other by passing needed supplies. For example, if the container is placed near one child, ask that child to pass it to a friend.

5. Comment on how friends help each other by saying:
   "What a good helper. You passed the oil pastels to a friend."
   Whenever possible, write the toddlers' names near the area they worked.
6. After the activity, remove the paper from the table. Then hang the picture on the wall or bulletin board for everyone to see.

☀ Highlighting Development

Sharing is an important interpersonal skill that children need to learn. However, by nature, young children are egocentric and territorial. Thus, sharing is difficult. As children mature, sharing becomes more common and it is easier for them to relinquish items they are still playing with. However, children at this stage of development find it easier to share with an adult than with their peers or siblings. Therefore, adults can teach children the concept of sharing through on-the-spot instruction.

VARIATION:

♡ Use other tools for marking such as crayons or nontoxic markers.

ADDITIONAL INFORMATION:

♡ When working with more than one toddler, chances are some children may want to make their own picture. To accommodate this desire, have additional paper available.

SOCIAL

Child's Developmental Goals

✓ To interact with another person

✓ To suggest an animal for the song

MATERIALS:

❑ Stuffed animals to correspond with the song

❑ Bag, box, or crate to house the stuffed animals

PREPARATION:

♡ Memorize the words to this nonsexist version of the popular children's song:

♬ Old MacDonald had a farm
♬ E-I-E-I-O
♬ And on that farm there was a cow
♬ E-I-E-I-O
♬ With a *moo, moo* here
♬ And a *moo, moo* there
♬ Here a *moo*, there a *moo*
♬ Everywhere a *moo, moo*
♬ Old MacDonald had a farm
♬ E-I-E-I-O.

Other verses: sheep (baa), pig (oink), dog (bow wow), horse (neigh), cat (meow), duck (quack), etc.

NURTURING STRATEGIES:

1. When a toddler needs a new experience, begin singing the song. Take out the stuffed animal that corresponds to the verse being sung.

2. If a child is hesitant to participate, provide a special invitation. To illustrate, say:
   "Ray, come sing with me."

3. After the first verse, ask the toddler for the next animal on the farm. Sing the song including the suggested animal. Encourage the toddler to hold the stuffed animal while singing.

4. Thank the toddler for a suggestion after singing verses.

5. If more than one child is participating, comment on how they are singing together. Comments to make include:
   "There are three of us singing."
   "Ray and Autumn both suggested we sing about a sheep."

6. Continue singing the song as long as the toddlers seem interested.

☀ Highlighting Development

Toddlers are becoming interested in classifying people as males and females. When singing songs, omit pronouns whenever possible. If omission is not possible, balance your presentation of pronouns. For example, the first time you sing a song, use "she" and the second time, use "he." Toddlers need to be exposed to the fact that males and females can engage in the same behaviors.

VARIATION:

♡ Cut animal shapes out of felt for the toddlers to place on a flannel board.

ADDITIONAL INFORMATION:

♡ As you may notice, the version of this traditional song printed above omits pronouns. The change is nonsexist, allowing both women and men to be land owners.

Emotional Development

THIRTEEN to EIGHTEEN MONTHS

Tearing Paper

MOTIONA

Child's Developmental Goals

✓ To express a sense of satisfaction when a task is completed

✓ To express emotions such as enjoyment or anger

MATERIALS:
- ❑ 2 plastic containers
- ❑ Lightweight colored paper for tearing
- ❑ Child-size table

PREPARATION:
♡ Set four pieces of paper on a child-size or coffee table in the place you want the child to sit. Place the plastic container next to the paper.

NURTURING STRATEGIES:
1. When a child chooses the activity, introduce it. To illustrate, say:
   "The paper is for tearing. How many pieces can you make? Let's count!"
2. To improve language skills, introduce descriptive words such as *tearing, ripping, small,* and *large* when appropriate.
3. Encourage the toddler to tear the paper. Comments include:
   "Sarah, use both of your hands to tear the paper."
   "How many pieces can you make?"
4. Comment on how the toddler is feeling while engaging in this activity by interpreting the child's nonverbal behavior, including facial expressions. To illustrate, say:
   "You are smiling. Do you like this tearing activity?"
   "What an angry look. Your nose is all crinkled."
5. Providing positive reinforcement may result in the continuation of the desired behavior. Comments include:
   "Sarah, you are tearing the paper."
   "You are working hard at this activity."
   "What a small piece of paper! It started out big and now it's small."
   "Thank you for putting the pieces in the plastic container."
6. To introduce the concept of one-to-one correspondence, count the number of pieces of paper. Given the age of the toddler, avoid counting beyond the numeral 4. You might say, for example:
   "One, two, three. You have three pieces of paper."
   "Look at all of these pieces of paper."
7. To conclude the activity, talk about how completing an activity feels. Comments include:
   "Sarah, you worked hard. You should be proud of your work."
   "Look at all the pieces. You worked hard today."

☀ Highlighting Development

Research tends to support the belief that females are more emotionally expressive than males. Girls cry and smile more than boys (Kostelnik, et al., 2002). Therefore, it is important that boys receive positive reinforcement for expressing emotions. They might even need more assistance in this developmental area.

VARIATION:
♡ Follow up this activity by using the torn paper to make a collage. Adhere the torn paper to clear self-adhesive paper.

ADDITIONAL INFORMATION:
♡ Some papers are more difficult to tear than others. Because toddlers lack the necessary strength to tear heavier-weight paper, select grades of paper that are developmentally appropriate.
♡ Toddlers typically enjoy tearing activities; therefore, you can expect an abundance of small pieces.

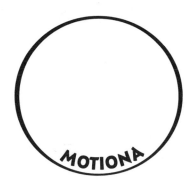

MOTIONA

Happy . . . !"

Child's Developmental Goals

✓ To connect labels of emotions with social behaviors

✓ To label emotions

MATERIALS:

❑ Index card

PREPARATION:

♡ If needed, prepare and place the index card in your pocket. Retrieve the card when you are ready to introduce the activity.

NURTURING STRATEGIES:

1. Sing this song with the child:

   ♫ If you're happy and you know it
   ♫ Clap your hands   (clap two times)
   ♫ If you're happy and you know it
   ♫ Clap your hands.   (clap two times)
   ♫ If you're happy and you know it
   ♫ Then your face will surely show it   (smile)
   ♫ If you're happy and you know it
   ♫ Clap your hands.   (clap two times)

   Other verses:

   . . . sad . . . Say "boo hoo" or "wipe your tears"
   . . . angry . . . Say "I'm mad" or "scowl"
   . . . happy . . . Say "hurray" or "smile"

2. If a child is performing one of the behaviors in the song, begin with that verse. For example, if a child is scowling, begin with "If you're angry and you know it."
3. Discuss the connection between emotions and behavior. To illustrate, say:
   "What do you do when you're sad?"
4. Respond to the toddler's verbalizations or gestures.
5. Close the activity by stating:
   "We talked about three different feelings: happy, sad, and angry."

☀ Highlighting Development

Adults play an important role in connecting emotional labels to social experiences. First, the child's emotions appear. Then you will need to help the child connect the emotion's label to the social behavior by tutoring. This involves describing the child's emotional expressions.

VARIATION:

♡ Repeat this activity with more than one toddler as a group activity.

ADDITIONAL INFORMATION:

♡ This song presents a simplistic expression of emotions. Toddlers quickly learn that one emotion can result in several social behaviors.

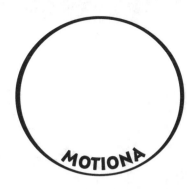

EMOTIONAL

Child's Developmental Goals

✓ To express a need or desire

✓ To find ways to get a need or desire met

MATERIALS:

None

PREPARATION:

None

NURTURING STRATEGIES:

1. Respond to a toddler's verbal or physical request for assistance.
2. Encourage elaboration of the toddler's needs so that you can better assist. Comments include:
   "Taj, what about your blanket?"
   "Show me. Take my hand and show me."
3. Work with the toddler to solve the problem.
4. Provide positive reinforcement when the need or desire is met. To illustrate, say:
   "You showed me what you needed. We solved your problem."
   "You used words to tell me what you needed. That was helpful, Taj."

☀ Highlighting Development

Most children at this age are attached to soft objects such as teddy bears and blankets. Cuddly toys serve as a source of security. They help children manage the stress associated with separation. The need for security items occurs at a period when the toddlers are increasing their psychological separateness from their primary caregivers.

VARIATION:

♡ Pay close attention to the child's nonverbal cues. This may allow you to quickly respond, thereby meeting the child's emotional needs.

ADDITIONAL INFORMATION:

♡ The use of physical gestures will begin to decline as verbal communication skills increase. Providing children with the necessary words to communicate will facilitate this process.

13 to 18 months

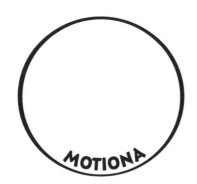

EMOTIONAL

Child's Developmental Goals

✓ To identify emotions

✓ To connect emotions with social behaviors

MATERIALS:

☐ 4 paper plates

☐ 4 popsicle sticks

☐ Multicultural colors of felt-tip markers or crayons

☐ Glue

PREPARATION:

♡ Draw faces on the paper plates to exemplify the following feelings: happy, sad, afraid, and surprised.

♡ Attach the popsicle stick to the bottom of the paper plate with the glue.

NURTURING STRATEGIES:

1. Introduce the activity to the toddler by saying: *"Let's play a guessing game. Guess how I'm feeling."*

2. Hold up a feeling mask.

3. Encourage the toddler to guess how you are feeling.

4. Reinforcing guesses may result in the toddler continuing the game. To illustrate, say: *"Ashanti, look at my mask. How am I feeling?"* *"Yes. I was wearing a mask with a surprised look."*

5. Discuss how people behave when they feel a particular way. For example, ask: *"What do you do when you are surprised?"*

6. Continue the conversation by expanding or elaborating on the toddler's verbal responses and gestures. For example, if the toddler begins jumping up and down, say: *"Ashanti, when you are surprised, you jump up and down."*

7. Use the masks as long as the toddlers appear interested.

☀ Highlighting Development

Children's emotional signals, such as smiling or crying, affect the behavior of other people in powerful ways. Similarly, emotional reactions of others regulate children's social behavior. In this experience, the toddlers will be able to alter their reaction based on the expression of the mask.

VARIATIONS:

♡ Encourage the child to imitate you by holding up a mask and behaving accordingly.

♡ Repeat this activity with a small group of children.

ADDITIONAL INFORMATION:

♡ Given toddlers' levels of cognitive development, they often express fear of masks. Reduce this anxiety by providing repeated exposure. Furthermore, hold the mask so that your face is always visible.

MOTIONA

Child's Developmental Goals

✓ To practice labeling complex emotions

✓ To continue identifying emotions

MATERIALS:

None

PREPARATION:

None

NURTURING STRATEGIES:

1. When you observe a toddler displaying an emotion, label and explain it. For example, the toddler may be hiding behind your leg. When this occurs, say, for example:

   "Antonio, you are feeling shy today. You are hiding your face from me."

2. If the toddler is crying, label the child's emotion by saying:

   "You are crying. You must be feeling sad."

3. If the child is smiling, again label the emotion by saying:

   "Antonio, you are smiling. You must be feeling proud because you stacked the blocks."

4. If the child looks frustrated, label the emotion by saying:

   "You look frustrated. The puzzle piece won't fit."

☼ Highlighting Development

More complex emotions such as shame, embarrassment, guilt, shyness, and pride begin appearing in the second year of life. These are called self-conscious emotions because each involves injury or enhancement to the sense of self. Toddlers need complex emotions labeled and explained to understand them.

VARIATION:

♡ Continue introducing the labels for new emotions whenever the toddler displays them.

ADDITIONAL INFORMATION:

♡ By labeling young children's emotions, you are a role model. Eventually, they will imitate your labeling when interacting with their peers.

13 to 18 months

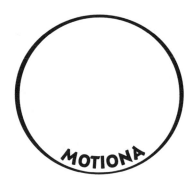

MOTIONAL

Child's Developmental Goals

✓ To express the emotion of caring through a hug or kiss

✓ To feel loved and valued

MATERIALS:

None

PREPARATION:

♡ In preparation for nap time, dim the lights and put on quiet music.

NURTURING STRATEGIES:

1. After gathering a toddler's comfort items, have the child sit on your lap in a rocking chair.
2. Gently rock and sing the following chant:

      Kelly, Kelly, you are so sweet.
      Kelly, Kelly, you are so sweet.
      Kelly, Kelly, you are so sweet.
      I'll rock, rock, and rock you
      Till you fall asleep.

3. Use your voice as a tool for communicating a quiet, restful time.
4. When the child is relaxed, carry and place the toddler in a crib or on a cot. Remain nearby until the toddler is comfortable.

☀ Highlighting Development

Expressing love for another is the basis for later prosocial or altruistic behavior. When children express love, they do so without the expectation of rewards for themselves. They may express their love through actions such as kissing, hugging, and even patting.

VARIATION:

♡ Sing this song again after the toddler wakes up from her nap. At this time, you can pick up the tempo and sing the song faster, communicating a more active time.

ADDITIONAL INFORMATION:

♡ If older children are present, encourage them to sing this song to or with the toddler.
♡ If caring for more than one child, ensure that you individualize the song for each child.
♡ If you are caring for other people's children, share the song with the parents or caregivers of those children.

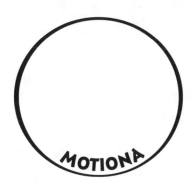

MOTIONA

Child's Developmental Goals

✔ To label emotional expressions

✔ To connect emotional labels with social behaviors

MATERIALS:

None

PREPARATION:

None

NURTURING STRATEGIES:

1. When working one-on-one with a toddler, introduce the activity by saying:
   "Mekhi, let's play a guessing game. Guess how I am feeling. Look at my face."
2. Make a face to illustrate one of the following feelings: happy, sad, surprised, or angry.
3. Encourage the toddler to guess how you are feeling.
4. Reinforcing guesses may result in the toddler continuing the game. To illustrate, say:
   "Mekhi, you are good at this game!"
   "Yes, I was making an angry face."
5. Continue the game as long as the toddler demonstrates signs of interest.

☀ Highlighting Development

Children at this age are extremely lovable. Moreover, they are sociable and friendly. Because of their understanding of the connection between behaviors and emotions, they observe other people's faces for cues. If others are sad and crying, they may cry. Likewise, they will be joyful when others are happy.

VARIATION:

♡ When the toddler has identified the emotions listed above, ask the child to act them out.

ADDITIONAL INFORMATION:

♡ Toddlers should be able to easily identify the four emotions of happiness, sadness, surprise, and anger.

13 to 18 months

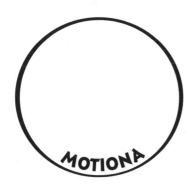

MOTIONA

Child's Developmental Goals

✓ To express the emotion of excitement

✓ To feel a sense of accomplishment

MATERIALS:

☐ 6 to 8 beanbags

☐ Laundry basket

PREPARATION:

♡ Select and clear an area that can be constantly supervised. Place three or four beanbags in the basket. Then place the basket in the area with the remaining beanbags lying alongside of it.

NURTURING STRATEGIES:

1. Introduce the activity if the toddler seems interested. To illustrate, say:
   "Yoko, today we have a beanbag toss game."
   Throw a beanbag into the basket and ask:
   "How many beanbags can you throw in the basket?"
2. Providing positive reinforcement for attempts and accomplishments helps the toddler to identify strengths. Make comments such as:
   "Yoko, you tossed one in the basket."
   "Look. You almost got the beanbag in the basket."
3. Encourage the toddler to keep working at the activity. Say, for example:
   "Keep trying. You almost got that one."
4. Modify the physical environment as necessary to increase the toddler's chance of success. This can be accomplished in one of two ways. Either move the basket closer to the toddler or verbally instruct the toddler to move closer to the basket.

5. Comment on emotional expressions displayed while playing this game. Comments include:
   "Yoko, what a big smile! You must be happy because you tossed the beanbag into the basket."
   "You have a sad face. Keep trying. I know you can do it."
   "You are jumping up and down. You are proud of yourself. You tossed in three beanbags."

☀ Highlighting Development

Toddlers learn to feel proud when adults provide them emotional instruction. In other words, adults define situations and reactions in terms of self-conscious emotions. Situations invoking pride vary considerably from culture to culture. For example, in some cultures, pride is associated with individual achievement, such as tossing a beanbag into a basket (Berk, 1997).

VARIATION:

♡ Cover boxes of assorted sizes with different colors of self-adhesive paper. Then provide directions to the child. To illustrate, you may encourage the toddler to throw the beanbag into the yellow box.

ADDITIONAL INFORMATION:

♡ Always arrange the environment and design activities to promote the child's success.

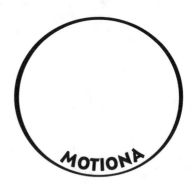

MOTIONA

Child's Developmental Goals

✔ To develop self-help skills as a means of independence

✔ To increase self-esteem

MATERIALS:

❑ Child-size pitcher

❑ 2 cups

❑ Sensory table, plastic tub, or quilt box

❑ Smock

PREPARATION:

♡ Fill the pitcher about halfway full of water and place it inside the sensory table, plastic tub, or quilt box. Sit the cups beside the pitcher. Then lay a smock where the child can see it and know it is needed for the activity. If more than one child is participating, increase the number of materials for the activity.

NURTURING STRATEGIES:

1. Observe the child's behavior after he chooses the activity.
2. If necessary, introduce the activity to the toddler. To illustrate, say:
   "Reed, you can practice pouring water. Pour the water into the cups."
3. Encourage the toddler to use both hands to hold the pitcher. This will increase the toddler's control and accuracy.
4. Provide assistance as necessary to help make this activity successful. For example, you may need to steady the cup while the child is pouring.

5. Provide positive reinforcement for pouring water into a cup. Say, for example:
   "Reed, look at you! You're pouring water into the cup."
   "You did it! You're good at pouring."

☀ Highlighting Development

According to Erikson (1950), toddlers face a crisis of autonomy versus shame and doubt. During this crisis, healthy resolution is reached when toddlers are able to choose and decide things for themselves. Of course, autonomy is fostered when adults permit a reasonable choice of activities and avoid shaming the toddler for accidents or lack of accomplishment.

VARIATION:

♡ When the toddler is ready, encourage the child to pour water, juice, or milk during snack by providing child-size plastic pitchers. Assist as necessary.

ADDITIONAL INFORMATION:

♡ Toddlers love helping. However, they lack the necessary fine motor skills to be successful at some tasks. Therefore, be selective when choosing tasks for promoting their independence and self-esteem.

♡ Toddlers may want to drink the water in the sensory table. This interest may be magnified due to the snack cups being used as part of the activity.

(CAUTION) To promote the child's health, safety and maintain sanitary conditions, have drinking water available.

13 to 18 months

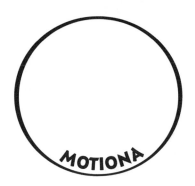

MOTIONAL

Diapering

✓ To assist in dressing

✓ To feel a sense of pride for an accomplishment

MATERIALS:

❑ Regular diapering supplies

PREPARATION:

♡ Arrange the supplies on or near the changing table.

NURTURING STRATEGIES:

1. While diapering the toddler, visually connect with the child.
2. Converse with the toddler about what you are doing. To illustrate, say:
   "Anita, I'm putting on my gloves now."
   "This wipe might be cold. I'm going to wash your bottom."
3. Enlist the child's assistance whenever possible during the diapering process. Given toddlers' large and fine muscle skills, they can easily and successfully participate in pulling up their pants after the clean diaper has been securely fastened. To assist the toddler, stand the child on the diapering table while securely holding her under the arms with both hands. Then encourage the toddler to assist by saying, for example:
   "Anita, pull up your pants."
   "Use both hands to grab your pants." Pause. *"Now pull."*
   Observe. The toddler will probably be able to pull up only the front of the pants.

4. Provide positive reinforcement for assisting. Comments to make include:
   "Anita, diapering goes faster when we work together."
   "What a good helper. You pulled up your pants."
5. Finish the diapering procedure.

☀ Highlighting Development

To assist children in dressing, demonstrating at the child's eye level usually is the most effective. For children at this stage of development, you may need to start an action and then allow the child to complete the process. For example, demonstrate to the child closing a zipper halfway. Then encourage the child to complete the task. Children take pride in developing self-help skills (Herr, 1998).

VARIATION:

♡ Encourage the toddler to assist in putting on her jacket or other clothing when getting ready to go outside, if needed.

ADDITIONAL INFORMATION:

♡ During the first year of life, diapering served as a way for the adult to build trust with the child. During the second year, the focus should shift to fostering the child's autonomy.

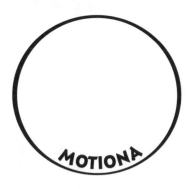

MOTIONAL

Child's Developmental Goals

✓ To express emotions through movement

✓ To associate feelings with behaviors

MATERIALS:

❑ Cassette tape or compact disc of fast-paced classical or jazz music

❑ Cassette tape or compact disc player

❑ One scarf for each toddler and adult participating

❑ Bag, basket, or other container for holding scarves

PREPARATION:

♡ Plug in the tape or compact disc player and place it on a shelf out of the child's reach.

♡ Insert the cassette or compact disc of desired music into the player.

♡ Place the scarves in the container.

NURTURING STRATEGIES:

1. Introduce the activity by saying:
   "We are going to dance to music today. We have scarves for moving to the music. Let me give you one."
2. Turn on the music and begin dancing. Model how to move the scarf to the music.
3. Suggest different ways for moving the scarf such as high or low, fast or slow, in waves or in circles. In addition, discuss how the music makes you feel. For example, quick, light sounds might make you excited whereas long, heavy sounds might remind you of times when you were angry.

4. Use children as models by commenting on their movements with the scarves. If more than one child is present, you might say:
   "Look at how Jonathan is moving his scarf. It is floating to the ground."
   "Graeme, you're walking around your carpet piece."
5. Assist the toddlers in calming down after the music has stopped by encouraging slow movements with the scarves. Ask, for example:
   "Who can move the scarf the slowest?"
6. Tell the children to return their scarves to the bag or basket.

☀ Highlighting Development

Moving to music can be an important way of expressing emotions. It also fosters the development of the whole child: physical, emotional, social, cognitive, and language. For example, creative movement experiences promote spatial relationships, emotional expression, social interactions, cause-and-effect relationships, and receptive language skills.

VARIATION:

♡ Using streamers or bells instead of scarves, dance to the music.

ADDITIONAL INFORMATION:

♡ Toddlers should be introduced to a wide variety of music. However, you will need to carefully select pieces for individual activities to ensure the goals of the experience are met.

13 to 18 months

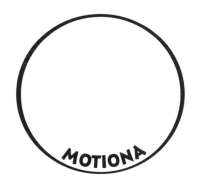

MOTIONA

Shaving Cream

Child's Developmental Goals

✓ To express one's emotions through art

✓ To feel a sense of satisfaction when performing a task

MATERIALS:

❑ Can of unscented shaving cream

❑ Sponge

❑ Nonbreakable container of lukewarm water

❑ Damp towel

❑ Smock

PREPARATION:

♡ Fill the container with lukewarm water and place a sponge in it. Immerse the towel in the container of water and wring it out so that it is slightly damp. Then place the water and towel within easy reach of the high chair.

♡ If the room is warm, remove the toddler's clothing. If the room is drafty, roll up the toddler's sleeves and pant legs. Then encourage the child to put on a smock to prevent wet clothing.

NURTURING STRATEGIES:

1. While preparing the toddler for the activity, talk about it. To illustrate, you might say:
   "Nadia, we have shaving cream today. The shaving cream is smooth. You can use your fingers to paint. Paint the tray."
2. Secure the toddler in the high chair. Lock the tray in place.
3. Squirt a small amount of shaving cream on the tray.
4. Observe the toddler's behavior with the shaving cream. Whenever the toddler raises the hands toward the face, restate the limit:
   "Paint the tray."
5. Describe how the child is manipulating the shaving cream and reacting to the experience. Comments include:
   "Nadia, you're pushing the shaving cream with your fingers."
   "What a puzzled look. Do you need more shaving cream?"
   "You are smiling. You must be proud of your work."

6. Add more shaving cream if needed. Then continue the activity as long as the toddler remains interested.
7. When the toddler is finished with the experience, remove the tray. Wipe the child with the damp cloth to remove as much of the shaving cream as possible. Take the child to the bathroom to continue the cleaning process.
8. Clean the tray of the high chair with the sponge.

☀ Highlighting Development

Consensus is lacking on materials that are appropriate for sensory experiences. Some people suggest using food. This may be an acceptable solution to the problem of children's oral exploration; however, food activities can cause confusion. Playing with food teaches young children that sensory materials are edible. Thus, they learn to put sensory material in their mouths. You must take responsibility for helping children to distinguish between play materials and edible substances.

VARIATIONS:

♡ Have the toddlers finger paint on a child-size table while standing up.

♡ For interest, add a few drops of food coloring to the shaving cream.

ADDITIONAL INFORMATION:

♡ Young children experience their world orally by tasting. This can be problematic when planning and supervising activities. Therefore, careful observation is needed.

 This experience requires constant supervision to ensure that the shaving cream is not accidentally wiped into the child's eyes or ingested. To prevent safety hazards, use the sponge to clean up spills as soon as they occur.

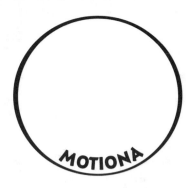

MOTIONAL

Child's Developmental Goals

✓ To practice self-help skills by putting on simple articles of clothing

✓ To develop independence

MATERIALS:

❏ Hats and shoes for dress up

❏ Child-size shelf

❏ Shatterproof, full-length mirror

PREPARATION:

♡ Display the hats and shoes on the child-size shelf.

NURTURING STRATEGIES:

1. Observe the toddler dressing in the shoes and hats.
2. Provide verbal, as well as physical, assistance as needed. Comments include:
   "It may be easier to take off your shoes when you are sitting down."
   "Can I help to untie your shoes?"
3. Encourage the toddler to try on several different pairs of shoes and hats. Suggest viewing the outfit in the mirror.
4. Provide positive reinforcement for attempts and accomplishments. Make comments such as:
   "What a neat hat you have on."
   "Fancy shoes. Are they new?"
5. Encourage the child to act out different roles while dressed in the clothing. To illustrate, say:
   "That looks like a shopping outfit. What will you buy at the store?"
6. If appropriate, suggest that two or more children play together. For example, say:
   "Tyler is going shopping for shoes. Should Darby come along to get a new pair?"
7. Observe the child undressing and provide any needed assistance.

☀ Highlighting Development

Play is important for young children's development. Play is children's work. The first stage in dramatic play is functional. In other words, they will use the prop in the traditional manner. For example, when provided dress-up clothes, they will explore, manipulate, and dress in them, thereby improving their self-help skills. As they progress developmentally, their play will change, becoming more imaginative or creative. To illustrate, eventually they may dress up and pretend to take a bus ride to the library.

VARIATION:

♡ Provide purses, wallets, and play money as accessories. Add simple articles of clothing such as pants with elastic bands and pull-on shirts.

ADDITIONAL INFORMATION:

♡ This activity provides time to practice self-help skills in a fun atmosphere.

♡ Let the child play and explore the clothing. Be respectful attentive by observing and assisting only when necessary.

 Carefully examine the shoes and hats before you put them out. Select low-heeled shoes that can easily be slipped on and off rather than being buckled or tied. Hats should be loose-fitting and without long strings. Check the hats to make sure there are no removable decorations that could pose a choking hazard.

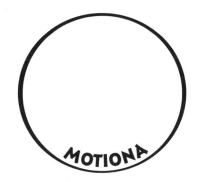

MOTIONAL

and Jelly

Child's Developmental Goals

✓ To improve self-help skills

✓ To feel a sense of pride when accomplishing a task

MATERIALS:

❑ Plastic knife for each person

❑ 2 teaspoons

❑ Creamy peanut butter

❑ Jelly

❑ Saltine crackers

❑ Pitcher of milk

❑ Cups and napkins

❑ 3 nonbreakable plastic bowls

PREPARATION:

♡ Spoon peanut butter and jelly into separate bowls, leaving the spoon in each of the bowls. Pour crackers into the third bowl. Place the bowls, cups, napkins, spoons, knives, and pitcher on a tray. Place the tray on the table.

♡ Clean and sanitize the snack table.

NURTURING STRATEGIES:

1. Assist the child in washing hands for snack. Then wash your own hands.

2. If more than one child is present, ask a toddler to assist in passing out cups, napkins, and knives. Work on one-to-one correspondence skills by providing one of each item to a child. To illustrate, say:
   "LaRonda, does everyone have a cup?"
   "Alex still needs a cup."

3. Pass around the bowl of crackers. Remind the toddlers of how many crackers can be taken at one time. Say, for example:
   "Two crackers. You may take two crackers. One for each hand."
   State how much food can be eaten by each person at this snack. For example, say:
   "You can have six crackers and two glasses of milk."

4. Offer the children peanut butter and jelly to spread on the crackers.

5. Encourage the toddlers to use a spoon to put peanut butter or jelly onto their cracker. Using the knife, spread the topping.

6. Provide positive reinforcement for spreading the topping. Comments might include:
   "LaRonda, excellent job spreading the jelly."
   "You spread out the peanut butter."
   "What a well-covered cracker."

7. Pour milk for the children to enjoy with the crackers.

☀ Highlighting Development

Toddlers' growing, active bodies need plenty of the healthy foods that form a balanced diet. By one year of age, diets should include all of the basic food groups. Toddlers' stomachs, however, are too small to consume the necessary nutrients at three main meals. Hence, they need to eat small amounts of food approximately every 2 to 2½ hours.

VARIATIONS:

♡ Make peanut butter and jelly sandwiches.

♡ Spread softened cream cheese or apple butter on graham crackers.

ADDITIONAL INFORMATION:

♡ Consider the serving size of the food provided for snack. You may need to limit the quantity consumed.

♡ A snack should be a small offering of food to sustain children between meals. It is important to avoid overeating at snack time because it reduces appetites at the next meal. If this occurs, the children may not consume a balanced diet.

♡ Check children's records to ensure there are no allergies to peanut butter.

♡ Informing the children of their limits at snack time is important. It teaches language, numerals and sharing.

 Peanut butter can be a choking hazard. To reduce the potential hazard, serve small quantities and provide plenty of fluids.

Physical Development

♡

NINETEEN to TWENTY-FOUR MONTHS

Jump, Frog, Jump

PHYSICAL

Child's Developmental Goals

✓ To practice jumping

✓ To improve balance skills

MATERIALS:

❑ Book, *Jump, Frog, Jump* by Robert Kalan

PREPARATION:

♡ Select and clear a large space for reading the book.

NURTURING STRATEGIES:

1. Gather the children in the selected area.
2. Read the book, *Jump, Frog, Jump.* This story contains repetitious phrases; therefore, read slowly so the toddler can join in, if desired.
3. Discuss how frogs move from one place to another.
4. Ask the children if they can move that way.
5. Remind the toddlers of any limits, such as jumping around their friends.
6. Let the jumping begin!
7. Using children as models may result in the other children imitating the behavior. Comments to make include:
   "What a safe jump. You waited until Dustin moved his body."
   "You're jumping up and down in place."
8. Assisting the children in calming down after the jumping is very important. Begin by encouraging the toddlers to jump slowly or to make small jumps. Use comments such as:
   "Who can move the slowest?"
   "What a tiny jump; you barely moved!"

☀ Highlighting Development

Toddlerhood is a time of rapid change. Large motor skills are continuing to develop. Likewise, improved balance skills and whole body coordination skills lead to the ability to jump in place. The first attempts at jumping occur at about 18 months of age. Observe them. Toddlers enjoy jumping off the bottom step of a staircase with assistance (Snow, 1998). At about 23 months of age, children are successful at jumping with a two-footed takeoff.

VARIATION:

♡ Play leapfrog by having the children jump over a teddy bear.

ADDITIONAL INFORMATION:

♡ Toddlers will attempt to jump for several months before they can master a two-footed takeoff and landing. Initially, the jumps look like a one-foot bouncing step.

🛑 CAUTION To promote safety, all attempts to jump from safe locations should be reinforced.

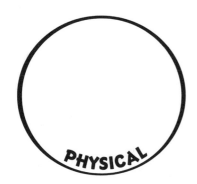

PHYSICAL

Child's Developmental Goals

✓ To move a wheeled toy vehicle

✓ To improve eye-foot coordination skills

MATERIALS:

❑ Plastic toy car that can be pushed or self-propelled

❑ Helmet

PREPARATION:

♡ Sweep sidewalk or slab of concrete to remove loose stones or pebbles. Park the car in the "parking" area. Finally, place the helmet on the seat of the car.

NURTURING STRATEGIES:

1. When a child moves close to the car, provide a reminder that a helmet is needed and assist, if necessary.
2. Set any necessary limits while buckling the helmet. Comments to make include:
   "Shanta, walk while pushing the car."
   "Push the car on the cement."
3. Encourage imaginative play by asking questions such as:
   "Where are you going in your car?"
   "Are you taking a trip?"
4. Describe what the toddler is doing with the car. Comments include:
   "You are pushing the car up the hill."
   "Shanta, you're driving the car, turning the steering wheel, and pushing with your feet."

5. Providing reinforcement may result in the continuation of positive behavior. To illustrate, introduce comments such as:
   "Shanta, you're riding the car slowly."
   "You're wearing your helmet. You're keeping your head safe."
6. Encourage the toddler to return the car to the parking area and place the helmet on the seat.

☀ Highlighting Development

Toddlers are naturally somewhat unbalanced because their heads are one-quarter of their total height. With practice and maturation, children walk with more balance. Toddlers' knees are less flexed and their feet are positioned closer together. Moreover, toddlers' toes are pointed in the direction the body is moving. Previously, they used wheeled toys for support and balance. Now they can independently move wheeled toys, using them in a functional manner.

VARIATION:

♡ When pushing or pulling a wagon, enlist the toddler's help.

ADDITIONAL INFORMATION:

♡ Provide the minimum amount of assistance so the child has the maximum opportunity to grow in independence, thereby promoting an "I-can-do-it" attitude.

 For safety purposes, make sure that wheeled toys are well balanced and move easily.

PHYSICAL

Child's Developmental Goals

✓ To improve eye-foot coordination skills
✓ To practice balancing skills

MATERIALS:

❑ 5 feet of masking tape

PREPARATION:

♡ Select and clear a flat, smooth area that can be easily supervised. Apply the tape to the flooring or carpet in a straight line.

NURTURING STRATEGIES:

1. When a toddler chooses the activity, observe the child's behavior.
2. If the toddler doesn't seem to know what to do, introduce the activity. To illustrate, say:
   "Jordan, walk on the tape. Can you walk all the way to the end of the tape?"
3. Suggest holding the arms out to the side to assist in balancing.
4. If necessary, model walking on the line. Walk while holding out your arms.
5. Provide support and encouragement for attempts and accomplishments. Comments include:
   "Jordan, keep going. You're doing it. You're walking on the line."
   "You took two steps on the line."

☀ Highlighting Development

Running, jumping, and climbing are activities toddlers enjoy. In observing them, you will note that they cannot run with ease because they are still having difficulty balancing themselves. Therefore, to maintain balance, they will often take a few rapid steps.

VARIATION:

♡ Arrange tape in the shape of a square, rectangle, or circle.

ADDITIONAL INFORMATION:

♡ If possible, use masking tape that is 2 or 3 inches wide. This will be easier for the toddler to see and, therefore, visually track.
♡ Because toddlers spend much of their time practicing their locomotion skills, to promote their safety, provide them plenty of open space indoors and outdoors.

19 to 24 months

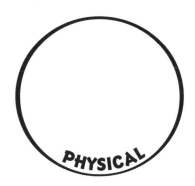

PHYSICAL

Child's Developmental Goals

✔ To increase eye-hand coordination skills

✔ To refine fine motor skills

MATERIALS:

☐ Ring toss game

PREPARATION:

♡ If a ring toss game is unavailable, you can make your own game. Begin by collecting six to eight plastic container lids and one margarine container. Cut the center out of the lids. Then cut a hole the size of a paper towel roll in the bottom of the container. If necessary, cover sharp edges with masking tape. Insert the paper towel roll into the container. Test each ring to be sure it easily fits around the tube.

♡ Select an area in the room or outdoors that has sufficient space for this activity. Then set the ring toss game in this area.

NURTURING STRATEGIES:

1. When a toddler selects the activity, observe the child's behavior. Note the child's ability at the game.
2. Providing support and encouragement may result in the toddler engaging in the activity for a longer period of time. Make comments such as:
   "Colette, almost. Try it again."
   "You're working hard at this game."

3. Modify the environment as necessary to decrease or increase the challenge by asking the toddler to step closer to or farther away from the ring toss.
4. Incorporate math into the activity by counting the number of rings that encircle the tube.
5. Provide positive reinforcement by clapping or smiling when the toddler gets a ring on the tube.

☀ Highlighting Development

To promote the development of toddlers, consideration needs to be given to choosing appropriate toys and materials. Unlike younger children who are used to grasping, shaking, and mouthing objects, toddlers are beginning to move objects from container to container. They also enjoy stacking or tossing objects. Then, too, toddlers prefer realistic-looking toys that encourage involvement such as transportation toys, dolls, or puzzles where they can cause a reaction.

VARIATION:

♡ To increase the challenge, use large-mouth canning rings to toss onto the tube.

ADDITIONAL INFORMATION:

♡ Often, games can be made from common household items. Not only is this inexpensive, but it teaches children creativity and recycling.

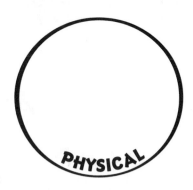

PHYSICAL

Child's Developmental Goals

✓ To improve eye-hand coordination skills

✓ To refine large muscle coordination skills

MATERIALS:

❑ 8-foot piece of wool yarn

❑ Masking tape

❑ Rubber or sponge ball at least 12 inches in diameter

❑ Tree or other structure

PREPARATION:

♡ Tie one end of the yarn piece to the ball and secure with masking tape as necessary. Tie the other end of the yarn to a low tree limb or structure so that the ball will be in reach of the child's hands.

NURTURING STRATEGIES:

1. Introduce the activity to the toddler by saying:
   "Ewan, the ball is for hitting. Hit it gently with your hand."

2. State additional limits as needed if other children are present. Comments include:
   "One person at a time" or "Stand still while hitting the ball."

3. Encourage the toddler to hit the ball with both hands by saying, for example:
   "Now use your other hand."

4. Discuss how the ball moves after being hit. To illustrate, say:
   "Ewan, look. The ball hit the tree trunk and bounced back."

5. Provide positive reinforcement for the child's behaviors. Use comments such as:
   "What a gentle hit."
   "Wow. The ball went higher that time."

6. If necessary, when other children are present, set a time limit for the child so that others can take a turn. An egg timer works great for this. Tell the child that when the timer rings it will be another's turn. Comments include:
   "Ewan, when the timer rings, it will be Bailey's turn. Bailey has been waiting for her turn."

☼ Highlighting Development

By six months, infants will begin to show a preference for handedness. Most of the time, infants will use their right hand. By two years of age, most toddlers show a preference for one hand. While 10 percent show a preference for their left hand, 90 percent prefer their right. To check children's handedness, observe their behavior in this activity. What hand are they repeatedly using to swipe at the ball? Some children at this stage will use both hands equally.

VARIATION:

♡ As the child's accuracy increases, reduce the size of the ball.

ADDITIONAL INFORMATION:

♡ Toddlers are more focused on ownership than sharing or taking turns. Therefore, you should always provide duplicate items to prevent conflicts. However, with this activity, it would be difficult to supervise two children at one time. As a result, helping the children to take turns will be necessary. Likewise, it is a starting point for learning the skills of sharing and problem solving.

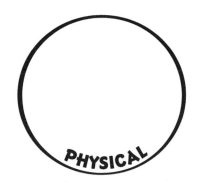

PHYSICAL

Child's Developmental Goals

✓ To improve balancing skills

✓ To practice eye-foot movements

MATERIALS:

❑ 2 to 3 beach balls

PREPARATION:

♡ Inflate the beach balls. Clear an open area, grassy, if available, of any obstacles.

NURTURING STRATEGIES:

1. Observe the toddler's behavior with the beach balls.
2. Suggest different ways to use the balls. For example, if the toddler is pushing or hitting the ball with a hand, suggest kicking the ball with a foot.
3. Encourage the toddler to kick the ball with both feet.
4. If the child is having difficulty kicking the ball, provide plenty of time to practice that skill. Comments include:
   "Emily, oops. You lost your balance. Keep trying."
   "You're getting it! I saw the ball move."
   "It takes time to learn something new."
5. Make a game of kicking the ball by suggesting that the toddler kick it to you.
6. Model suggestions that would improve the toddler's kicking. Connect your actions to words by verbally describing your actions. If the toddler loses balance, model kicking the ball with your arms out to your side while saying:
   "Holding out my arms helps to keep me balanced."
   If, on the other hand, the toddler is trying to run and kick the ball, stand still and say:
   "I'm going to kick the ball while standing still. That works better for me."
7. Play the kicking game as long as the toddler seems interested.

☀ Highlighting Development

Toddlers at this stage are typically showing a preference for one side of their body over the other. The child's handedness is related to the dominant side of the body. Observe. Right-handed people use their right hand and ear. Moreover, they kick using their right foot.

Toddlers like rolling, kicking, and tossing balls. To prevent injuries, choose a foam or soft rubber ball that is about the size of a volleyball. Because toddlers are passive in their first efforts to catch, throw the ball gently.

VARIATION:

♡ If caring for more than one child, encourage two toddlers to kick the ball back and forth.

ADDITIONAL INFORMATION:

♡ For success, children need large, lightweight balls to kick.

♡ At this stage, toddlers also enjoy playing roll-and-catch with an adult.

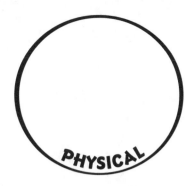

PHYSICAL

Child's Developmental Goals

✔ To increase body awareness

✔ To exercise large muscles

✔ To develop healthy habits

MATERIALS:

☐ Rag doll

PREPARATION:

None

NURTURING STRATEGIES:

1. If more than one child is present, gather the children in a group.
2. Introduce your rag doll and the activity. To illustrate, say:
   "I brought a special friend with me today. His name is Yuji. Yuji likes to move his body. Let's see if you can do what he can do."
3. Move the rag doll while verbally describing the movement. Introduce actions such as jumping in place, touching your toes, nodding your head, moving your arms in circles, stretching to touch the sky, and turning in a circle.

4. If other children are present, use them as models by providing positive reinforcement for desirable behaviors. Comments to make include:
   "Yuji, look at how Lydia is jumping. Up and down."
   "Patrick, you're moving your arms in little circles."
5. Assist the children in calming down by introducing slow movements such as sitting on the floor, clapping hands, or tapping toes.
6. If the toddlers want to continue the activity, have other dolls available for them to manipulate.

☀ Highlighting Development

Obesity has been related to lack of regular exercise. Obese children have a higher incidence of health-related problems. Although toddlers should not be labeled as overweight, they should be taught skills for healthy living. You should model exercising and eating low-fat foods.

VARIATION:

♡ Exercise to music.

ADDITIONAL INFORMATION:

♡ If you model the importance of being physically fit, children will imitate you.

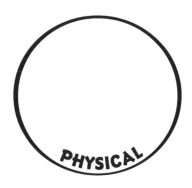

PHYSICAL

Child's Developmental Goals

✔ To improve eye-foot coordination skills

✔ To strengthen large muscles

MATERIALS:

❑ Toddler-size wagon

❑ 2 stuffed animals

PREPARATION:

♡ Place the stuffed animals in the wagon

NURTURING STRATEGIES:

1. When a toddler chooses the activity, observe the child's behavior.
2. If necessary, introduce the activity. To illustrate, say: *"Jacinta, the stuffed animals want to go riding. Pull the handle of the wagon and walk. Stay on the cement."*
3. Explain that the stuffed animals are riding today. Provide a choice for the toddler. Ask if the child wants to push or pull the wagon.
4. Describe the toddler's behavior with the wagon. For example, comment:
   "Jacinta, you're pulling the wagon up the hill."
5. Restate limits as necessary to protect the safety of the toddler.
6. Provide positive reinforcement for following the limits and, when applicable, working with another person. Use comments such as:
   "You remembered to keep the wagon on the sidewalk."
   "Jacinta, you are taking the animals for a walk."
   "We are working together to give the animals a ride."

☀ Highlighting Development

Toddlers are becoming increasingly independent. Because they are interested in pursuing their own purposes and enjoy movement, they lack the ability to make safe judgments. They love climbing into, on top of, or out of almost anything—a shelf, a wagon, or even a dresser. To protect them, you must constantly supervise them.

VARIATIONS:

♡ Provide infant strollers for pushing.

♡ Take the toddler for a ride in the wagon.

ADDITIONAL INFORMATION:

♡ Pulling wagons will help build the child's strength and endurance.

🚫 Carefully observe toddlers to prevent potential accidents, especially when they are turning corners. They will often turn too sharply and dump the contents of the wagon.

Cotton Balls

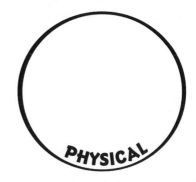

PHYSICAL

Child's Developmental Goals

✓ To improve eye-hand coordination skills

✓ To practice fine muscle skills

MATERIALS:

❑ 2 nonbreakable bowls

❑ Bag of cotton balls

❑ 2 pairs of tongs

❑ Child-size table or coffee table

PREPARATION:

♡ Clear an area on a child-size table. Place several cotton balls and a pair of tongs in each bowl. Scatter approximately 20 cotton balls on the table in front of the bowls.

NURTURING STRATEGIES:

1. When a toddler chooses the activity, observe.
2. If necessary, introduce the activity. To illustrate, say:
    "Nigel, use the tongs to pick up the cotton balls. Then put the balls in the bowl."
3. Suggest different ways, such as one hand versus two hands, to hold the tongs.
4. Model different ways to hold the tongs, if necessary. Reinforce your actions with words by saying, for example:
    "I'm holding the tongs with both of my hands."
5. Count the number of cotton balls the toddler puts in the bowls with the tongs.
6. Provide positive reinforcement for attempts and accomplishments. Comments include:
    "Nigel, you're getting it. Keep trying."
    "You put nine cotton balls in the bowl. That is a lot of cotton balls."
7. Encourage the toddler to work independently by saying:
    "Come and get me if you need something."

☀ Highlighting Development

Large muscle skills develop first. They are also easier to master than small muscle skills. Observe toddlers' developmental progression holding tools. At first, the children hold marking tools such as pencil, crayons, and chalk with their fists to scribble. Later, they will hold the tools with their thumb and finger. At this time, tongs can be introduced to continue strengthening and developing control of the hand and finger muscles.

VARIATION:

♡ Use different tools such as large spoons or pliers to pick up the cotton balls.

ADDITIONAL INFORMATION:

♡ When handing materials to toddlers, position them in either the right or left side of their body as opposed to the middle. This will encourage the children to rotate the body and cross their midline as they reach to obtain the materials.

 Closely supervise toddlers when they are working with tongs. Be prepared to quickly set limits for the proper use of tongs, if necessary. Say, for example, "Use the tongs to pick up the cotton balls."

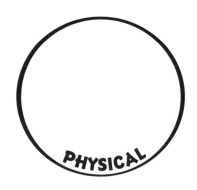
PHYSICAL

Taking Off Lids

Child's Developmental Goals

✓ To practice eye-hand coordination skills
✓ To improve fine muscle skills

MATERIALS:

❑ 4 to 5 plastic nonbreakable containers with snap-on lids
❑ Basket

PREPARATION:

♡ Clean the containers, checking each for sharp edges. If any sharp edges are discovered, cover them with masking tape.
♡ Put all containers in the basket and then place it in a convenient location for the child.

NURTURING STRATEGIES:

1. Observe the child's behavior with the materials.
2. If necessary, introduce the activity. To illustrate, say:
   "Zhu, find the lids that fit on the containers."
3. Provide support and encouragement as the toddler is working. Comments include:
   "Push with your fingers. It will fit."
   "Keep trying. The lid is almost on."
4. If the toddler is having difficulty finding a lid that fits, verbally assist by saying:
   "Zhu, try the red lid. It might fit."
   "The container is small. Look for a small lid. Let me help you."

5. Providing positive reinforcement may result in the toddler spending more time at the activity. Use statements such as:
   "Zhu, you've matched three lids and containers."
   "You're working hard at this activity."
6. Continue the activity as long as the toddler shows interest.

☀ Highlighting Development

Motor development continues to mature during this period as children master small muscle skills. Although there are variations among child-rearing practices in different cultures, the sequence of motor development proceeds at about the same rate and sequence. Milestones include making more controlled marks on paper. With their increased ability, children's accuracy in using nesting boxes, placing shapes in sorters, and placing lids on containers is also increasing.

VARIATION:

♡ Increase the challenge by using nonbreakable containers with screw-on lids.

ADDITIONAL INFORMATION:

♡ Toddlers revel in opening and closing containers, as well as filling and emptying them. Therefore, be sure to have objects available for filling and spilling.

Puddle Jumping

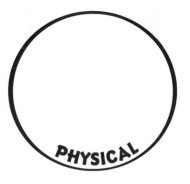

PHYSICAL

Child's Developmental Goals

✓ To improve balance skills
✓ To practice jumping

MATERIALS:

☐ Blue butcher paper
☐ Transparent adhesive tape
☐ Scissors

PREPARATION:

♡ Clear a large area on the floor.
♡ Cut six "puddles" from the butcher paper. Arrange the puddles on the floor, placing them approximately 8 to 12 inches apart. Tape the puddles to the floor.

NURTURING STRATEGIES:

1. Introduce the activity as a toddler chooses it. To illustrate, say:
   "Tyee, look here. These are pretend puddles. See if you can jump in all of them."
   "Watch me jump. Now show me how you can jump."
2. Encourage the toddler to jump to another puddle. Enthusiastically say, for example:
   "Jump. Jump. Jump to another puddle."
3. Describe how the toddler jumps. Comments include:
   "Tyee, you jumped with both feet."
   "You swung your arms while jumping."
4. Provide positive reinforcement while the toddler is engaged in the activity. Comments to make might include:
   "What a long jump. You landed right in the middle of the puddle."
   "Wow! You jumped high that time."

5. If present, invite another toddler to join in the activity.
6. If two or more toddlers are playing together, comment by saying:
   "Tyee and Oshima are puddle jumping together."

☀ Highlighting Development

Normal development assumes many different forms and proceeds at a pace appropriate to each child. Although you need to carefully observe for completion of developmental milestones, avoid creating a climate of comparison or competition (Greenman & Stonehouse, 1996).

VARIATIONS:

♡ Tape two different shapes such as squares or triangles on the floor. Encourage the toddlers to jump to the triangle or square. This activity could also be designed to include puddles of different colors.
♡ Provide plastic raincoats, hats, and galoshes to wear while jumping.

ADDITIONAL INFORMATION:

♡ Observe the child. Typically, toddlers thoroughly enjoy moving their bodies. When the child appears to particularly enjoy an activity, consider repeating it.

19 to 24 months

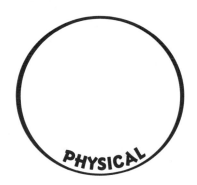

PHYSICAL

Footprints

Child's Developmental Goals

✓ To improve balancing skills

✓ To practice eye-foot coordination skills

MATERIALS:

❑ Several pairs of adult-size shoes

❑ Construction paper

❑ Scissors

❑ Transparent self-adhesive paper

❑ Bag

PREPARATION:

♡ Trace the shoes onto two or three pieces of construction paper. Cut out the footprints. Then cut rectangles that are larger than the footprints from the transparent, self-adhesive paper.

♡ Clear a path on the vinyl floor or carpet from one door to another. Lay the footprints on the floor about 6 inches apart in a stepping fashion. Adhere each footprint to the floor with the transparent self-adhesive paper.

♡ Put adult-size shoes in the bag and set them at the end of the footprints.

NURTURING STRATEGIES:

1. Observe the reactions to the footprints. Are they being noticed immediately? If so, are the footprints being followed?

2. Begin introducing the activity by saying:
   "Look, someone came into our room last night. They left tracks or footprints behind. What can we do with the footprints?"

3. Encourage creative thinking by asking open-ended questions such as:
   "Why do you think the person was here?"
   "Do you think the person left something for us?"

4. Suggest that the toddler follow the footprints from beginning to end.

5. Provide positive reinforcement for walking on the footprints. Comments to make include:
   "You're stepping on each footprint. Left, right, left, right."
   "You're using your arms for balance. You're holding them out to your sides."

6. If more than one child is participating, use a child as a model. For example, say:
   "Look at the way Junie is using her arms. She holds them that way for balance."

7. When you reach the end of the footprints, ask the toddlers if they can see anything new.

8. If necessary, provide clues to encourage the discovery of the bag of shoes.

9. Encourage each toddler to pick out a pair of shoes, put them on, and follow the footprints again.

10. Discuss whether moving in the adult-size shoes is harder or easier than walking in their own shoes.

☀ Highlighting Development

Gradually, children improve their balancing skills. Watch them. They enjoy imitating another person's walk in the sand or snow. You can foster balancing and eye-foot coordination skills by providing a path for the toddlers to track.

VARIATION:

♡ Cut out animal or dinosaur footprints to follow.

ADDITIONAL INFORMATION:

♡ This activity, although designed for physical development, emphasizes creative thinking. Asking open-ended questions with an activity can encourage toddlers to think about things in a variety of ways, even though they may lack the ability to clearly communicate what they are thinking.

Popping Bubbles

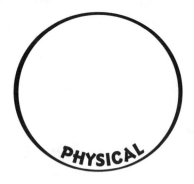

PHYSICAL

Child's Developmental Goals

✔ To practice jumping up and down

✔ To improve whole-body coordination skills

MATERIALS:

❑ 2-foot-square piece of bubble wrap

❑ Wide masking tape

PREPARATION:

♡ Clear a surface that can be easily supervised. If available, a carpeted area is preferred for safety purposes. Secure the bubble wrap to the floor with the masking tape.

NURTURING STRATEGIES:

1. Introduce the activity to the toddler. To illustrate, say:
   "Look, here is bubble wrap. These bubbles have air in them. They make noise when they are popped. How could we pop these bubbles?"

2. Converse with the toddler about his answers. If necessary, ask, for example:
   "Rashid, what would happen if we jumped on the bubbles?"

3. Encourage the toddler to jump on the bubble wrap and find out.

4. Act surprised when a bubble pops.

5. Encourage the toddler to join in the jumping. Carefully supervise the activity and set limits as needed.

6. If there is only one child jumping, you can join in the play. Begin by holding on to the toddler's hands while jumping. Swing your arms while jumping to promote the toddler's whole-body coordination.

7. Provide positive reinforcement for jumping. Comments include:
   "Rashid, you're jumping up and down in the same spot."
   "Listen. The bubbles are popping."

8. If present, invite another child to join in the jumping.

☀ Highlighting Development

Remember that norms represent the average performance of a group of children. Before children can jump off the floor, they walk backward and up stairs. Typically, they can perform a two-footed takeoff by about 23 months of age. Watch them. Once they have mastered this skill, they will enjoy repeating it over and over again.

VARIATION:

♡ Tape bubble wrap to serving trays and provide wooden hammers for popping the bubbles.

ADDITIONAL INFORMATION:

♡ This is a very noisy activity. Therefore, make it available only for short periods of time. If you can devise a safe way for introducing the activity outdoors, then do it outside. The noise level will be lower.

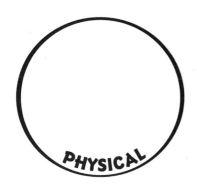

PHYSICAL

"Hokey Pokey"

Child's Developmental Goals

✓ To improve balancing skills

✓ To refine whole-body coordination skills

MATERIALS:

❑ Index card

❑ Pen

PREPARATION:

♡ Clear a large space on the carpet for this activity.

♡ Write the words to the song on the index card, if desired. Put the card in your pocket.

♪ You put your arm in   (arm in a circle)
♪ You put your arm out   (arm out of a circle)
♪ You put your arm in   (arm in and shake)
   and you shake it all about.

♪ You do the hokey pokey   (twist body)
♪ And you turn yourself   (walk in circle)
   about
♪ That's what it's all about.   (clap to beat)

♡ For additional verses, substitute the leg, elbow, hand, foot, head, and/or whole body.

NURTURING STRATEGIES:

1. Gather the toddlers and introduce the activity and model, if necessary. Begin by saying:
   "We are going to sing. Singing is fun. Stand up. Put your arms out to your side. For this song, we need plenty of space. If you touch someone, move your body. Good. Now everyone has enough space. Let's sing."

2. Begin to sing the song at a very slow pace, allowing the toddlers to join in.

3. Provide positive reinforcement throughout the activity. Comments to make include:
   "You're really good at singing this song."
   "This is fun!"
   "You are keeping your body safe."

4. Continue the activity as long as the toddlers seem interested.

☀ Highlighting Development

By the end of the second year, toddlers are able to control their bodies remarkably well. They enjoy jumping, running, and dancing. Additionally, they can identify body parts with ease. Therefore, activities that combine these skills may soon become favorites that are frequently repeated. Moreover, these activities are beneficial because they stimulate toddlers' sensory and motor systems.

VARIATION:

♡ Weather permitting, introduce this activity outdoors, preferably on a grassy area, if available.

 For safety purposes, if more than one toddler is participating, each toddler will need plenty of space. Therefore, you will need to assist the toddlers in positioning themselves a safe distance from their peers.

Language and Communication Development

NINETEEN to TWENTY-FOUR MONTHS

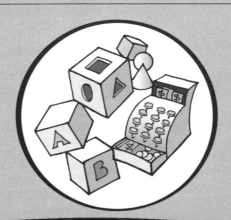

a Story

& COMM

Child's Developmental Goals

✓ To improve receptive language skills

✓ To practice reading along with a book

MATERIALS:

❏ Tape or compact disc player

❏ Headphones

❏ Tape or compact disc book set

PREPARATION:

♡ Select an area for this activity that has a child-size table and chairs and is near an electrical outlet.

♡ To promote independence, tape a green dot on the play button and a red dot on the stop button.

♡ Place the electronic device and headphones on the table.

♡ Insert the tape or compact disc into the player and lay a book next to it. To ensure it is working properly, test the player.

NURTURING STRATEGIES:

1. When a child selects the activity, introduce it by saying:
   "Eloise, this is a new way to read a book. You can listen to the words with the headphones. Turn the page when you hear a beep."

2. Help the toddler put on the headphones. Talk about how the headphones feel. Say, for example:
   "The headphones are heavy."

3. Demonstrate turning on the tape. While pointing to the green dot, say:
   "Green means go. Press the green button."

4. Reinforcing your words with actions may be necessary. If so, press the green button while saying:
   "Green means go. Push down on the button. Now the tape will play."

5. Observe the toddler "reading" the book. If the child is not turning the pages, put on a set of headphones and model this. Verbally describe your actions. Comments to make include:
   "Eloise, I turned the page because the tape beeped."
   "When the tape beeps, I turn the page."

6. When the toddler is finished with the listening activity, help the child remove the headphones. While doing so, talk about the activity by saying:
   "This is a new way to listen to stories. Do you like it?"

7. Encourage the toddler to repeat the activity later. To illustrate, say:
   "This player and book will be here. Come and listen to the story again."

☼ Highlighting Development

Language is the most important method of communication. When reading to a child, respond to any vocalizations that are made. Greet the child's language with a smile or nod or verbally acknowledge it by expanding the child's words into a sentence. These strategies will reinforce the value of language as well as encourage the child to repeat the words.

VARIATION:

♡ Read and tape the recordings of the children's favorite stories.

ADDITIONAL INFORMATION:

♡ Provide two or more headphones if several children are present.

♡ Some children will not like how the headphones feel. Encourage them to try the headphones on. However if they feel uncomfortable, allow the child to remove them.

♡ Stories on tape should be used to supplement reading stories to the child. They should never be used as a substitute for daily reading.

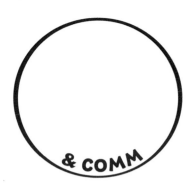

& COMM

Locating "Spot"

Child's Developmental Goals

✓ To increase receptive language skills

✓ To demonstrate expressive language skills

MATERIALS:

❑ Book, *Where Is Spot?* by Eric Hill

❑ Felt-tip marker

❑ Buff-colored paper

❑ Dog stencil

PREPARATION:

♡ Trace and cut a dog shape for the toddler. If more children are present, prepare one shape for each child. Then prepare at least two extra dog shapes. Print the toddler's name on a dog shape.

NURTURING STRATEGIES:

1. Signal that it is time to pick up the toys by singing a cleanup song. See Appendix G for a list of songs.
2. Model cleanup skills by assisting the toddler in picking up toys.
3. Briefly introduce the book by saying:
   "I have a book about Spot. He is hiding. Let's see if we can find him."
4. Read the story. Ask the child to describe where Spot might be hiding. Look where the child suggests.
5. Provide positive reinforcement for guesses whether correct or not. Use comments such as:
   "Troy, what a thoughtful guess."
   "Good guess!"

6. When the story is complete, show the child a dog shape. When the child's eyes are closed, hide the dog someplace in the area where it will be visible.
7. Encourage the child to guess where the dog is hiding.
8. If the child remains interested, hide the dog again.
9. To end the activity, provide each child participating with a dog shape.

☀ Highlighting Development

New words are learned by young children through conversing and reading. Reading helps encourage an enjoyment of books and promotes the development of language skills. As in other developmental areas, growth in language is asynchronous. It has intermittent spurts, and these spurts vary with each individual child (Deiner, 1997). However, by 24 months, most children are using two-word phrases.

VARIATION:

♡ Play "Hide the Bone" game by providing a rubber bone, which can be purchased from a pet store.

ADDITIONAL INFORMATION:

♡ Depending on the child's understanding of object permanence, carefully select a location for hiding the toys. For some children, the dog will need to be visible positioned. For others, select a more challenging location.

Teddy Bear

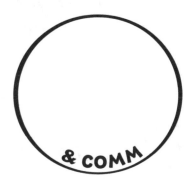

& COMM

Child's Developmental Goals

✓ To interact with an adult

✓ To practice following directions

MATERIALS:

❑ 2 to 3 teddy bears

PREPARATION:

♡ Place teddy bears in an open area.

NURTURING STRATEGIES:

1. When a toddler is carrying a teddy bear, suggest playing a game with the toy.
2. Introduce the game by saying:
   "Aida, this is a tickle game. I'm going to tell you what to do. Then you do it to the teddy bear."
3. Recite areas for the toddler to tickle. Include toes, nose, eyes, mouth, chin, fingers, arm, leg, knee, ear, and tummy.
4. Periodically provide positive reinforcement for accuracy. Comments include:
   "Aida, you found the teddy bear's knee."
   "The teddy bear likes having its tummy tickled."
5. Converse with the toddler about being tickled. Start the conversation by asking, for example:
   "Aida, do you like to be tickled?"

6. Encourage the toddler to repeat the label for the area being tickled by asking questions such as:
   "What are you tickling now?"
7. Continue the game as long as the toddler remains interested.

☀ Highlighting Development

Children at this stage possess the necessary receptive language skills to follow a simple directive. It is necessary, however, to tailor your directions to the abilities of the child. To illustrate, you may tell one child to touch only a body part. You may tell another child, who is more advanced, to touch two body parts. Thus, you have made the activity developmentally appropriate for both children.

VARIATIONS:

♡ Repeat similar activities using a baby doll.
♡ Tickle a toddler's body area and encourage the child to name it.

ADDITIONAL INFORMATION:

♡ Toddlers enjoy moving items from one area of a room to another. This gives them power and control over their environment. Therefore, avoid discouraging this behavior until it is time to clean up.

19 to 24 months

& COMM

Taking a Trip

Child's Developmental Goals

✔ To practice using expressive language skills

✔ To engage in functional play

MATERIALS:

❑ 1 small suitcase with flip latches or 1 child-size back-pack per child

❑ 1 or more of the following items: shirts, hats, pairs of shoes, small dolls, or stuffed animals

PREPARATION:

♡ Arrange all materials neatly. In a child care center, place the items on a shelf or sturdy coat rack in the dramatic play area.

NURTURING STRATEGIES:

1. Observe the toddler. Ask yourself, "Is the child using the suitcase?"

2. If the toddler is not using the suitcase, think how it can be integrated into the child's current play. You may suggest that the child pack a suitcase for a visit to granny's house, if appropriate. If the suitcase doesn't fit into the play, return at a later time and see if it does.

3. When the child is packing the suitcase, to prevent distraction, engage in minimum dialog. Use comments such as:

   "Steve, here is a shirt. Do you need to pack a shirt?"
   "What do you have packed?"
   "Are you ready to leave on your trip?"

4. When the child gets to the destination, encourage unpacking the suitcase. Focus on promoting language skills while the child is unpacking. Assist the toddler in labeling unfamiliar items.

☀ Highlighting Development

Listen to the children. The words they use are the names of people, objects, or actions. Favorite words in their vocabulary refer to toys, people, animals, and food. Common mistakes during this period are underextension and overextension. To illustrate, an underextension is defining a word too narrowly. The child may use the word *bear* to refer only to a favorite teddy bear. The opposite problem, over-extension, occurs when the child uses a word too broadly; for example, *kitty* may refer to all four-legged animals. As children refine their word meanings, underextensions and overextensions gradually will disappear.

VARIATION:

♡ Discuss real-life props that could be packed in a suitcase for a trip.

ADDITIONAL INFORMATION:

♡ Use language to extend, elaborate, or prompt play by following the toddler's cues.

♡ Toddlers tend to engage in functional play without interacting with others. Avoid forcing toddlers into interactions before they are developmentally ready.

Miss Muffet"

& COMM

Child's Developmental Goals

✓ To combine actions and words

✓ To repeat a familiar nursery rhyme

MATERIALS:

❑ Spider puppet

❑ Small stool or pillow

❑ Tagboard

❑ Felt-tip markers

❑ Bowl and spoon

PREPARATION:

♡ Create a poster that contains the words to the nursery rhyme, if desired. See Appendix F for the words. Hang the poster where the child can view it at eye level.

♡ Clear an area to display the rest of the material.

NURTURING STRATEGIES:

1. When a toddler selects the activity, ask:
   "What could these be used for?"
   "Do you know a nursery rhyme that has a spider in it?"
2. Introduce the activity. To illustrate, say:
   "Jin, these are things for acting out 'Little Miss Muffet.' There is a spider, puppet, pillow, bowl, and a spoon."
   "Would you like to be Little Miss Muffet or the spider?"
3. Discuss the nursery rhyme and encourage the toddler to recite it with you. Ask, for example:
   "What did the spider do in the nursery rhyme?"

4. Begin to act out the nursery rhyme. Support the toddler's behavior. Use comments such as:
   "So Little Miss Muffet runs away at the end."
   "The spider moves quickly."
5. If present, invite another toddler to join in the activity. Then continue reciting the nursery rhyme.
6. Continue as long as the child seems interested.

☼ Highlighting Development

Children need to be exposed to a wide variety of language-stimulating activities beginning at birth. Listening and speaking skills can be encouraged through the use of nursery rhymes. By adding a new twist or variety to a familiar nursery rhyme, you will captivate the child's interest and encouraging active participation.

VARIATION:

♡ Act out other familiar nursery rhymes such as "Jack and Jill," "Humpty Dumpty," etc. Repeat nursery rhymes as often as the child desires.

ADDITIONAL INFORMATION:

♡ If more than one child is present, rotate the parts of the nursery rhyme so that each child wishing to participate has an opportunity. You may need to have more than one Little Miss Muffet to keep this activity running smoothly.

& COMM

to Rest

Child's Developmental Goals

✓ To use books for relaxation

✓ To look at a book independently

MATERIALS:

❑ Calm, soothing story such as *The Sleepy Little Lion* by Ylla

❑ Box of other "nap" books

PREPARATION:

♡ Review the nap books. These should be familiar stories that can be used independently by the toddlers. Be sure the books have good illustrations. See the criteria in Appendix A for choosing books for infants and toddlers.

NURTURING STRATEGIES:

1. Prepare the child for the transition to nap time by finishing diapering, brushing teeth, and drinking water. Make sure the child's security items are available.
2. Dim the lights in the room and begin moving at a slower pace.
3. While reading the story, use your voice as a tool for calming the child. Refrain from asking questions or engaging the child in the story.
4. Show your affection by hugging, kissing, or rubbing the child's back.
5. Encourage the child to rest quietly by choosing and looking at books in the "nap box."
6. Observe. If the child falls asleep, discontinue reading.

☀ Highlighting Development

When choosing books for children, consider content, illustrations, vocabulary, length, and durability. Children enjoy looking at books that repeat and add to their own experiences. For example, books related to potty training; messy eating; caring for pets; and separating from parents, grandparents, and siblings are all appealing at this stage of development.

VARIATION:

♡ Play soothing music instead of reading a story.

ADDITIONAL INFORMATION:

♡ If caring for children other than your own, discuss with each family how the toddler likes to relax and how the nap routine is handled at home. Following each routine as closely as possible will help reduce frustration for you and increase the length of nap time for the toddler.

♡ Toddlers like and need routines for predictability and consistency as much as they did when they were infants. Create a routine and stick to it as much as possible.

Puppet Show

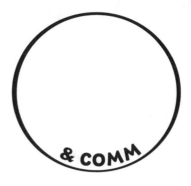

& COMM

Child's Developmental Goals

✓ To talk through a puppet

✓ To practice expressive language skills

MATERIALS:

❑ 6 multigender, multicultural hand puppets, if available

❑ Puppet stands: 6 cylindrical blocks or empty dish detergent bottles

PREPARATION:

♡ Clear an area for the puppets. Set each puppet on a stand.

NURTURING STRATEGIES:

1. Observe the behavior of a toddler after choosing a puppet.
2. Select a puppet and join the toddler in play sitting on the floor. If other children are present, placing your back toward a wall will enable supervision of the room.
3. Model the puppet talking to the toddler and yourself. For example, talk about what is happening. Address the toddler's puppet by asking a question.
4. Encourage the toddler to converse using the puppet.

5. Whenever necessary, state the limit such as: *"Pedro, talk with the puppet."*
6. Provide positive reinforcement when the toddler makes the puppet talk. Comments to make include:
   "You're making the puppet talk."
   "Your puppet is talking about the blocks."
7. If available, invite another toddler to play with the puppets.

☀ Highlighting Development

Puppets are wonderful tools for promoting language development. Using a puppet to tell a story adds variety. Puppets are beneficial for gaining children's attention and adding novelty. Puppets are useful for encouraging children to talk and retell their experiences and stories. Furthermore, puppets can be valuable tools for expressing emotions.

VARIATION:

♡ Use animal puppets.

 To eliminate a potential choking hazard, check the eyes on the puppet to ensure they are securely attached.

& COMM

Child's Developmental Goals

✓ To identify other people's voices

✓ To practice language skills by speaking into a microphone

MATERIALS:

❑ Blank cassette tape

❑ Cassette tape recorder that is powered by batteries

❑ Paper and pen

PREPARATION:

♡ Insert the tape into the recorder. Then run an audio test to ensure the recorder is working properly.

NURTURING STRATEGIES:

1. Carry the tape recorder and approach each toddler. Begin by introducing the activity. To illustrate, you may say:
   "I want you to talk. Then I can save your words on this machine. When you are finished, we will listen to your words."
2. Show the toddler how the machine works. For example, demonstrate that when the record button is pushed, the tape moves.
3. Ask the toddler a couple of questions to elicit speech such as:
   "What is your name?"
   "What do you like to play with?"
4. Rewind and play the tape of the toddler's voice.
5. Discuss how the child sounded on the tape.
6. If more than one child is participating, write the names of the children on the paper in the order that they were taped.

7. Then repeat the taping process with other children. If other children are not present, tape your own voice.
8. After everyone has had a chance to be taped, gather in one area and play the tape.
9. Encourage the children to guess who is speaking on the tape.
10. Provide positive reinforcement for attempts and accomplishments. Comments include:
    "You're right! That is Felicity talking on the tape."
    "Keep guessing. It wasn't Dorian that time."

☼ Highlighting Development

Auditory and visual discrimination are both continuing to rapidly develop during this stage. Children are learning to associate people by verbal and nonverbal cues. When recognizing a sound or voice, they become outwardly excited. Nonverbal cues may confuse them. For example, a child whose mother is a police officer may see another female uniformed officer and greet her by saying "mama."

VARIATION:

♡ Tape a toddler or group of children singing a favorite song. Play back the tape and sing along with it.

ADDITIONAL INFORMATION:

♡ Show the children how to stop and start the tape recorder using visual cues. To do this, cut a red circle and tape it onto the stop button. Likewise, cut a green circle and place it onto the start button.

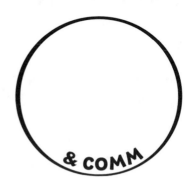

& COMM

Child's Developmental Goals

✓ To identify, compare, and contrast fruit according to shape and color

✓ To discuss how fruit tastes

MATERIALS:

❑ Fresh fruit such as pineapple, banana, apple, orange, and grapes

❑ Large, nonbreakable plastic bowl

❑ Knife

❑ Cutting board

❑ Tray

PREPARATION:

♡ Clean the fruit and place it with other supplies on a tray. Place the tray on the table.

♡ Then encourage the toddler to wash hands for snack.

NURTURING STRATEGIES:

1. Introduce the activity by saying:
   "Look at what we are having for snack. I'm going to cut some fruit. Watch me."
   "After I cut the fruit, we can taste it."
2. Set limits as necessary. Limits may include:
   "Only I can touch the knife."
   "Stay seated while the fruit is being cut."
3. Hold up a piece of fruit. Encourage the toddlers to identify the fruit by asking:
   "What is the name of this fruit?"
4. Discuss the appearance of the fruit. Talk about size, color, shape, etc.
5. Cut the piece of fruit and share some with the children. Encourage each of the children to taste each type of fruit.
6. Converse about how the fruit tastes.
7. Cut another type of fruit and repeat steps 3 through 6.

8. Encourage the toddlers to discuss the fruit they have tasted by asking:
   "Which fruit was crunchy?"
   "Which fruit was sweet?"
   "Which fruit was sour?"
9. Place the untouched pieces of fruit in the bowl. They can be enjoyed later as a fruit salad.

☀ Highlighting Development

A study shows that questioning is one effective method for teaching young children the meaning of words. Two groups of parents were compared. One group just read to their children and had the children listen. The other group of parents read the book and stopped after reading certain parts to ask "where" and "what" questions. When asked, the children responded with the targeted words. After the experience, the children who answered questions were more likely to reproduce the words contained in the story (Sénéchal, Thomas, & Monker, 1995; Kail, 1998). Therefore, when engaging in activities, ask questions to focus the children's attention and maintain their involvement.

VARIATIONS:

♡ Introduce new types of fruits such as kiwi or papaya.

♡ Cut vegetables for a salad and eat with lunch.

ADDITIONAL INFORMATION:

♡ Before making your selection, ensure that the child does not have an allergy to the fruit.

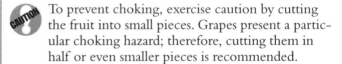 To prevent choking, exercise caution by cutting the fruit into small pieces. Grapes present a particular choking hazard; therefore, cutting them in half or even smaller pieces is recommended.

& COMM

Teapot"

Child's Developmental Goals

✓ To continue developing expressive language skills
✓ To act out a song using nonverbal communication

MATERIALS:

❑ Index card
❑ Felt-tip marker

PREPARATION:

♡ Write the song's words on the index card, if desired. The words are:

♫ I'm a little teapot
♫ Short and stout
♫ Here is my handle   (put hand on hip)
♫ Here is my spout.   (bend arm and hand
                              away from body)

♫ When I get all steamed up
♫ Hear me shout
♫ Just tip me over and
♫ Pour me out.   (lean over)

NURTURING STRATEGIES:

1. When a toddler needs something to do, invite the child to sing with you.
2. Introduce the activity to the toddler by saying, for example:
   "Brendan, I would like to teach you a new song. We can act it out while singing. Let's start with the motions."
3. Model each movement in sequence. Connect your actions with words by describing each movement. State, for example:
   "Here is my handle."
   "Tip me over."

4. When the toddler successfully completes the movements, begin to sing the song and perform the movements.
5. Sing the song slowly to encourage the toddler's participation.
6. Providing positive reinforcement may result in the child practicing the behaviors. To illustrate, say:
   "You're singing along with me. You know the words."
   "Brendan, you are acting like a teapot."
7. Repeat the song as long as the toddler appears interested.

☼ Highlighting Development

Children, like adults, communicate the majority of their messages nonverbally. Watch them. Toddlers will gesture while babbling or engaging in telegraphic speech. Music is another important form of communication. Use it to provide a background for playing. It can help enhance the child's expression of feelings. Furthermore, it can help the child build vocabulary, release pent-up feelings, and relax.

VARIATION:

♡ Tape the song using a cassette recorder and replay it for the child.

ADDITIONAL INFORMATION:

♡ Music experiences are beneficial to young children. Make music a natural part of daily experiences. As children participate in music, language skills build.

Match

& COMM

MATERIALS:

❑ Poster board

❑ Glue

❑ Magazines

❑ Black construction paper

❑ Scissors

❑ Clear adhesive paper

PREPARATION:

♡ Cut out pictures of animals from magazines. Trace around each animal on the black construction paper and cut out the shapes. Using glue, adhere the black animal shapes to the poster board. Then cover the poster board with clear adhesive paper. Finally, cover each of the individual animal pictures with adhesive paper and trim the excess.

♡ Clear a spot on the floor and lay out the poster board and animal pictures.

NURTURING STRATEGIES:

1. When a toddler selects the activity, provide time for exploring the materials. During this process, observe the child's behavior.

2. If necessary, introduce the activity using comments such as:
   "Krista, match the shapes. Which shape on the board looks like a bird?"

3. Ask the toddler to verbally label the animals by asking:
   "What animal is this?"

4. Assist the toddler with matching by describing the shapes:
   "This animal has four legs and a long tail. Look for a black shape with a long tail."

5. Provide positive reinforcement when a child makes a match. Smiling and clapping are ways to non-verbally reinforce the toddler. Verbally reinforce the child by saying, for example:
   "Krista, you did it! You matched the cow."

6. Encourage the toddler to converse about the animals. Questions to ask might include:
   "What do kittens drink?"
   "What do dogs like to eat?"

☀ Highlighting Development

Toddlers need a rich, stimulating environment to promote their cognitive, social, emotional, language, and physical development. Observe them. Staring is one of their most time-consuming activities. Take advantage of these opportunities for promoting language skills. Labeling and describing what they are looking at will develop their vocabulary.

VARIATION:

♡ Create shadow matches for different shapes such as eating utensils, forms of transportation, toys, etc.

ADDITIONAL INFORMATION:

♡ Choose animals that are familiar and often seen in the children's environment. This will increase the chances of the toddlers having the necessary language skills to successfully label the animals.

19 to 24 months

& COMM

Developmental Goals

✓ To act like animals

✓ To make animal sounds

MATERIALS:
- ❑ Headbands
- ❑ Brown paper
- ❑ Scissors
- ❑ Stapler or glue

PREPARATION:
- ♡ Cut "ears" from the brown paper and attach them to the headbands.
- ♡ Clear a large space on the floor to allow plenty of room for movement.

NURTURING STRATEGIES:
1. Gather the toddlers and introduce the activity by saying:
   "We are going to pretend to be dogs. What noise do dogs make?"
2. Converse with the toddlers about dogs. Talk about things such as how dogs look, feel, and act.
3. Put a pair of ears on your head. Then hand the children a pair of ears. Help put them on, if necessary.
4. Model acting like a dog. For example, crawl on the floor and bark.

5. Comment on the children's behavior. Comments include:
   "Shane, you're a fast-moving dog."
   "What a loud bark."
6. Provide positive reinforcement for acting and sounding like dogs. To illustrate, say:
   "You are barking like dogs."
   "Look at all the dogs moving on the carpet."

☀ Highlighting Development

Engaging in creative drama fosters the development of cognitive, imaginative, and language skills. Moreover, imitating animals in this activity involves the production of sounds, resulting in the children exercising and strengthening muscles in the tongue, mouth, and vocal chords.

VARIATION:
- ♡ Act like different animals such as a cow, pig, elephant, cat, pony, or monkey.

ADDITIONAL INFORMATION:
- ♡ When acting like animals, be sure to crawl on the floor.
- ♡ Children this age need props to help them pretend; hence, the ears will contribute to the success of this activity.

Child's Developmental Goals

✔ To continue increasing vocabulary skills

✔ To practice expressive language skills

MATERIALS:

❑ Duct tape

❑ Several large cardboard boxes

PREPARATION:

♡ Tape the boxes together to make a tunnel. Select and clear an area that can be easily supervised. Place the tunnel in the cleared area.

NURTURING STRATEGIES:

1. When a child chooses the activity, position your body to supervise the area. To view the child inside the tunnel, you will need to sit on the floor at one end.

2. Set limits to protect the safety of the child. For example, if a toddler is climbing on the outside of the boxes, tell the child to crawl inside the tunnel.

3. It may be necessary to reinforce your words with actions. If this occurs, pat the inside of the box while repeating,
   "Crawl inside the tunnel."

4. Use other children, if present, as models of appropriate behavior by saying:
   "Look at Tovah. She is crawling inside the tunnel."

5. Describe the child's behavior in and around the tunnel, focusing on three words: inside, outside, through. To illustrate, say:
   "You are crawling outside the tunnel."
   "Tovah crawled through the tunnel."

6. Converse with the toddler about the experience or about pretending during the experience. Ask, for example:
   "What did you see inside the tunnel?"

7. Providing positive reinforcement may result in the toddlers increasing the time engaged in the activity. Comments include:
   "You crawled through the tunnel with a friend."
   "You are crawling slowly. It took you a lot of time to crawl through the tunnel."

☼ Highlighting Development

The relationship between understanding and producing language is asymmetrical. By 24 months, toddlers typically understand approximately 300 words. In comparison, they can produce approximately 250 words. In the beginning, there is a five-month lag between comprehension and production. However, "fast mapping" virtually eliminates this time lag. With maturity, the child is able to connect a new word with an existing concept after a brief encounter (Berk, 1997; Santrock, 1993).

VARIATION:

♡ Create other obstacles for the toddler to move around and through. Use a clothesline, blanket, and clothespins to create a tent.

ADDITIONAL INFORMATION:

♡ The best way to introduce new vocabulary words is to create experiences and then describe the children's behavior. In other words, children more easily learn words that reflect or describe their lives.

♡ When using children as models, equally distribute your attention. Children can recognize adults' preferences at very young ages.

19 to 24 months

& COMM

Story Quilt

MATERIALS:

❑ Quilt

❑ Container such as a crate, box, bag, or basket

❑ 6 to 8 books for toddlers; see Appendix A for a list of toddler books.

PREPARATION:

♡ Spread out the quilt in an open area. Lay the books on the quilt. Keep the container nearby for easily storing the books and quilt when finished.

NURTURING STRATEGIES:

1. Observe the toddler's behavior after choosing the activity.
2. Avoid interrupting the toddler while reading. However, when the toddler is finished reading, ask questions about the book. Questions to ask include:
   "Who was in the story you read?"
   "What was the story about?"
3. Encourage the toddler to read another story independently. But, if asked, read a story to the toddler.
4. If you notice that a toddler is becoming very excited and needs to relax or calm down, direct the child to the quilt.
5. Encourage the toddler to pick out a book for you to read. Sit on the quilt beside the toddler. Use your body and voice as tools for calming the toddler while reading the story.
6. Converse about the book during and after reading it.
7. Suggest that the toddler select another book to read. Excuse yourself and allow the child to read independently.

☀ Highlighting Development

Early experiences have an influence on children's literacy development. Children who are read to during the early years typically enjoy higher levels of success in learning to read than their peers who have not had these experiences. Evidence suggests that hearing and responding to stories read from books is probably the most important literacy experience for children. However, the importance of talking and conversing should not be overlooked (Rice, 1997).

VARIATION:

♡ Set up a story area inside a tent or tepee.

ADDITIONAL INFORMATION:

♡ You may need to set limits for using books while outdoors. For example, to prolong the life of the books, they must stay on the quilt.

Cognitive Development

♡

NINETEEN to TWENTY-FOUR MONTHS

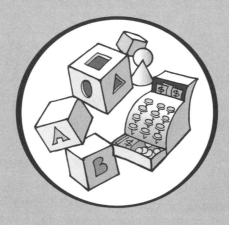

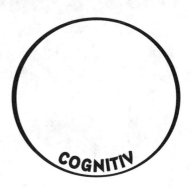

COGNITIV

Child's Developmental Goals

✓ To match similar objects

✓ To discriminate between objects visually

MATERIALS:

❑ 6 pairs of different-colored socks such as white, red, and black

❑ Basket to hold socks

PREPARATION:

♡ Mix up the socks. Place the socks in the basket. Then set the basket on a table or place it on the floor where it is easily accessible to the child.

NURTURING STRATEGIES:

1. When a toddler selects the activity, observe the child's behavior. Note how the toddler is exploring or arranging the socks.

2. Comment on the child's behavior. Comments to make include:
   "Benito, you put the two green socks close together."
   "You're sorting the socks."

3. Use your knowledge of the child's skills to guide your behavior. If, for example, the toddler can correctly label some colors, point to a sock and ask:
   "What color is this sock?"
   If the child has not begun to label by colors, introduce them. Begin by labeling the color of the sock the child is touching or manipulating. Say, for example:
   "Benito, you are touching a black sock."
   "You have two socks in your hand. This one is brown and this one is green."

4. Encourage the toddler to match the socks by color. While holding up a sock, make comments such as:
   "Let's match up the socks. Find the other sock that looks like this."

5. Provide positive reinforcement when a match is made. Clapping or smiling indicates you are proud of the toddler's accomplishments. Additionally, you could say:
   "Benito, you made a match. Both socks are red."
   "You're fast at finding matches!"

6. If the toddler desires, mix up the socks and begin again.

☀ Highlighting Development

At this stage, children become more actively involved in developing classification skills by physically grouping objects into classes or categories based on one attribute: color, size, shape, function, or pattern. One form of classification is matching. This process involves putting together like objects. Toddlers are capable of simple matching activities. That is, they can put two identical objects together such as the socks in this activity (Herr, 1998).

VARIATION:

♡ Sort baby shoes, scarves, or shirts.

ADDITIONAL INFORMATION:

♡ Whenever possible, elicit the child's assistance when sorting laundry, nonbreakable dishes, groceries, blocks, etc.

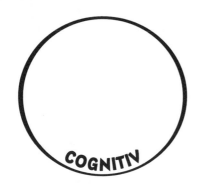

COGNITIV

Child's Developmental Goals

✓ To observe and discuss transformations.

MATERIALS:

❑ Several plastic containers of varying sizes
❑ Water
❑ Water table or a minimum of two quilt boxes
❑ Smocks

PREPARATION:

♡ Fill each container with water and freeze to make large ice cubes.
♡ Lay towels on the floor to prevent slipping in splashed water.
♡ Sanitize water table and move to desired location. Fill with 2 to 3 inches of water.
♡ Remove ice from container when ready to use (this may require cutting the plastic) and place it in the water table.
♡ If working in a child care center, you may want to place a Hand Washing sign on the table. This serves as a visual reminder to encourage hand washing before the beginning of the activity.

NURTURING STRATEGIES:

1. Assist the toddler, as necessary, with washing hands.
2. As the toddler is putting on her smock, discuss the experience. To illustrate, say:
   "There are large blocks of something in the water. Can you guess what they are?"
   Pause to allow answer/discussion.
3. Encourage the toddler to test her hypothesis. Use comments such as:
   "Touch them, Bailey, and see if they are hard."
   "I don't know. Move them around to see if they roll like a ball."

4. When necessary, set limits on behavior. For example say:
   "Splash gently so the water stays on the table."
   "Use the towel to clean up the spill so no one slips and falls."
5. Encourage the toddler to talk about what is happening to the blocks of ice. During the discussion, introduce vocabulary words such as *melting, solid, liquid, changing,* and/or *transforming.* Connect with child's past experience whenever possible.

☀ Highlighting Development

Toddlers, like preschoolers, focus on beginning and ending states and tend to ignore any transformations in between (Berk, 1999). Furthermore, they often treat the initial and final states as unrelated. Providing toddlers with the opportunity to manipulate, observe, and discuss transformations assists them in reaching a higher level of understanding.

VARIATIONS:

♡ Add food coloring to the water before freezing.
♡ Do this activity outdoors on a warm day.
♡ Add small toys, such as a car or a golf ball, to the water before freezing.

ADDITIONAL INFORMATION:

♡ Most children are delighted with experiences related to water. It is a satisfying medium for young children that can promote the development of many science concepts. Through water play children learn that water makes objects wet, it takes many forms, and it can be held in a container.

CAUTION Using large chunks of ice is safer than using small ice cubes for very young children.

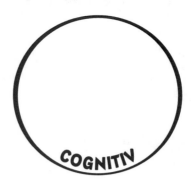

COGNITIV

Child's Developmental Goals

✓ To find similar colors in the environment

✓ To discriminate between objects visually

MATERIALS:

None

PREPARATION:

None

NURTURING STRATEGIES:

1. Invite a toddler who needs an activity to play this game with you. To illustrate, say:
   "Dan, let's play a game. It is a color matching game. I'll point to something. You then point to something different that is the same color. Here we go."

2. Point to an object in the room and verbally describe it, emphasizing the color. For example, say:
   "Dan, this is a yellow apple."

3. Remind the toddler of his part of the game by stating:
   "Now you look around the room. Find something else that is yellow."

4. Provide positive reinforcement when the toddler identifies another object of the same color. Comments might include:
   "The bus is yellow. Good match!"
   "You found a yellow plate. Good eye!"

5. Support and give encouragement to a toddler who is having difficulty finding a similar color. Use comments such as:
   "Blue is a hard color to find; keep looking."
   "Would you like to carry the red crayon to match to other items?"
   "Have you looked at the books?"

6. Repeat the game as long as the toddler is interested.

☀ Highlighting Development

Color matching is considered a mathematical activity. These experiences help children develop cognitively by refining their discrimination skills. Color matching experiences also help promote language development—children are generating a visual image with a name.

VARIATION:

♡ Provide the child with a piece of colored paper for matching.

ADDITIONAL INFORMATION:

♡ Use color searching to follow up after reading a story. Color searching can be practiced anywhere. It can be done while walking outside or waiting for your food in a restaurant.

♡ When playing this game, choose the color of your object carefully. Avoid shades of colors that would be difficult to match easily.

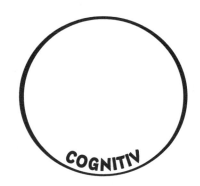

COGNITIV

Child's Developmental Goals

✓ To follow simple directions

✓ To observe and discuss transformations

MATERIALS:

- ❑ 1 English muffin per person
- ❑ 1 jar of pizza sauce
- ❑ 1 bag of shredded mozzarella cheese
- ❑ ¼-cup measuring cup
- ❑ Metal or plastic mixing bowls
- ❑ Plates
- ❑ Napkins
- ❑ Masking tape
- ❑ Felt-tip markers
- ❑ Tagboard
- ❑ Toaster oven

PREPARATION:

♡ If desired, prepare a recipe board that uses pictures as well as words to outline step-by-step directions for making a pizza. Hang the recipe board in the area that you will be using to prepare the pizza.

♡ Plug in the toaster oven.

♡ Pour the pizza sauce into one of the mixing bowls and the cheese in the other. Put the ¼-cup measuring cup in the cheese. Gather all equipment and ingredients, including bowls, spoons, plates, English muffins, cheese, and napkins. Place them in the area that you will be working.

NURTURING STRATEGIES:

1. Assist the toddler, as necessary, with washing hands.
2. While pointing to the recipe board, introduce the activity by saying:
   "We are going to make pizzas for our snack. The recipe or directions are right here. What do you like on your pizza?"
3. Explain to the toddler how to make the pizza as you work. Refer to the recipe board as needed.
4. Discuss how the English muffins, pizza sauce, and cheese taste by themselves. Speculate on how they might taste together.
5. As you put on the cheese, describe what it looks like. Talk about what happens to cheese when it is heated. Introduce and explain the word *melts*.

6. When it is time to bake the pizza, set any limits related to the toaster oven. Comments include:
   "The oven is hot. Stand near this end of the table."
   "The oven could burn you. Sit in your chair."
7. Allow the pizzas to cool slightly before eating.
8. While eating the snack, discuss how the pizzas were made, how they taste, and how they look now. Do so by asking questions such as:
   "How did you make your pizza?"
   "What does the cheese look like now?"
   "What else could we put on our pizza?"

☀ Highlighting Development

Toddlers discover and learn through concrete, hands-on experiences. To do this, they need to be provided a rich environment with opportunities for examining, exploring, manipulating, and experimenting with objects. Hence, cooking activities are a method for facilitating toddlers' cognitive growth.

Toddlers, like preschoolers, fail to recognize transformations. They treat the initial and final states as completely unrelated, ignoring the dynamic transformation between them (Berk, 1997). Therefore, observing and discussing the transformation will help their cognitive and language development.

VARIATION:

♡ Prepare one large pizza for everyone to share.

 Use extreme caution once the toaster oven becomes hot. Never leaving it unattended as well as setting and following through on limits may prevent accidents. If necessary, have the child turn the chair with the back facing the heat source. Sitting on the chair in this position may prevent the child from reaching forward and possibly touching a hot appliance.

 For safety purposes, avoid using an extension cord, if possible. If that isn't possible, tape the extension cord to the floor to reduce the possibility of tripping.

Match

COGNITIV

Child's Developmental Goals

✓ To discriminate between objects visually

✓ To identify people in photographs

MATERIALS:

❑ Camera

❑ Tagboard

❑ Glue or tape

❑ Scissors

❑ Basket

PREPARATION:

♡ Take pictures of the toddlers working independently. When developing the film, request double prints.

♡ Cut the tagboard slightly larger than the pictures. Adhere one picture to each piece of tagboard by gluing or taping. Place sets of pictures in a basket and put it on a child-size table.

NURTURING STRATEGIES:

1. When a child selects the activity, observe the toddler's behavior.

2. If necessary, introduce the activity. To illustrate, say: *"Look at these pictures of us. Match the pictures that are alike."*

3. Providing verbal assistance may help the toddler to match the photographs. Comments include: *"Tamara, here you are wearing a red shirt. Look for a red shirt."* *"Look for another picture with lots of books."*

4. Encourage the toddler to identify other people in the photographs. Questions to ask include: *"Who is in this picture?"* *"Where is the picture of Noel?"*

5. Provide support and encouragement when a toddler is having difficulty finding a particular picture. Make comments such as: *"Keep looking. You're working hard."* *"Who is that? What are they doing in this picture?"*

6. Reinforce the toddler when he makes a match. To illustrate, say: *"Tamara, those two pictures are identical!"* *"You found two pictures that match."*

7. Encourage the toddler to continue playing the game independently. Check on the child periodically to provide support, encouragement, or reinforcement as necessary.

☀ Highlighting Development

The toddlers' ability to remember, although not efficient, continues to improve. Toddlers are able to recognize family members in photographs before they are able to recognize themselves. However, by age two, recognition of the self is well established (Berk, 1997). To facilitate the toddlers' recognition, provide mirrors and photographs.

VARIATION:

♡ If in a classroom setting, ask the parents or guardians for duplicate photographs of their family. Repeat the activity by matching the family photos.

ADDITIONAL INFORMATION:

♡ Toddlers delight in seeing themselves in photographs. Therefore, they probably will want to repeat the activity several times. Furthermore, they may want to carry their photographs for looking at and sharing with others.

19 to 24 months

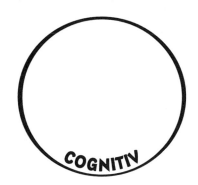

COGNITIV

Child's Developmental Goals

✔ To classify objects by color

✔ To discriminate between objects visually

MATERIALS:

☐ 1½ dozen egg carton

☐ 12 plastic milk jug lids, 6 of one color and 6 of another

PREPARATION:

♡ Place the lids in an egg carton. After this, set the carton in an easily accessible location.

NURTURING STRATEGIES:

1. When a child chooses the activity, observe the child's behavior.

2. Ask the toddler how the lids are being grouped. For example, you may comment by saying:
   "Tell me about the lids. How do you decide where to put them?"

3. If the child is using the lids in a different way, allow the toddler time to explore. After that, talk about the lids. Discuss, for example, the color of the lids. Comments include:
   "Chen, I see two colors of lids: red and green."
   "I see red lids and I see green lids."

4. If necessary, encourage the toddler to continue sorting the lids by asking:
   "How can you group the lids?"

5. Provide positive reinforcement for sorting the lids by color. Make comments such as:
   "Chen, you've sorted the lids by color."
   "I see two groups of lids: one group is red and the other group is green."

☀ Highlighting Development

Toddlers typically are able to follow simple directions, classify objects by color, and discriminate between objects visually. Notice how hard toddlers concentrate when playing. Likewise, notice how the children keep you informed of your role. For example, while sorting lids, a child may reverse the roles, assuming a leadership role by showing or telling you what to do. Reinforce the behavior by following the child's lead.

VARIATION:

♡ Sort objects, such as cars and airplanes, by color.

 Sometimes toddlers continue exploring their world orally. Therefore, it is necessary to verify that the objects you provide are not choking hazards.

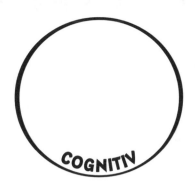

COGNITIV

Child's Developmental Goals

✔ To connect parts to make a whole

✔ To match pictures

MATERIALS:

❑ 4 to 6 magazine or catalog pictures with a related theme such as animals, vehicles, or clothing

❑ Self-adhesive paper

❑ Tagboard or heavy cardboard

❑ Scissors

PREPARATION:

♡ Cut pictures from magazines or catalogs and mount them on tagboard or heavy cardboard. Then cover them with self-adhesive paper. Cut each picture in half.

♡ Shuffle the pictures and lay them out on a child-size table.

NURTURING STRATEGIES:

1. Invite a toddler to the table and point out the pictures. Introduce the activity by saying, for example:
   "Noelle, help me put these pictures together."

2. Observe the child working with the puzzle pieces.

3. Providing encouragement and support while the toddler is working may result in longer participation. Comments include:
   "Noelle, keep going. You've matched two pictures."
   "That is almost a match. Both of the animals are black, but they look different. Look for a long tail."

4. Assist the toddler as necessary with completing the puzzles. Comments to make include:
   "Here is a dog's head. Let's find a picture with a dog's tail."
   "This animal is brown. Look for a picture with brown in it."

5. Provide positive reinforcement when the toddler completes a puzzle. Clapping or smiling may reinforce the desired behavior. In addition, examples of verbal reinforcement include:
   "You did it! You put together all of the puzzles."
   "Noelle, what a hard worker. You've completed three puzzles."

6. Mix up the pictures and begin the experience again if the toddler shows interest.

☀ Highlighting Development

By the end of the second year of life, toddlers have made many cognitive advances. While playing now, children are able to draw on information already learned. To illustrate, body parts, objects, and familiar people can be recognized. Likewise, when the objects are named, children are able to point to them. Hence, the picture puzzle and other related puzzle activities will promote problem-solving skills.

VARIATION:

♡ Use store-bought puzzles with knobs.

ADDITIONAL INFORMATION:

♡ Mounting the pictures on tagboard makes them easier for the toddler to grasp and pick up.

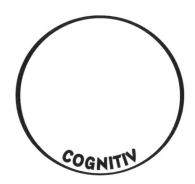

COGNITIV

Basket?

Child's Developmental Goals

✓ To refine object permanence skills

✓ To develop auditory memory skills by remembering and identifying a missing object

MATERIALS:

❏ Tightly woven basket

❏ 3 favorite identically colored objects that fit in the basket

PREPARATION:

♡ Place the three objects inside the basket. Then place the basket out of the child's reach.

NURTURING STRATEGIES:

1. When a toddler needs a new activity, get the basket and invite the child to play a game with you.
2. Introduce the activity to the toddler by saying: *"Look. I have three things here: a ball, a car, and a block. All of these are colored red. I'm going to hide one of them under the basket. Then you can guess which one is missing."*
3. Instruct the toddler that eyes need to be closed while you hide one item under the basket.
4. Ask the toddler to open his eyes and guess the missing item.

5. Provide support and reinforcement for guesses. Comments include:
   "The red ball is right here. What else could be in the basket?"
   "Good guessing! The red block was in the basket."
6. Continue the game as long as the toddler seems interested. Changing the objects being hidden may sustain the toddler's interest in the game.

☀ Highlighting Development

Children love the game of hide-and-seek. At this stage, they will remember where items are hidden. In fact, they may even want to reverse roles. They will hide the item and have you look for it.

VARIATION:

♡ Increase the challenge by placing one item inside the basket and keeping the other items out of sight. Provide hints, if necessary, to help the toddler guess which item is under the basket.

ADDITIONAL INFORMATION:

♡ Reinforce the child's efforts as well as accomplishments.

Making Play Dough

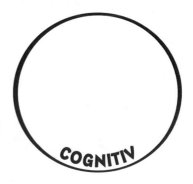

COGNITIV

Child's Developmental Goals

✔ To observe transformations

✔ To discuss similarities and differences

MATERIALS:

❏ Play dough recipe

❏ Supplies for recipe

❏ High chair or child-size table

PREPARATION:

♡ Choose a noncooked play dough recipe from the list located in Appendix I. Then gather the necessary supplies. For this age group, it is preferable to premix the dry and liquid ingredients in separate containers so that the toddler mixes only two things together.

NURTURING STRATEGIES:

1. Assist the toddler, if necessary, in hand washing.
2. Sit the toddler in the high chair, securing the safety straps.
3. Introduce the activity. To illustrate, say: *"Ginger, today we're going to make play dough. You can help. You can mix the play dough."*
4. Discuss and elaborate on the toddler's responses.
5. Pour the dry ingredients onto the toddler's tray. Encourage the child to explore the ingredients using her fingers.
6. Introduce and reinforce the appropriate vocabulary words such as *bumpy, gritty,* and *dry.*
7. Pour the wet ingredients onto a corner of the tray. Again, encourage the toddler to explore the wet substances with her fingers.

8. Introduce and reinforce vocabulary words such as *wet, oily,* and *smooth.*
9. Suggest mixing the substances together. Discuss what happens to the dry ingredients when liquid is added. In addition, talk about how the dough now feels and looks.
10. Encourage the toddler to continue exploring the dough once it is mixed.

☀ Highlighting Development

Most children enjoy using play dough, which is material that can be formed, molded, and reshaped. They enjoy the tactile appeal and the response to touch. Typical behaviors include pushing, pulling, squeezing, and rolling. Observe them during this process. When they are ready, provide them with tools such as small rolling pins and cookie cutters to use with the play dough.

VARIATION:

♡ If more than one child is present, encourage the children to work together to prepare one recipe of play dough.

ADDITIONAL INFORMATION:

♡ Play dough typically is a messy activity. Control the mess by placing the high chair on a vinyl tablecloth and having damp towels available to wash the child's hands.

19 to 24 months

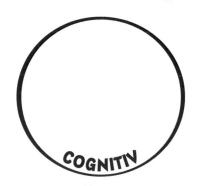

COGNITIV

Child's Developmental Goals

✓ To use sensory stimulation to distinguish between objects by texture

✓ To compare and contrast objects

MATERIALS:

☐ Pita bread
☐ Yeast rolls
☐ Bagels
☐ Italian bread
☐ Cutting board and knife
☐ Napkins
☐ Cups
☐ Pitcher of milk or juice

PREPARATION:

♡ Clean and sanitize a child-size table. Gather the snack ingredients and place them on the tray.

NURTURING STRATEGIES:

1. Encourage the child to engage in hand washing. If necessary, provide assistance.
2. Carry the supplies to the table and ask the child to sit down.
3. Show the child one type of bread. Verbally label it and elicit descriptions by asking, for example:
   "What is this?"
   "What does this look like?"

4. Discuss the size, shape, and color of the bread.
5. Cut the bread and encourage the child to taste it.
6. Converse about how the bread feels and tastes.
7. Choose another type of bread and repeat steps 3 through 6.
8. Compare and contrast how the bread feels and tastes.
9. Continue with the rest of the breads.
10. Provide positive reinforcement for comparing and contrasting the breads. Comments to make include:
    "Yes, Lamar. The bagel and Italian bread are both chewy."
    "Good observation! The pita bread and yeast rolls both have holes."

☀ Highlighting Development

Tasting experiences are important because young children learn through their senses—feeling, smelling, seeing, hearing, and tasting. By observing and tasting the breads, children learn the color, texture, smell, feel, and taste of each. Moreover, you can assist in the development of cognitive skills such as comparing and contrasting by asking questions.

VARIATION:

♡ Make bread in a bread machine.
♡ Introduce other types of bread such as tortillas, waffles, pancakes, and crepes.

 Safety always comes first. As a result, set limits for using the knife.

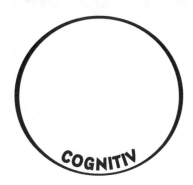

Child's Developmental Goals

✓ To make a secondary color by mixing two primary colors

✓ To observe transformations

MATERIALS:

❑ Recipe for Rainbow Stew; see Appendix I for a list of recipes

❑ Red and blue food coloring

❑ Tray

❑ Resealable plastic bags

❑ Supplies and equipment needed to prepare the stew

PREPARATION:

♡ Prepare the Rainbow Stew. Allow it to cool to room temperature and then spoon it into the plastic bags. Place bags and food coloring onto a tray.

♡ Clean a child-size table and place the tray in the center.

NURTURING STRATEGIES:

1. When the child shows interest in the activity, move to the table.

2. Explain the experience by saying, for example:
   "This bag is for mixing colors. I'm going to put in blue and red food coloring. Help me. Hold the bag while I put in the food coloring."

3. Drop the food coloring into different sides of the bag.

4. Remove as much air from the bag as possible and seal it.

5. Encourage the toddler to talk about what is happening to the Rainbow Stew. Discuss, for example, the movement of the colors in the bag.

6. When a third color emerges, act surprised and say, for example:
   "What happened here? We added the colors red and blue. Look, now I see purple. What happened?"

7. Converse with the toddler about the transformation.

☼ Highlighting Development

Color is all around young children. Children can describe their world through naming colors. Many children by the age of two can also match a color to a sample. One approach for teaching children color concepts is to mix colors. Mix two primary colors to create a secondary color.

VARIATION:

♡ For an outdoor activity, place the Rainbow Stew in a wash tub or quilt box. Add food coloring and encourage mixing.

 Many toddlers continue exploring their world through their mouths. All of the materials used to make the Rainbow Stew, as well as the food coloring, are nontoxic. However, consuming large quantities may cause an upset stomach. Therefore, close supervision is recommended.

19 to 24 months

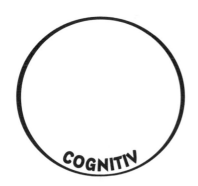

COGNITIV

MATERIALS:

❑ Bath towels

❑ Plastic container

❑ Basket

❑ Items to put in water such as cork, fishing bobber, wood, boat, plastic car, golf ball

❑ Smocks

PREPARATION:

♡ Clear off a child-size table. Spread out one towel and set the plastic container on it. Fill the container with 1 to 2 inches of water.

♡ Place the sink and float items in the basket. Then place the basket beside the container of water on the table. Lay the smocks on the corner of the table.

♡ Keep other towels handy in case of spills.

NURTURING STRATEGIES:

1. When a toddler selects the activity, move closer and observe the child's behavior. Note how the toddler is interacting with the available materials.

2. Discuss the items the toddler has placed in the water. Point out items that are floating and those that are sinking to the bottom. To illustrate, say:
   "The cork and wood pieces are floating on top of the water. See how they stay on top? But look at the car. It sank to the bottom."

3. When the toddler picks up another item from the basket, ask the child if the item will sink or float. Use comments such as:
   "Katrina, do you think the golf ball will sink or float?"
   "What will happen to the boat when it's put in the water? Will it sink or float?"

4. Repeat the toddler's guess and then encourage the child to test the hypothesis.

5. Provide support and reinforcement when the results are discovered. State, for example:
   "Look. The ball sank. You thought it would."
   "The boat floated. It stayed on top of the water."

6. Encourage the toddler to create and test hypotheses for the remaining items.

☼ Highlighting Development

Children at this age are anxious to explore their world using a hands-on approach. By exploring, they construct knowledge. Provide them a stimulating environment containing hands-on materials. When playing with the materials, they will observe and solve problems. Hence, complex science concepts can be introduced through simple activities such as Sink or Float.

VARIATION:

♡ Provide large rocks and boats in the water table. Discuss why some objects sink and others float.

ADDITIONAL INFORMATION:

♡ If the toddlers are more interested in just playing in the water, encourage this behavior by removing the sink and float items.

and Bolts

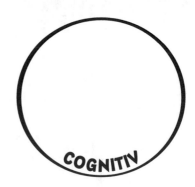

COGNITIV

Child's Developmental Goals

✓ To differentiate sizes
✓ To match objects

MATERIALS:

❑ 6 different sizes of plastic, color-coded nuts and bolts
❑ Basket

PREPARATION:

♡ Place the nuts and bolts in the basket and put it on a child-size shelf.

NURTURING STRATEGIES:

1. When a toddler selects the activity, observe the child's behavior.
2. If necessary, introduce the activity by saying and pointing to each:
   "Roberto, there is one nut for each bolt. See if you can match them up."
3. Providing verbal assistance may reduce the toddler's frustration with the activity. Comments include:
   "The bolt in your hand is very big. Let's look for the biggest nut and try it."
4. If necessary, assist the toddler with placing the nut on the bolt.
5. Encourage the toddler to match up all of the nuts and bolts.

6. Provide positive reinforcement for attempts and accomplishments. Make comments such as:
   "Roberto, you're working so hard at matching the nuts and bolts."
   "Two more matches to go. You've almost matched them all!"

☀ Highlighting Development

Even at this stage, children are learning math concepts. Math can be defined as the science of shapes and numbers. Children can learn shapes by playing with the color-coded plastic nuts and bolts. They also can practice sorting by colors while using these materials.

VARIATIONS:

♡ When developmentally ready, provide appropriate-size wrenches for working with the nuts and bolts.
♡ To focus on fine motor skills, provide nuts and bolts of the same size.

ADDITIONAL INFORMATION:

♡ Modify your interactional style to meet the individual needs of the toddlers. For example, one toddler may desire your physical presence only, while another toddler may desire verbal assistance as well.
♡ Supervise the activity to ensure that the child uses the nuts and bolts as intended.

19 to 24 months

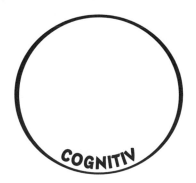

COGNITIV

It Under?

MATERIALS:

☐ 3 cans of different sizes

☐ 1 toy that will easily fit inside the smallest can but large enough not to be considered a choking hazard

☐ Masking tape

PREPARATION:

♡ Cover any sharp edges on the cans with masking tape. If desired, decorate the outside of the cans with self-adhesive paper, wrapping, or construction paper.

♡ Clear an area on a child-size table and place the cans there.

♡ Hide the toy under one can.

NURTURING STRATEGIES:

1. When the toddler selects the activity, ask:
   "Sioux, what are these cans for?"

2. Converse with the toddler about the purpose of the cans. While talking, lift up each can. Act surprised when the toy is uncovered as this may pique the child's interest.

3. Show the toddler what container you're hiding the toy under and then shuffle the cans.

4. Have the toddler guess which can the toy is under.

5. Provide support and reinforcement for guesses. Comments include:
   "Sioux, you found the toy. It was under the tall, skinny container."
   "Keep guessing. I know you'll find the toy."

6. Switch roles in the game by allowing the toddler to hide the toy, shuffle the cans, and have you guess where the toy is hidden.

☀ Highlighting Development

Between 18 and 24 months, growth spurts occur in cognitive development. This coincides with the increasing development of representational thought, memory, and language skills (Berk, 1997). Current research emphasizes the importance of a rich, supportive environment that promotes such development (Shore, 1997).

VARIATION:

♡ Hide two objects and have the toddler find a specific object to increase the challenge if the child is developmentally ready.

ADDITIONAL INFORMATION:

♡ When you switch roles, to promote the child's self-esteem, purposefully choose the container that does not contain the toy.

Social Development

NINETEEN to
TWENTY-FOUR MONTHS

Beanbag

SOCIAL

Child's Developmental Goals

✓ To interact with others

✓ To participate in a group game

MATERIALS:

❑ 2 to 3 identical beanbags

❑ Tape or compact disc player

❑ Musical cassette or compact disc

PREPARATION:

♡ Select an area that has an electrical outlet for this activity. Plug in the tape or compact disc player. Then fast forward or rewind the tape to obtain the desired song.

♡ Place the beanbags on the floor in the selected area.

NURTURING STRATEGIES:

1. When a toddler selects the beanbags, discuss their purpose. Ask for example:
   "Andrew, what are these beanbags for?"
   "What can we do with these?"

2. Providing positive reinforcement may encourage more creative responses or divergent thinking. Comments include:
   "Good idea. I didn't think about taking them shopping."
   "Wow! You thought of four things to do with the beanbags."

3. If a child suggested the activity of passing the beanbag around, say:
   "Let's play what Andrew suggested. Let's pass the beanbag to each other."

4. Encourage and give suggestions for playing the game. Ask, for example, if the game should be played while standing up or sitting down.

5. Pass the beanbag back and forth to the child.

6. If available, invite other children to join in the game.

7. After the beanbag has been passed, suggest playing the game to music. Say, for example:
   "Let's turn on some music while we pass the beanbag."

8. Begin the game again. When not holding a beanbag, clap or dance to the beat of the music to express your enjoyment of the music.

9. Continue as long as the toddlers seem interested.

☀ Highlighting Development

During infancy, peer sociability begins emerging. In infancy, early social gestures are followed by peer-directed smiles and vocalizations. By two years of age, however, children are beginning to develop preferences for particular people and, as a result, seek them out (Spodek, 1993).

VARIATIONS:

♡ Use other items to pass such as a hand-size stuffed toy, block, or car.

♡ Play "freeze" while passing the beanbag to music.

ADDITIONAL INFORMATION:

♡ If working with more than one child, promote everyone's self-esteem by ensuring all children have an equal opportunity to participate.

 To promote safety, place the tape player out of the children's reach.

19 to 24 months

SOCIAL

Spray Art

Child's Developmental Goals

✓ To participate in a group project

✓ To interact with others

MATERIALS:

☐ Large piece of white butcher paper

☐ Masking tape

☐ 4 small spray bottles set to a fine stream

☐ Food coloring and water

PREPARATION:

♡ Adhere the butcher paper to a fence or wall with the masking tape.

♡ Prepare the spray bottle by filling it half full with water and adding several drops of food coloring. Prepare two spray bottles with solutions of each color you choose. Adjusting the spray to a fine stream will prevent the paper from getting soggy.

NURTURING STRATEGIES:

1. When a child chooses the activity, introduce it. To illustrate, say:
   "This is a new way to make a picture. Squeeze the trigger while pointing at the paper. Colors will spray on the paper."

2. While speaking, reinforce your words with actions by showing the child how to squeeze the bottle. State limits positively and clearly. Say, for example:
   "Ada, spray the paper."

3. Describe the child's picture. Comments to make include:
   "You're using green."
   "You're spraying at the top of the page. Look, it is dripping down."

4. Restate limits when necessary. If the limit continues to be violated by a child, state a logical consequence for the behavior. State, for example:
   "Ada, spray on the paper. Otherwise, you will need to find another activity."
   Follow through with the consequence as necessary.

5. Providing positive reinforcement may result in the desired behavior being repeated. If several children are participating, comments might include:
   "Ada is spraying the paper to make a picture."
   "Squirt. Squirt. Squirt. Maria is squirting colors on the paper."

☀ Highlighting Development

Toddlers engage in solitary play—playing independently and alone—more than any other type of play. They also engage in parallel play such as the spray art activity. By observing them, you will note that they are engaged in the same activity but independently using the materials and equipment. To promote desirable social behaviors as well as minimize undesirable behaviors, adults need to provide duplicate materials.

VARIATION:

♡ If appropriate, repeat the activity during the winter by painting the snow with colored water.

ADDITIONAL INFORMATION:

♡ Children delight in spray art because they can see the immediate effect of their actions. Limits regarding spraying the paper must be consistently enforced. If limits are repeatedly violated, enact logical consequences such as taking the spray bottle away and finding a new activity.

Playground Picnic

SOCIAL

Child's Developmental Goals

✓ To engage in functional play

✓ To interact with an adult

MATERIALS:

❑ Blanket
❑ Picnic basket
❑ Stuffed animals
❑ Plastic plates and cups
❑ Assorted plastic food

PREPARATION:

♡ Select a flat area that is easy to supervise and spread out the blanket. Sit the stuffed animals on the blanket.

♡ Put the plates, cups, and food inside the picnic basket.

NURTURING STRATEGIES:

1. While preparing the children to go outside, show them the picnic basket. Ask, for example:
   "Tito, what is this for?"
2. Briefly discuss their answers. If necessary, state:
   "We're going to have a pretend picnic on the playground. Some friends are already waiting for us."
3. Enlist the help of the toddlers to carry out the picnic basket.
4. Encourage the toddlers to engage in functional play by asking questions such as:
   "Tito, what do people do on a picnic?"
   "What do people eat on a picnic?"
   "Do you think the bear is hungry?"
5. Verbally describe the children's actions. If more than one child is present, comments might include:
   "Tito, you're feeding the lion spaghetti."
   "Rosie, you stacked two pieces of bread together. You made a sandwich."

6. Whenever possible, focus on social interaction between the children. Discuss how two or more children are engaging in the same activity. Say, for example:
   "Tito and Rosie are feeding the animals."
   "There are four of us on a picnic right now."

☼ Highlighting Development

Toddlers are beginning to engage in functional play. They particularly enjoy imitating others' behaviors, which is part of their learning process. Watch. Their play behavior is changing. Previously, they may have played with a ring of keys by just shaking or manipulating them. Now they are beginning to use objects, such as the keys, for their intended use or function. To illustrate, now toddlers will try to insert the keys into a door lock or a pretend car.

VARIATION:

♡ Plan an indoor picnic on a rainy day by serving snack on a blanket.

ADDITIONAL INFORMATION:

♡ Functional play involves children using props for their intended purpose, such as feeding and dressing. As children continue developing socially and cognitively, their play begins involving toys such as dolls and animals. Therefore, you will want to have these props readily available.

⚠ Whenever pillows or blankets are used, constant supervision is necessary to prevent the possibility of suffocation.

SOCIAL

Child's Developmental Goals

✓ To participate in a small group activity

✓ To sing a song with others

MATERIALS:

❑ Stuffed animals or plastic figurines that you want to sing about

❑ Bag

PREPARATION:

♡ Place the animals in the bag. When you are ready to introduce the activity, move the bag to the area where you want the children to interact with you.

NURTURING STRATEGIES:

1. Gather the toddlers and introduce the activity by saying:
   "Let's sing a song about animals that live in a zoo. This is a new song, so I'm going to sing part of it to you."

2. Remove the first animal from the bag and sing:

   ♫ The lions in the zoo
   ♫ Go roar, roar, roar
   ♫ The lions in the zoo
   ♫ Go roar, roar, roar
   ♫ All around their home.

   Additional verses include: snakes—hiss; monkeys—hee; parrots—swack; gorillas—hoo; donkeys—hee haw; bears—growl.

3. Encourage each child to remove one animal from the bag at a time. While singing the verse related to the animal, the child can stand beside you.

4. Provide positive reinforcement to the children at the end of the song. To illustrate, say:
   "Thank you for helping to sing the song. You helped by selecting an animal from the bag. We worked together to sing this song."

5. Leave the bag and animals in a place where the toddlers can continue exploring and singing the song, if desired.

☀ Highlighting Development

At this stage, toddlers are aware of themselves as being separate from caregivers, parents, siblings, and peers. Toddlers frequently are referred to as being egocentric or self-centered. From their standpoint, everyone thinks like they do. As a result, toddlers have difficulty interacting with others. To promote healthy interactions between two or more children, model by sharing or taking turns.

VARIATIONS:

♡ Sing about farm animals or pets.
♡ Add actions to the song.

ADDITIONAL INFORMATION:

♡ Toddlers are constantly gaining independence. Encouraging them to participate in related activities will foster a sense of pride and self-worth as well as independence. This occurs because they are able to perform the task on their own.

SOCIAL

Child's Developmental Goals

✔ To explore the physical environment

✔ To hold a person's hand when walking

MATERIALS:

❑ Lunch-size paper bag for each child

❑ Felt-tip markers

❑ Field trip supplies such as tissues, first aid kit, and medical release form(s)

PREPARATION:

♡ Walk the route you will take to look for dangers. If possible, fix dangers; otherwise, alter your route as necessary.

♡ Write the child's name on a paper bag. If there is more than one child present, provide a bag for each.

♡ Gather all supplies needed for the field trip, including medical release form(s), a first aid kit, and tissues, and put them in one bag.

NURTURING STRATEGIES:

1. While transitioning to go outside, discuss the nature walk you will be taking. To illustrate, say: *"Today we are going to do something special. We are going to take a walk. We are going to a park with lots of trees. We need to hold hands."*

2. Assist the child in holding hands.

3. Begin walking. Conversing with the children may help improve their observation skills, especially when you are talking about things around them. Comments to make include:
"Mikko, what are you looking at?"
"Here comes a car. Look, it is red."
Focus on objects and people at the toddler's eye level.

4. Once you arrive at your destination, give each toddler a bag and explain its use. To illustrate, say: *"If you find something special that you want to keep, put it in your bag. We'll use these treasures tomorrow for art."*

5. Verbally label items being put into each bag, being as descriptive as possible. For example, say: *"What a shiny blue rock"* rather than *"You found a rock."*

6. On the trip back, talk about the objects observed or gathered.

7. If the children are tired of conversing, singing a favorite song may be effective.

☼ Highlighting Development

Because toddlers are curious by nature, they enjoy taking walks around their neighborhood. Watch them. They use their senses in an effort to understand their world.

VARIATION:

♡ Take a walk just to enjoy nature.

ADDITIONAL INFORMATION:

♡ As the toddlers fill their bags, encourage them to leave some items behind for others to enjoy.

♡ Follow up on your nature walk by using the items gathered in an art collage.

♡ Toddlers can tire easily, making the return trip challenging. Therefore, you may need to use strollers.

 Caution needs to be continuously exercised on walks. If toddlers observe some object or person that interests them, they typically lack judgment concerning safety hazards. Therefore, they need very careful supervision.

SOCIAL

Child's Developmental Goals

✓ To engage in imitating another's play
✓ To interact socially with a toy

MATERIALS:

❑ 2 stuffed animals
❑ Favorite books

PREPARATION:

♡ Place the books in an area that will attract the child's attention or display them neatly on a child-size shelf.
♡ Sit the stuffed animals on both sides of the books.

NURTURING STRATEGIES:

1. When a toddler chooses a book, observe the child's behavior.
2. If the child invites you to participate by handing you the book, read it.
3. While reading, move the stuffed animal closer or even on your lap. Reinforce your actions with words by saying, for example:
   "The teddy bear can't see the pictures. Teddy also wants to read the story."
4. When the story is completed, tell the toddler you must do something else and encourage reading another story. To illustrate, state:
   "I need to check the charts. Teddy still wants to read. What book are you going to read to your teddy bear?"

5. Periodically observe the toddler.
6. Provide positive reinforcement after the toddler finishes the activity. Use comments such as:
   "The teddy bear really enjoyed the story."
   "You read two stories."

☀ Highlighting Development

A growing tenderness toward toys will begin to emerge. Children at this stage of development often show a fondness for a particular stuffed toy, doll, etc. They will begin playing affectionately with it by hugging, smiling, and kissing it. When this occurs, it is a healthy sign. Children who have been properly nurtured have the capacity to demonstrate this behavior.

VARIATION:

♡ Encourage the toddler to look at books before napping.

ADDITIONAL INFORMATION:

♡ Reading to others serves to increase the toddlers' self-esteem and independence.
♡ Some toddlers enjoy having a book in their bed. They may look at the book before falling asleep or when they wake up.

SOCIAL

Child's Developmental Goals

✓ To interact with others

✓ To control one's body

MATERIALS:

❑ Tape or compact disc player

❑ Tape or compact disc of favorite song

PREPARATION:

♡ Plug in the tape or compact disc player and place it on a shelf out of the children's reach. Fast-forward or rewind the tape or compact disc to the song you wish to dance to.

♡ Clear a space for dancing.

NURTURING STRATEGIES:

1. Direct the toddler to the open space.
2. Introduce the activity by saying:
   "We're going to dance to music. When there is no music, stop moving."
3. Turn on the tape or compact disc player. Model dancing to the music.
4. Set and enforce limits as necessary. If supervising more than one child, you may need to have the dancers remain in one area so that others can work undisturbed.
5. Turn off the music and stop dancing. You probably will need to gently remind the child to stop moving. If several children are participating, one way to do this is to use a child as a model by saying:
   "Hailey, you stopped moving as soon as the music stopped."

6. Turn the music on again and begin dancing. Express your enjoyment of the activity by smiling or laughing. This may encourage the toddler to express her feelings.

☀ Highlighting Development

With self-orientated motives, toddlers have difficulty acting in a prosocial manner. Adults need to help them develop an awareness and recognize when another person needs support or assistance. In addition, toddlers have difficulty understanding the intentions of others. Therefore, during this activity, you may need to explain why a behavior occurred. For example, if one child accidentally bumps into another, say, "That was an accident. Sometimes when we are dancing too close, we bump each other."

VARIATION:

♡ Vary the type of music for dancing by including fast, slow, jazz, country, or ethnic songs.

ADDITIONAL INFORMATION:

♡ The benefits of this activity include promoting social skills and fostering the development of large muscle skills. Toddlers are working on how to stop movements once started. Therefore, it will take them a few seconds to "freeze." In addition, they are learning to keep their balance. Hence, limit the "freeze" to only 10 to 15 seconds. Once the children demonstrate a readiness, slowly increase the time.

SOCIAL

Color Hop

Child's Developmental Goals

✓ To engage in parallel play
✓ To initiate play

MATERIALS:

❑ Mat from Twister game, if available; otherwise, see the Variation section
❑ Clear, wide tape

PREPARATION:

♡ Select an area that can be easily supervised. Clear this area and lay down the mat. Securing the mat with tape may prevent falls.

NURTURING STRATEGIES:

1. When the toddler chooses the activity, observe the child's behavior.
2. Comment about the child choosing the activity by saying:
   "Elijah, you picked this activity. What do you do here?"
3. Converse about possible uses of the mat. If the child doesn't mention jumping from color to color, suggest this behavior.
4. Encourage the toddler to stand on a color on the mat and then jump to another circle. Describe the circles the child stood on. Comments include:
   "You jumped from a red to a green circle."
   "You jumped from one red to another red circle. You jumped to the same color."
5. Given your knowledge of the toddler's understanding of color concepts, you may want to encourage the child to jump to a particular color by saying:
   "Now jump to a green circle."

6. If more than one child is present, comment on how they are using the mat in similar or different ways. Statements to use include:
   "You're both jumping from color to color."
   "Elijah is on a red circle and Tangine is on a blue circle."
7. Providing positive reinforcement may result in the toddlers extending their parallel play. Use comments such as:
   "You two are having so much fun jumping on the mat."
   "Two friends are jumping and playing together."

☼ Highlighting Development

The three types of play typically seen during this stage are solitary, parallel, and associate. Solitary and parallel play dominate, while associate play is seen less frequently. In associate play, children interact by exchanging toys and/or commenting on one another's behavior. To illustrate, they may smile, talk, and offer each other toys.

VARIATION:

♡ Create a map by adhering circles of different colors to a piece of vinyl. Another approach would be to cut circles from construction paper and tape them on the floor.

ADDITIONAL INFORMATION:

♡ Check the distance the child is able to jump.

 Periodically check the mat to make sure it is securely taped to the floor. Given the toddlers' balance and full-body coordination, they are very likely to lose their balance and fall if the mat moves.

Cozy Quilt

SOCIAL

Child's Developmental Goals

✓ To share a space with another child

✓ To read a book to a doll or an adult

MATERIALS:
❑ Large, fluffy quilt
❑ Pillows
❑ Dolls
❑ Books

PREPARATION:
♡ Spread out the quilt in an open area of the room. Place the pillows, dolls, and books on top of the quilt.

NURTURING STRATEGIES:
1. When a toddler shows interest in the activity, move closer to provide assistance.
2. Ask what the quilt is for. Expand upon the child's answer. For example, if the child says, "books," reply with *"Yes, this quilt is a place for reading books."*
3. Encourage the toddler to read a story to one of the dolls.
4. If other children are present and want to join the activity, discuss ways to share the space by saying: *"The quilt is large enough for three children. Where can Reina sit?"*

5. Assist the children in solving and implementing a solution to the problem of limited space.
6. If more than three children want to be on the quilt, make a waiting list and redirect the additional children to another activity. Reassure these children that you will call them when it is their turn.

☼ Highlighting Development

At this stage, toddlers are struggling between wanting independence and needing dependence. This struggle is evident in their behavioral incongruencies. At one moment toddlers will model independent behavior. At this time, it is important for them to do things independently. Then the next moment, the toddlers model dependent behavior and solicit your assistance.

VARIATION:
♡ Lay the quilt, dolls, and books outside for an outdoor activity.

ADDITIONAL INFORMATION:
♡ Toddlers need opportunities to explore materials before they are able to use them for the intended purpose.

 Whenever pillows or blankets are used, constant supervision is necessary to prevent the possibility of suffocation.

19 to 24 months

SOCIAL

Child's Developmental Goals

✓ To engage in parallel play

✓ To interact with an adult

MATERIALS:

☐ Play dough recipe; see Appendix I for a list of dough recipes

☐ 4 place mats

☐ Identical plastic animal figures such as dinosaurs, monkeys, dogs

☐ Child-size table or coffee table

PREPARATION:

♡ Select a child-size table for the experience and lay out place mats. Divide the play dough equally and lay it on the place mats with two animal figures.

NURTURING STRATEGIES:

1. When a toddler chooses the activity, observe the child's behavior.
2. Encourage sensory exploration through the use of the fingers and hands.
3. Describe the toddler's actions with the dough. Comments include:
   "Goran, you're squishing the dough through your fingers."
   "You're poking the dough with your finger."
   "You're rolling the dough with your palms."
4. Suggest that the toddler incorporate the animals in playing by asking:
   "What are the animals for?"
5. If necessary, modeling imprinting the animal's feet in the dough may increase the child's level of play.

6. Invite another child, if present, to join the activity.
7. Comment on the similarities and differences of the children's work, if several are present. To illustrate, say:
   "Goran is making dinosaur prints, and Dale is flattening the dough with her fist."

☀ Highlighting Development

To promote a healthy self-concept, positive guidance is necessary. Guidance can be described as the direct or indirect actions used by adults to help children develop socially acceptable behavior. During parallel or associative play, children might invade others' physical space or take their property. When this occurs, you need to set and maintain limits. If necessary, you may need to enact a consequence for negative behavior. For example, if a child pretends his animal bites another, say, "Sarah doesn't like it when you are pretending to bite her. If you do that again, you will need to give me the animal."

VARIATION:

♡ Spread out a vinyl tablecloth on the floor for a working surface.

ADDITIONAL INFORMATION:

♡ Experiment with various play dough recipes because each has a slightly different texture. Compare and contrast the doughs.

♡ Use different animals, small rolling pins, or cookie cutters.

SOCIAL

Child's Developmental Goals

✓ To imitate another's behavior

✓ To participate in a game

MATERIALS:

None

PREPARATION:

None

NURTURING STRATEGIES:

1. When a toddler loses interest in an activity, suggest playing a game. To illustrate, say:
   "Amber, let's play a game. It is called 'Follow the Leader.' Listen and do what I say or do. Are you ready?"
2. Begin with something easy, such as clapping hands or rubbing your tummy. Alternate between doing the behavior and providing verbal instructions. Behaviors may include walking around the room, crawling under a table, jumping/hopping in place, stamping your feet, flapping your arms, wiggling your nose, or shaking your head.
3. Providing positive reinforcement may result in the toddler imitating or paying more attention. Comments might include:
   "Amber, excellent job listening to my words. You crawled under the table. This time walk around the table."
   "You're good at this game. You do everything that I do."

4. If the child is ready, increase the difficulty and silliness of the game by trying to do two things at once. Laugh at yourself for not being able to do both tasks. Discuss how silly you look, for example, when crawling and shaking your head.

☀ Highlighting Development

Toddlers are very skilled at observing and imitating people that surround and are important to them. Use this to your advantage. Demonstrating prosocial behaviors results in the toddlers imitating them. For example, when the child hands you something, respond by saying "thank you." Likewise, when asking the child to hand you an object, include the word "please." Gradually, they will incorporate these words into their vocabulary.

VARIATIONS:

♡ Follow the child's lead.

ADDITIONAL INFORMATION:

♡ As discussed earlier, encourage toddlers to crawl during activities like these. Crawling exercises both sides of the brain at once and should be encouraged often.

♡ Respect the child's attempts by laughing "with" and not "at" the child.

19 to 24 months

SOCIAL

Child's Developmental Goals

✓ To interact with at least one other person

✓ To participate in a game

MATERIALS:

❏ 6 two-liter bottles

❏ Lightweight, plastic ball

PREPARATION:

♡ Set up the six bottles in a triangle. Lay the ball several feet away on the sidewalk. If several children are present, set up a second bowling game and ball in a separate area.

NURTURING STRATEGIES:

1. When a toddler chooses the activity, observe the child's behavior.
2. Introduce the activity to the child by saying:
   "This is a bowling game. Roll the ball and knock down the bottles. When you knock them down, set them back up. Then you can roll the ball again."
3. Observe the toddler playing the game. If other children are present, invite them to join.
4. If more than one child is participating, assist the toddlers in working together. Comments to make include:
   "Cooper, you can roll the ball after Sania has a turn."
   "Set up the bottles so your friend can have a turn."

5. Provide positive reinforcement both for individual skills and working together. To illustrate, comment:
   "Wow! You knocked down all six bottles."
   "You're sharing the bowling game. Cooper goes and then Sania goes next."

☀ Highlighting Development

Toddlers often find transitions to or from another activity stressful. Observe. Transition frequently involves waiting. This is difficult for toddlers, who are used to being busy. Sometimes they test your limits. To illustrate, when told to pick up the game, toddlers may refuse to clean up, cry, or throw toys. To prevent this behavior, warn them several minutes before cleanup time. The warning will provide time to finish current activities and for mental preparation for the next transition. To reduce potential guidance problems, avoid a waiting time during a transition.

VARIATION:

♡ Play the game inside in a hallway or open area of a room.

ADDITIONAL INFORMATION:

♡ Depending on the number of children present and interested, you may need to set a limit of two to three children per bowling game.

Going Camping

SOCIAL

Child's Developmental Goals

✔ To share physical space with another person

✔ To engage in functional and/or pretend play

MATERIALS:

❑ Tent for two to four children

❑ Backpacks

❑ Adult-size flannel shirts

❑ Items to carry in backpacks

PREPARATION:

♡ Select and clear an area that can be constantly supervised. Set up the tent in this area. Place the flannel shirts, backpacks, and other items near the tent.

NURTURING STRATEGIES:

1. Introduce the activity to the toddler. To illustrate, say:
    "We are going to pretend to go camping. You can go inside the tent. There are backpacks for carrying supplies."
2. Observe the toddler exploring the available materials.
3. Assist with putting on shirts, zipping and unzipping backpacks, and putting on the backpacks. Encourage the toddler to assist in helping as much as possible. Comments to make include:
    "Push your arm through the sleeve."
    "I'll hold it while you pull the zipper."
4. Suggest that two toddlers, if present, get inside the tent.

5. Provide positive reinforcement for sharing the space. Use comments such as:
    "You are sharing the tent."
    "You two are inside the tent."
6. Encourage the toddler to engage in pretend play by asking questions related to camping. For example, say:
    "What are you taking camping?"
    "Where are you going camping?"

☀ Highlighting Development

Toddlers need to be responsible for caring for toys and maintaining the environment. Therefore, participating in cleanup activities is an important routine. Set expectations that are developmentally appropriate. For a child of this age, putting away two toys may be sufficient. As the toddler matures, expectations should be raised accordingly.

VARIATION:

♡ Set up an area outdoors for the camping activity.

ADDITIONAL INFORMATION:

♡ Toddlers enjoy private spaces such as those provided by tents.

♡ Tents are safe yet adventurous toys. To encourage participation in functional or pretend play, place accessories in the tent such as flashlights, portable radios, and sleeping bags.

19 to 24 months

SOCIAL

Child's Developmental Goals

✓ To engage in parallel play
✓ To interact with an adult

MATERIALS:

❑ 2 rubber balls

PREPARATION:

♡ Lay the balls in a grassy and/or open area outdoors.

NURTURING STRATEGIES:

1. Observe the toddler playing with the ball.
2. Suggest new ways to use the ball. For example, if the toddler is rolling the ball, suggest that the ball be kicked with the feet.
3. In addition, suggest that the child kick the ball to you. When you receive the ball, gently kick it back to the child.
4. Comment on how the child or group of children is playing with the ball. Comments include:
   "You are kicking the balls."
   "Shelby and Darby are chasing the balls."
5. Providing positive reinforcement may result in the toddler spending more time at the activity. To illustrate, say:
   "You kicked that ball to me."
   "What a good kick."
6. The toddlers may be uncoordinated in their initial attempts at kicking. Therefore, you will need to provide much support and encouragement.

 Highlighting Development

Selecting an appropriate ball is important to the success of this activity and, therefore, the children's view of themselves. Balls should be lightweight and approximately the size of volleyballs. If the ball is too small, the children may lack the necessary eye-foot coordination to successfully kick it when swinging their leg. Ensuring success is important because one way children evaluate themselves is in relationship to their physical abilities.

VARIATION:

♡ Encourage the toddler to kick the ball to another person.

ADDITIONAL INFORMATION:

♡ If several children are present, be sure to divide your time equally among them. It is important for all children to receive positive attention to make them feel valued as individuals.

Emotional Development

NINETEEN to TWENTY-FOUR MONTHS

Paper Crunch

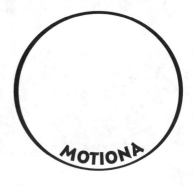

MOTIONA

Child's Developmental Goals

✓ To express emotions such as anger or enjoyment

✓ To coordinate behaviors with emotions

MATERIALS:

❑ Used wrapping paper of different sizes and designs

PREPARATION:

♡ Cut large sheets of paper into smaller pieces, if necessary. Place the wrapping paper in the center of a child–size table.

NURTURING STRATEGIES:

1. When a toddler chooses the activity, observe the child's behavior.

2. If necessary, introduce the activity. To illustrate, say: *"Randall, this paper is for crumpling and crunching. You can wad it into a ball."*

3. Describe the emotions displayed by the child while working. Use comments such as:
   "You are smiling. Crunching paper must make you happy."
   "You have a frightened look. Does the noise scare you?"

4. Encouraging the toddler to express different emotions may result in a greater understanding of them. Say, for example:
   "If you were mad, how would you crunch the paper?"

5. Follow up by providing positive reinforcement that connects the child's behaviors with the displayed emotion. To illustrate, say:
   "I can tell that you are mad. You are scrunching the paper hard. You are also scrunching your nose."

6. If necessary, model crunching the paper to express different emotions such as happiness, fright, anger, or sadness. Ask the child to guess how you are feeling.

7. Continue the activity as long as the toddler seems interested.

☼ Highlighting Development

Toddlers display anger more frequently, with more intensity, and in more situations than do infants. This change is linked to growth in cognitive development. As they engage in more intentional behavior and are better at identifying the source of their blocked goals, their expressions of anger may be particularly intense (Berk, 1997).

VARIATION:

♡ Toss paper balls into a laundry basket to practice eye-hand coordination skills.

ADDITIONAL INFORMATION:

♡ Young toddlers delight in the cause and effect as well as the sounds created by crunching paper. Keeping paper available for this purpose will assist when redirecting the child's inappropriate behaviors with materials such as the daily paper or pages in a book.

19 to 24 months

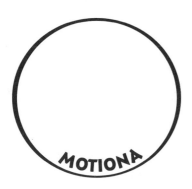
MOTIONA

Sad Little Spider

Child's Developmental Goals

✓ To associate emotions with behaviors
✓ To express emotions through a song

MATERIALS:
❑ Felt-tip pen
❑ Index card

PREPARATION:
♡ See Appendix G for the song, "The Itsy Bitsy Spider." If desired, copy the song on an index card.

NURTURING STRATEGIES:

1. When you notice a toddler wandering in search of an activity, extend an invitation for singing by saying:
   "I feel like singing. Would you like to sing with me?"
2. Sing the song, "The Itsy Bitsy Spider."
3. Tell the child that you'd like to sing the song about a sad spider.
4. Converse briefly about some things that make you and the toddler sad.
5. Ask the toddler to show you what she looks like when she is sad.
6. Describe the facial and bodily gestures made by the child. For example, say:
   "When you are sad, you stick out your bottom lip. You also look at the floor. Let's do those movements while singing about the spider."
7. Sing the song again, substituting the "sad little" instead of the "itsy bitsy" spider.
8. Provide positive reinforcement for singing and performing the movements of the song. Comments include:
   "Your spider was so sad."
   "You made all of the motions in the song."
   "You sang along with me."

☀ Highlighting Development

At this stage, toddlers experience a wide variety of emotions. To assist them, adults can provide verbal and nonverbal support when the child is experiencing success, frustration, or failure. Responding to a child's accomplishments with gestures such as smiling or nodding can convey an important emotional understanding. When the child is frustrated, try saying "Try it again. It is hard." Likewise, when the child is failing to complete a task such as inserting a puzzle piece, you may say, "Turn the piece around. Then it will fit."

VARIATIONS:
♡ Change words to reflect different emotions such as anger, happiness, or excitement.
♡ While singing the song, make facial expressions corresponding to the emotions being sung. Then ask the child to identify the emotion.

ADDITIONAL INFORMATION:
♡ Observe and assess the toddler's body language while singing. Is the child able to associate emotions with behaviors? If not, continue focusing on these skills. Otherwise, begin introducing more complex emotions.

Popping Popcorn

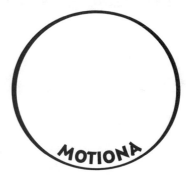

MOTIONA...

Child's Developmental Goals

✓ To develop self-control when excited

✓ To express emotions while singing

MATERIALS:

❑ Hot air popper

❑ Popcorn

❑ Metal or plastic mixing bowl

❑ Extension cord (if necessary)

PREPARATION:

♡ Gather all the necessary supplies and place them out of the children's reach.

♡ Clear a spot on the floor for popper and children.

♡ Gather all other supplies needed for snack and place in the snack area.

NURTURING STRATEGIES:

1. Introduce the activity to the children by saying: *"Today we are going to make popcorn for snack. Have any of you eaten popcorn before?"*

2. Discuss limits to prevent safety hazards. Comment, for example: *"The machine gets hot. It could burn us. Stay sitting."*

3. Plug in and turn on the popcorn machine. Then pour the popcorn into the appliance.

4. Talk about the sound of popping corn.

5. Sing the following chant and clap to the rhythm: (Tune: "Hot Dog Song")

   🎵 Three little kernels
   🎵 In the pan
   🎵 The air got hot
   🎵 And one went bam! (Continue until zero kernels: "The air got hot and the pan went bam!")

6. The children will become excited as the popcorn begins to pop.

7. Provide positive reinforcement for remaining seated. Comments to make include:
   "What a good listener."
   "You were safe because you followed the rules."

8. Wash hands and enjoy the snack.

☀ Highlighting Development

Children at this age are more skilled at imitating your actions. Observe them as you introduce this new chant. They may try clapping to the beat and repeating some of the words.

VARIATIONS:

♡ Act out what it would be like to be a kernel of corn.

♡ See Appendix F for other popcorn chants.

ADDITIONAL INFORMATION:

♡ Children enjoy eating foods they have participated in preparing. In some instances, they may even try new foods because of their involvement.

 Popcorn can be a choking hazard for children. Therefore, introduce this activity only if the toddlers are 24 months or older. Pay close attention to children who tend to not chew their food well because they might be at a higher risk for choking, even if they are over 24 months of age.

 Keep popcorn kernels out of the children's reach.

19 to 24 months

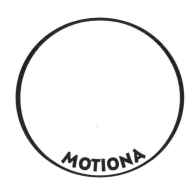

MOTIONA

Playground

Child's Developmental Goals

✔ To express enjoyment during an activity

✔ To experience a sense of satisfaction

MATERIALS:

❑ Bucket for each child

❑ 2-inch paintbrush for each child

❑ Water

PREPARATION:

♡ Fill the bucket half full of water. Then place a brush in the bucket. Set the bucket on a sidewalk. Repeat the process as necessary for additional children.

NURTURING STRATEGIES:

1. Introduce the activity by saying:
   "Kiri, you can paint. Here is a brush and a bucket of water."
2. Observe the child's behavior.
3. Be prepared to redirect the toddler, if necessary. For example, if the child is painting the slide, suggest painting the fence.
4. Describing the child's behavior will assist in connecting actions with language. Comments include:
   "Kiri, stretching. You're stretching your body to reach the top of that pole."
   "You're painting side to side."
5. If two or more children are painting, comment on how they are working together. Say, for example:
   "Everyone is painting. You're working hard."
   "The fresh paint makes everything look so new."

6. Describe the emotions being displayed by the children. Use comments such as:
   "Kiri, you're smiling. You like painting."
   "Josiah, you're stopping. You must be finished."

☀ Highlighting Development

Children's view of themselves comprises two separate yet related components—self-worth and competence (Berk, 1997). Self-worth is the belief that you are important as a person (Herr, 1998). Competence, on the other hand, is the belief that you can do things well (Berk, 1997). Therefore, you need to consider both components when helping toddlers to develop a healthy view of themselves. It is too limiting to focus on just the children's evaluation of their self-worth. Creating developmentally appropriate experiences is one way to help toddlers view themselves as being competent individuals.

VARIATION:

♡ Providing brushes of different sizes may result in experimentation.

ADDITIONAL INFORMATION:

♡ This is a wonderful activity to do on warm summer days. Repeat the activity as long as it appeals to the child.

MOTIONA

Child's Developmental Goals

✓ To practice self-help skills

✓ To develop healthy living habits and skills

MATERIALS:

❑ Sink

❑ Toothbrush and toothpaste

❑ Paper towels

❑ Basket

PREPARATION:

♡ Store the toddler's toothbrush and toothpaste on a child-size shelf or cabinet. In a child care center, you may want to clearly label the child's personal belongings.

NURTURING STRATEGIES:

1. After eating a meal or snack, direct the toddler to the sink to brush her teeth. Accompany the child to the sink and provide assistance, if needed.

2. Assist the child in selecting the basket holding the supplies. Say, for example:
   "Keiji, K, K, K—Where is Keiji's basket? Here it is." (while pointing to the label)

3. Ask the toddler to help you by holding the toothbrush while you squeeze out a small amount of toothpaste.

4. Instruct the toddler to begin brushing.

5. Sing the following song while the toddler brushes:

   ♫ Brush, brush, brush your teeth
   ♫ Until they're nice and strong
   ♫ Brush, brush, brush your teeth
   ♫ While we sing this song.

6. Provide positive reinforcement for brushing teeth. Comments include:
   "You cleaned your front and back teeth."
   "You cleaned the fronts and backs of your teeth."

7. Encourage the toddler to spit out the toothpaste rather than swallowing it. To do this, comment by saying:
   "Keiji, spit the toothpaste in the sink."

8. After rinsing the toothbrush, have the toddler return it to its proper place. To remove remaining toothpaste, wiping the face and hands with paper towels may be necessary.

☀ Highlighting Development

Children differ in their response to requests made by adults. Some children easily comply, while others resist. When resisting, children typically feel frustrated. The frustration may be expressed through a temper tantrum. This is the toddlers' way of communicating that they have had enough. Observe them. They may throw themselves on the floor, scream, and kick. When this occurs, simply ignoring the tantrum can be effective. Otherwise, distraction is one of the most effective techniques for diverting attention. Because these emotions need to be expressed, however, distraction should not be immediately introduced.

VARIATION:

♡ Encourage the child to wash his face after a meal by providing a warm, damp washcloth.

ADDITIONAL INFORMATION:

♡ Preventing tooth decay is necessary and important. Once the child's first tooth erupts, it should be brushed after meals or bottles. Until the infant/toddler is able to stand unassisted, you will need to do the brushing. Teaching lifelong habits for healthy living is a necessary role of adults.

19 to 24 months

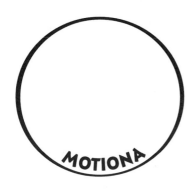

EMOTIONAL

Happy and Sad

Child's Developmental Goals

✔ To label emotions

✔ To associate emotions with behaviors

MATERIALS:

☐ Masks with different expressions (if unavailable, make your own with paper plates and felt-tip markers)

PREPARATION:

♡ If using commercially manufactured masks, select a happy face and a sad face. If you wish to make your own, draw a happy face on one side of the paper plate and a sad face on the other side. Decorate the masks with the felt-tip markers so the faces are easy to see.

NURTURING STRATEGIES:

1. Gather the masks and introduce the activity by saying:
   "I have a story to tell you today. It is about two children. Sometimes the children are happy, and sometimes they are sad. Let's look and see how the children feel."
2. Begin telling your story. Parallel your story with the lives of the children in the audience. For example, discuss a recent incident in which a child had hurt feelings.
3. During the story, hold up a mask while describing an emotion.
4. Ask the children to label the emotion being described. Ask, for example:
   "How is Sonya feeling now?"
5. Close the activity by asking the children to describe something that makes them sad and happy.

☀ Highlighting Development

Toddlers learn emotional display rules, which are guidelines that specify when, where, and how it is culturally appropriate to express emotions, through both direct and indirect instruction. Toddlers may be told or encouraged, for example, to express anger in self-defense such as when a friend grabs their toy or hits them. Indirectly, children learn how to behave emotionally by watching others control or express their feelings (Kostelnik, et al., 2002).

VARIATION:

♡ Cut out faces from magazines that represent different emotions such as surprised, scared, or angry. Mount the pictures on poster board and share them with the children.

ADDITIONAL INFORMATION:

♡ Toddlers are often frightened of masks because they lack a clear understanding of transformations. They fail to see the relationship between beginning and ending states. Therefore, avoid holding the mask directly in front of your face during this activity.

Helping with Lunch

MOTIONA

Child's Developmental Goals

✓ To experience a sense of self-satisfaction

✓ To improve self-help skills

MATERIALS:

❑ Fresh green beans

❑ Salt and pepper

❑ Basket

❑ Water

❑ Saucepan with lid

PREPARATION:

♡ Wash, drain, and place the green beans in the basket. Then place the basket on a child-size table. Finally, set the saucepan in the middle of the table.

NURTURING STRATEGIES:

1. Sit at the table and begin snapping the stems off the beans.
2. Invite a child to help you. To illustrate, say:
   "Darrell, I'm snapping beans to cook for lunch. Would you help me? Wash your hands first."
3. Discuss how and why you are breaking the stems from the beans. Comment, for example:
   "The stems are tough. We need to take them off. Watch me. See how I am bending the end of the bean. The end will break off. I'm placing the stems in this pile."
4. While handing the child a bean, encourage the toddler to join in the snapping by saying:
   "Darrell, try snapping this bean."
5. Provide positive reinforcement for attempts and accomplishments. Comments to make include:
   "Darrell, you broke off the stem. You are helping me."
   "No stems here. You're working hard."

6. Before putting the bean into the saucepan, model breaking each bean in half.
7. Talk about how the beans are easier to eat when smaller. That is why you are breaking them in smaller pieces.
8. Count the number of beans the toddler makes. Comment, for example:
   "You now have two beans to put into the pan."
9. Thank the child for snapping the beans.
10. Wash, season, and cook the beans. Serve for lunch or snack.

☀ Highlighting Development

Toddlers enjoy imitating and assisting adults. It is important that they participate in routine activities such as helping with lunch, eating, dressing, and caring for the environment. When these activities are first introduced, expect that they usually will be time intensive. With maturity and practice, children will become more proficient. In the meantime, they need time, instruction, encouragement, and praise.

VARIATIONS:

♡ Shell large peas or kidney beans.

♡ Plant a garden and, when the food ripens, prepare fresh salads.

ADDITIONAL INFORMATION:

♡ While eating the cooked beans, introduce raw beans for comparison tasting. Discuss the differences. Interject comments on how the toddler assisted in preparing the beans for lunch. To improve memory skills, recap the steps in snapping the beans.

19 to 24 months

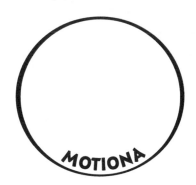

EMOTIONAL

Child's Developmental Goals

✓ To express caring emotions
✓ To learn ways for meeting needs

MATERIALS:

None

PREPARATION:

None

NURTURING STRATEGIES:

1. Observe a toddler at work, noticing how the child is feeling about the day.
2. If the child is feeling frustrated, sad, or tired, move closer and position yourself at the toddler's eye level.
3. Involve yourself in the toddler's play without disrupting it. For example, if the toddler is feeding a doll, begin feeding a doll of your own.
4. When that play episode is over, say to the toddler:
   "Oksanna, I'm sad and need a hug. Can I have a hug?"
5. While hugging, say, for example:
   "Hugs always make me feel better."
6. Thank the child for making you feel better. Comments include:
   "Thank you, Oksanna. I feel much better now."
   "Thanks for the wonderful hug, Oksanna. You helped me to feel better."
7. Converse with the toddler about ways of positively getting needs met. To illustrate, say:
   "When I'm sad and need a hug, I ask someone. Do you ask others for hugs?"
8. Comment on the toddler's answer and then encourage the child to practice asking for a hug. Respond by hugging the child.

☀ Highlighting Development

To direct their behavior, children at this stage often continue to rely on cues from others. They search for cues, such as facial expressions from parents, caregivers, siblings, and peers. This phenomenon is referred to as social referencing. To illustrate, when an adult appears afraid, the child will pick up on the nonverbal clues and move away from what the adult views as fearful. Likewise, chances are the child will also move closer to the adult for support.

VARIATIONS:

♡ Provide dolls or stuffed animals for hugging.
♡ If the child is feeling happy, offer a hug.

ADDITIONAL INFORMATION:

♡ Toddlers are battling the conflict between autonomy and dependence. On one hand, they want to do everything themselves and, on the other hand, they lack some of the necessary skills. Therefore, toddlers consistently need love and support.
♡ Be open and flexible in meeting the immediate needs of the child. If the child needs help, always try to provide assistance. Typically, tasks you are engaged in can temporarily wait.
♡ Show you care. Love and hugs are contagious. If a child feels loved, the child will hug others in return.

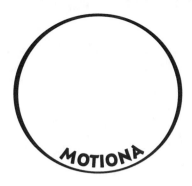

MOTIONA

Child's Developmental Goals

✓ To express caring to others

✓ To receive caring emotions from others

MATERIALS:

❑ Index card

❑ Felt-tip marker

PREPARATION:

♡ Write out the following words to the song on an index card, if preferred:

♫ Skinamarink, a rink, a dink (roll hands in circle)

♫ Skinamarink, a doo (roll hands in circle)

♫ I love you. (point to self, cross arms over chest, point to child or group)

♫ I love you in the morning and in the afternoon (roll hands in circle)

♫ I love you in the evening and underneath the moon. (roll hands in circle)

♫ Oh . . . (clap)

♫ Skinamarink, a rink, a dink (same as first verse)

♫ Skinamarink, a doo.

♫ I love you.

NURTURING STRATEGIES:

1. Introduce this song during a routine waiting time such as before mealtime. Begin by saying:
   "I have a new song for you. The song is about the feeling I have for you."

2. While rolling your hands in a circle, ask:
   "Can you do this?"

3. Provide positive reinforcement by commenting:
   "Good job."
   "Excellent. You can do it!"

4. Move on to the next movement but allow sufficient time for the child to imitate your actions.

5. After all movements have been introduced, say:
   "Let's put some words with the movements."
   Then begin to sing the song. Sing the song slowly the first couple of times. Ensure that the toddler can sing the song with you.

6. Repeat as time allows or introduce again throughout the day. Repetition will assist the toddler in learning the words and movements.

☀ Highlighting Development

The ways adults treat young children have been found to have a profound impact in the development of empathy. Adults who are nurturing and encouraging and show a sensitive, empathic concern have children who are more likely to react in a concerned way to the distress of others. Relatedly, harsh and punitive caregiving is related to disruptions in the development of empathy (Berk, 1997).

VARIATION:

♡ Sing the song to children when they are calming down prior to nap time.

ADDITIONAL INFORMATION:

♡ This song will quickly become a favorite for toddlers and teachers. The song has emotional appeal because it makes a person feel good. If working with children in a center, share the words in a printed form with parents and guardians.

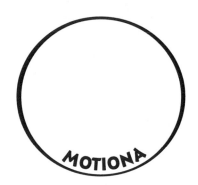

MOTIONAL

Child's Developmental Goals

✓ To associate emotions with behaviors

✓ To express emotions such as excitement

MATERIALS:

❑ Bottle of bubble solution or prepare own solution; see Appendix I for a list of recipes

❑ Bubble wands

❑ Paper towels

PREPARATION:

♡ If desired, prepare a bubble solution.

♡ Select a safe outdoor area for this activity.

♡ When planning an area to stage the activity, consideration needs to be given to the ground cover. Young children are developing balance and coordination skills. While chasing the bubbles, they may fall. Cement should be avoided; a soft grassy area would offer the most protection.

NURTURING STRATEGIES:

1. Observe the child playing. When a change of activity is apparent, get the bubble solution and wand.

2. The position of your body is important for this activity. Sit so you can see everyone you might be supervising. If the wind is blowing, position yourself so the wind carries the bubbles over the selected area.

3. Begin blowing the bubbles. Observe to see if the toddler notices. If so, continue. Otherwise, gain the attention of the toddler by using the child's name.

4. Often toddlers want to participate in blowing the bubbles. For safety purposes, encourage the child to chase the bubbles by saying:

   "Austin, go catch the bubbles. See how many you can get."

5. Describing the child's reactions to the activity may help in promoting understanding of emotions. Comments include:

   "You caught one. What a big smile. You must be proud!"
   "Oh, what a sad look. Are you disappointed because the bubble got away?"

6. Offering support and encouragement promotes participation. To illustrate, say:

   "Austin, almost. You almost got that one. Keep trying."
   "Here comes another bubble. Try to catch this one."

7. Providing positive reinforcement may result in the toddler chasing the bubbles longer and, therefore, allowing you to engage in more "emotion talk." Use comments such as:

   "Austin, you are working so hard to catch a bubble."
   "Wow! You've caught three bubbles now!"

☀ Highlighting Development

The beginnings of self-control emerge after the first birthday. At this time, children are aware that they must react to other people's demands. By two years of age, they have internalized some self-control. To illustrate, if the toddler is told not to touch something, the child may inhibit the desire. At this stage, the child may remember being told not to touch it. However, close supervision is always necessary because of lapses in memory and recall as well as the excitement of the moment.

VARIATIONS:

♡ Use a variety of tools such as a berry basket, large wand, or slotted kitchen spoon to create the bubbles.

♡ When children are skilled at blowing, encourage them to create their own bubbles.

 Exercise caution when playing with bubbles. The bubble solution can be irritating if it makes contact with the eyes. Therefore, encourage the children to stand away from the tool when you're actually blowing the bubbles. The children should also periodically wipe their hands with a paper towel, especially if they've caught several bubbles.

Child Feel?

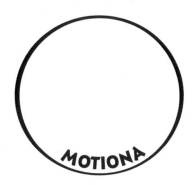

MOTIONA

Child's Developmental Goals

✓ To associate emotions with behaviors

✓ To identify and label emotional expressions

MATERIALS:

❏ Pictures of children from books, magazines, or catalogs

❏ Transparent self-adhesive paper

❏ Basket

PREPARATION:

♡ Select and cut out pictures of people expressing different emotions from books, magazines, or catalogs. Covering each picture with transparent self-adhesive paper will help preserve it.

♡ Place the pictures in the basket and put it on a shelf out of the reach of the children.

NURTURING STRATEGIES:

1. When you notice a child needing a new activity, retrieve your basket. Then sit on the floor close to the child.

2. Introduce the activity by saying:
   "Cami, I have some pictures for us to play with today. Look. The children are making different faces. Let's see if you can tell how each child must be feeling."

3. Hold up the first picture and say, for example:
   "Let's take a good look at this child."
   Allow time for visually exploring the picture.

4. To promote labeling emotions, ask the toddler:
   "Cami, how is the child feeling?"

5. If the child says "angry," nod and ask:
   "Does the child look really mad?"

6. Next, ask the child to tell you how she knew the child was sad. Focusing on the association between behavior and emotions may increase the toddler's understanding.

7. Lastly, ask the child for possible reasons why the child might be happy. Questions to ask include:
   "Cami, why is the child happy?"
   "What could have made this child happy?"

8. Move on to a second picture. Continue as long as the toddler is interested.

☀ Highlighting Development

Emotions emerge throughout childhood. By nine months of age, infants have experienced all four core emotions—joy, anger, sadness, and fear. During the second year, five additional emotions are added, including pride, guilt, affection, jealousy, and defiance.

Observe. One task facing young children is emotional self-regulation. As toddlers mature, their emotional responses become more differentiated. The children's responses grow in complexity as well. They may cry, scream, pout, hit, grab, and shove when angry. Moreover, they move into or out of situations depending on their needs. As children continue developing cognitive and language abilities, they begin using words for expressing their emotions. Likewise, they recognize the emotions of others. They may say, "Mama happy," "Tommy sad," or "baby cry" (Kostelnik, et al., 2002).

VARIATION:

♡ Repeat the activity while reading a picture book.

ADDITIONAL INFORMATION:

♡ Toddlers use telegraphic speech for several months. Continue expanding their language development by elaborating on their sentences. For example, if a toddler says, "Toy broke," you could expand it by saying, "The child was sad because her toy broke."

♡ Adults need to frequently ask questions. At times, they also need to provide the answers to these questions.

19 to 24 months

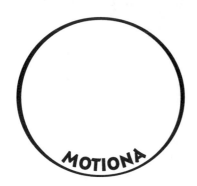

MOTIONAL

Child's Developmental Goals

✓ To express one's feelings through art
✓ To discuss feelings

MATERIALS:

☐ Tape or compact disc player
☐ Tape or compact disc containing instrumental music such as classical or jazz
☐ 8½ × 11–inch sheet of light-colored construction paper for each child
☐ Basket for each child
☐ Box of chubby crayons for each child

PREPARATION:

♡ Place one sheet of construction paper on a child-size table. Place a basket of chubby crayons beside each piece of paper. If there is more than one child, provide paper and crayons for each child.
♡ Plug in the tape or compact disc player and set it on a shelf beyond the toddler's reach. Insert the tape or compact disc you selected.

NURTURING STRATEGIES:

1. When a toddler chooses the activity, begin playing the music.
2. Observe the toddler's behavior.
3. If the toddler is coloring with the music, describe the child's behavior. Say, for example:
   "Amit, you are drawing quickly, just like the music."
4. If the toddler is ignoring the music, you may need to model. Begin by drawing scribbles in response to the music. Reinforce your actions with words by making comments such as:
   "Amit, the music is slow, so I'm slowly drawing a large circle."
   "Now the music is fast, so I'm drawing lots of short lines."

5. Allow the toddler to work in silence by minimizing conversation.
6. After the toddler is finished coloring, discuss the drawing. Describe what you see. Comments include:
   "Amit, you used lots of red."
   "Look at these long lines. They go from side to side."
7. Expand your conversation by commenting on how the song made the toddler and you feel. Elicit the child's feelings by asking, for example:
   "Amit, how did you feel when you heard that music?"

☀ Highlighting Development

During play, children display emotions. Depending on the circumstances, these emotions can be intense. As a result, children need appropriate self-expression skills. Often this requires adult assistance and guidance. For children to learn skills, adults need to set clear limits and enforce them as necessary. To illustrate, when a child throws a toy, adults need to intervene. They can respond by saying, "You are angry. I cannot let you hurt others." Adults need to reinforce the concept that the child's feelings are acceptable; however, their actions are unacceptable.

VARIATION:

♡ Experiment by providing different types of instrumental music.

ADDITIONAL INFORMATION:

♡ When modeling working with the music, avoid drawing objects. Toddlers will scribble. They lack the skills to create representational drawings.

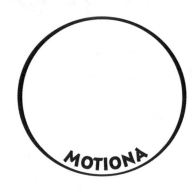
MOTIONA

Child's Developmental Goals

✔ To associate behaviors with emotions

✔ To express one's feelings through art

MATERIALS:

❑ Unused pizza boxes
❑ Construction paper
❑ Masking tape
❑ Paint
❑ Damp sponge
❑ Golf ball for each child
❑ Nonbreakable paint container for each child
❑ Spoon for each child
❑ Smock for each child

PREPARATION:

♡ Cut construction paper to fit inside the top and bottom of the pizza box. Using two pieces of tape, secure the paper to the top and bottom of the pizza box.

♡ Mix the paint to the desired thickness by using liquid soap to help facilitate cleanup. Pour paint into the container. If more than one child is participating, divide the paint equally among containers. Then put a golf ball and a spoon in each container.

♡ Place one pizza box and container at a child–size table for each child. Lay a smock over the back of each chair.

NURTURING STRATEGIES:

1. When a child chooses the activity, introduce it while assisting the child with putting on the smock. To illustrate, say:
   "Mulan, roll the ball in the paint and then place it in the box." Pause and wait for the child to follow the directions. "Now close the lid and shake the box. You will make two pictures at once. Try it!"

2. Assist the toddler, if needed, with getting the golf ball into the box.

3. Encourage the toddler to shake the box using different motions such as from side to side, fast, and slow. Then ask the toddler to act out different feelings by asking questions such as:
   "How would you shake the box if you were happy?"
   "How might you shake the box if you were sad?"

4. Provide positive reinforcement for the toddler associating behaviors with emotions. Use comments such as:
   "Mulan, I can tell you are angry. Your forehead is crinkled and you're shaking the box hard."
   "You are smiling and shaking the box firmly. You look happy."

5. Use the sponge to wipe a spill or dirty hands.

☀ Highlighting Development

During this stage of development, toddlers are learning referential and expressive speech. Referential speech includes the child's objects, actions, and location. Basically, this speech describes what is occurring. Expressive speech, on the other hand, includes feelings, emotional content, and social experiences. During art activities, children who use an expressive style will talk about their feelings and needs. In contrast, those preferring referential speech may focus their language on the materials, tools, or outcomes.

VARIATIONS:

♡ Introduce other types of art activities such as sponge painting or cookie cutter prints.

♡ For an outdoor activity, line a refrigerator box with butcher paper. Provide large items such as basketballs, footballs, or baseballs coated with paint. Encourage two or more toddlers to work together to shake the box.

ADDITIONAL INFORMATION:

♡ Whenever using paint, keep a damp sponge near the activity. If paint spills, wipe it up immediately.

"You Are Special"

Child's Developmental Goals

✓ To feel pride in oneself
✓ To recognize oneself as someone special

MATERIALS:

☐ Index card
☐ Felt-tip marker

PREPARATION:

♡ Either memorize the words to the song or write the words on an index card. If recorded, the words can be carried in your pocket:
(Tune: "Where is Thumbkin?")

♫ I am special, I am special
♫ Yes I am, yes I am (nod head)
♫ I am very special, I am very special
♫ Because I'm me, (point to self) because I'm me.

(Or)

♫ You are special, you are special
♫ Yes you are, yes you are
♫ You are very special, you are very special
♫ Because you're you, because you're you.

NURTURING STRATEGIES:

1. Introduce the song before napping or during a quiet time.
2. This can be sung to the child using your voice as a tool to soothe and calm. If more than one child is in your care, sing the song individually to each.
3. Further assist the toddler in calming down by rubbing the stomach or back.
4. Repeat the song several times until the toddler is ready to rest.

☀ Highlighting Development

The development of self-conscious behavior emerges as a result of adult instruction. Among some cultures, pride is evoked by generosity, helpfulness, and sharing. Situations that may evoke pride in one culture, however, may evoke shame or embarrassment in another. Pride may be shown for achievements of an entire group in one culture. In another, individual accomplishments result in pride (Kail, 1998).

Self-conscious emotions play an important role in children's achievement-related and moral behavior later in life. Therefore, adults need to help children develop an understanding of these complex emotions early in life (Berk, 1997).

VARIATION:

♡ Talk about the specific traits that make the toddler special.

ADDITIONAL INFORMATION:

♡ Toddlers often have a difficult time calming down at nap time. Making modifications to the environment or transitions to nap time can greatly help to reduce problem behaviors.
♡ As with infants, toddlers need predictability and consistency. Therefore, routines are important for guiding their behavior.

Berk, L. E. (1997). *Child development* (4th ed.). Boston: Allyn & Bacon.

Berk, L. E. (1999). *Infants, children, and adolescents* (3rd ed.). Boston: Allyn & Bacon.

Bukato, D., & Daehler, M. W. (1992). *Child development: A topical approach.* Boston: Houghton Mifflin.

Cowley, G., & Foote, D. (1997). The language explosion. *Newsweek,* 16–17.

Cromwell, E. (2000). *Early childhood education.* Needham Heights, MA: Allyn & Bacon.

Damon, W. (1988). *The moral child: Nurturing children's natural moral growth.* New York: Free Press.

Deiner, P. L. (1997). *Infants and toddlers: Development and program planning.* Clifton Park, NY: Delmar Learning.

Erikson, E. H. (1950). *Childhood and society.* New York: Norton.

Greenman, J., & Stonehouse, A. (1996). *Prime times: A handbook for excellence in infant and toddler programs.* St. Paul, MN: Redleaf Press.

Herr, J. (1998). *Working with young children.* Homewood, IL: Goodheart-Wilcox.

Kail, R. U. (1998). *Children and their development.* Upper Saddle River, NJ: Prentice Hall.

Kratcoski, A. M., & Katz, K. B. (1998). Conversing with young language learners in the classroom. *Young Children, 53*(3), 30–33.

Piaget, J. (1952). *The origins of intelligence in children.* York: International Universities Press.

Piaget, J. (1977). The role of action in the development of thinking. In W. F. Overton & J. M. Gallagher (Eds.), *Knowledge and development* (Vol. 1). New York: Plenum.

Rice, F. P. (1997). *Child and adolescent development.* Saddle River, NJ: Prentice Hall.

Santrock, J. W. (1993). *Children* (3rd ed.). Madison, WI: Brown and Benchmark.

Sénéchal, M., Thomas, E., & Monker, J. (1995). Children's acquisition of vocabulary during storybook reading. *Journal of Educational Psychology, 87,* 218–229.

Shore, R. (1997). *Rethinking the brain: New insights into early development.* New York: Families and Work Institute.

Snow, C. W. (1998). *Infant development* (2nd ed.). Upper Saddle River, NJ: Prentice Hall.

Spodek, B. (Ed.). (1993). *Handbook of research on the education of young children.* New York: Macmillan.

Young children need to be immersed in a literacy-rich environment. A foundation for reading success begins as early as the first few months of life. Exposure to books and caring adults nourishes literacy development. Books and oral language are tools to help toddlers become familiar with language. Young children enjoy handling books and listening to stories. Toddlers enjoy the visual and auditory stimulation of having books read to them over and over again.

Books help very young children by:

- Developing visual discrimination skills
- Developing visual memory skills
- Developing listening skills
- Developing auditory memory skills
- Presenting new and interesting information
- Introducing new vocabulary
- Stimulating new thoughts and ideas
- Helping children learn book-handling skills such as turning pages and reading text versus pictures

Books that are developmentally appropriate for toddlers are abundant. Some of the best examples feature various physical formats combined with clearly developed concepts or a simple story and distinctive art or photographic work.

Books for toddlers feature a scaled-down size and sturdiness. Other features may include interactivity such as touch-and-feel, lift-the-flaps, and detachable or cling-on pieces. Concept development remains paramount, and simple stories predominate. Recently, several picture book stories have been redone in board book format, greatly expanding the availability of quality literature for toddlers.

SELECTING BOOKS

Careful consideration should be given to selecting age-appropriate books for young children. When choosing books, begin by looking for award winners. You can ask the librarian at your local library to give you a list of award-winning picture books; likewise, do not hesitate to ask the salesperson at a local bookstore to provide this information. Chances are they will have a list of these award-winning books or can complete a computer search to obtain this information for you. On-line merchants should also be able to provide you this information.

You should also review the illustrations for size and quality before selecting a picture book. Study them carefully. You will notice a wide variety of illustration types in books for toddlers. There are photographs, watercolors, line drawings, and collages. As you review books, remember that toddlers need to have large, realistic illustrations. Realistic illustrations serve two purposes: They help the young children maintain their interest in the book and they help develop concept formation.

Other questions beside award-winning status and quality of illustrations to ask yourself while evaluating books for young toddlers include:

- Is the book developmentally appropriate for the child or group of children?
- Does the book have visual appeal?
- Are the pages thick, durable, and easy to clean?
- Are the illustrations large and brightly colored?
- Do the illustrations contain pictures of familiar objects, routines, or people?
- Does the story reflect the children's own experiences?
- Is the vocabulary appropriate?

For older toddlers, ask yourself the following questions:

- Is the story simple and easy to follow?
- Does the book contain rhyming or repetitive phrases to entice toddlers to join in the reading?
- Does the book accurately depict children and/or people of different races, cultures, and abilities?

TRANSITIONING TO PAPER BOOKS

Older toddlers may be ready to transition to paper books. At first, provide paper copies only when you can constantly supervise their use. Toddlers' fine motor skills can still be somewhat jerky, resulting in torn pages. In addition, until they have been taught how to appropriately handle paper pages, toddlers tend to treat paper books in the same manner as they would cardboard books. With your guidance, they can learn to read a paper book "just like a big kid."

SUGGESTIONS FOR READING TO TODDLERS

There are seven steps to making reading an enjoyable and educational experience for toddlers.

everyone

♡ Ask questions to engage children in conversation. The experience should be as much about speaking skills as listening skills for young children.

♡ Pause to encourage children to read along with you. You will find that toddlers will supply words or phrases. These experiences also serve to reinforce the development of turn-taking skills.

♡ Follow their lead. For example, encourage children to turn the pages. Do not worry if pages are skipped. It is highly likely that whatever you miss now will be covered in future readings of the book.

♡ Encourage children to read the story to you.

♡ Read for as long as children enjoy it. Forcing young children to remain in a situation when they are finished only serves to diminish their "love of books."

♡ Share your enthusiasm for the book through your voice and facial expressions. Children learn to love books when an adult shares their own enjoyment.

CLOTH BOOKS

Animal Play. Dorling Kindersley, 1996.

Briggs, Raymond. *The Snowman.* Random House, 1993.

Cousins, Lucy. My First Cloth Book series. Candlewick Press.
   Flower in the Garden. 1992.
   Hen on the Farm. 1992.
   Kite in the Park. 1992.
   Teddy in the House. 1992.

Harte, Cheryl. *Bunny Rattle.* Random House, 1989. (Has a rattle in it)
   Ducky Squeak. Random House, 1989. (Has a squeaker in it)

Hill, Eric. *Clothes-Spot Cloth Book.* Putnam, 1993.
   Play-Spot Cloth Book. Putnam, 1993.

My First Notebook. Eden International Ltd. (Has a rattle inside and plastic spiral rings.)

Pienkowski, Jan. Jan Pienkowski's First Cloth Book series. Little Simon.
   Animals. 1995.
   Friends. 1995.
   Fun. 1996.
   Play. 1995.

Pienkowski, Jan. *Bronto's Brunch.* Dutton Books, 1995. (Has detachable pieces. Ages 3+)
   Good Night, Moo. Dutton Books, 1995. (Has detachable pieces. Ages 3+)

Ulrich, George. *Baby's Peek A Boo.* 1989.

Tong, Willabel L. Cuddly Cloth Books. Andrews & McMeel.
   Farm Faces. 1996.
   My Pets. 1997.
   My Toys. 1997.
   Zoo Faces. 1997.

Tucker, Sian. My First Cloth Book series. Simon & Schuster.
   Quack, Quack. 1994.
   Rat-A-Tat-Tat. 1994.
   Toot Toot. 1994.
   Yum Yum. 1994.

VINYL COVER AND BATH BOOKS

Bracken, Carolyn. *Baby's First Rattle: A Busy Bubble Book.* Simon & Schuster, 1984.

De Brunhoff, Laurent. *Babar's Bath Book.* Random House, 1992.

Hill, Eric. *Spot's Friends.* Putnam, 1984.
   Spot's Toys. Putnam, 1984.
   Sweet Dreams, Spot. Putnam, 1984.

Hoban, Tana. *Tana Hoban's Red, Blue, Yellow Shoe.* Greenwillow Books, 1994.
   Tana Hoban's What Is It? Greenwillow Books, 1994.

I. M. Tubby. *I'm a Little Airplane.* Simon & Schuster, 1982. (Shape book)
   I'm a Little Choo Choo. Simon & Schuster, 1982. (Shape book)
   I'm a Little Fish. Simon & Schuster, 1981. (Shape book)

My First Duck. Dutton, 1996. (Playskool shape book)

Nicklaus, Carol. *Grover's Tubby.* Random House/Children's Television Workshop, 1992.

Potter, Beatrix. Beatrix Potter Bath Books series. Frederick Warne & Co.
   Benjamin Bunny. 1994.
   Jemima Puddle-Duck. 1988.
   Mr. Jeremy Fisher. 1989.
   Peter Rabbit. 1989.
   Tom Kitten, Mittens, and Moppet. 1989.

Reichmeier, Betty. *Potty Time.* Random House, 1988.

Smollin, Michael J. *Ernie's Bath Book.* Random House/Children's Television Workshop, 1982.

Tucker, Sian. Sian Tucker Bath Books series. Simon & Schuster.
   Animal Splash. 1995.
   Splish Splash. 1995.

Hanna, Jack. *Let's Go to the Petting Zoo with Jungle Jack.* Doubleday, 1992.

Hill, Eric. *Spot's Touch and Feel Day.* Putnam, 1997.

Kunhardt, Dorothy. *Pat the Bunny.* Western Publishing, 1968.

Kunhardt, Dorothy & Edith. *Pat the Cat.* Western Publishing, 1984.

Pat the Puppy. Western Publishing, 1993.

Lodge, J. *Patch and His Favorite Things.* Harcourt Brace, 1996.

Patch in the Garden. Harcourt Brace, 1996.

Offerman, Lynn. *Puppy Dog's Special Friends.* Joshua Morris Publishing, 1998.

Scarry, Richard. *Richard Scarry's Egg in the Hole Book.* Golden Books, 1997.

Witte, Pat & Eve. *The Touch Me Book.* Golden Books, 1946.

CHUNKY AND CHUBBY BOOKS

Barton, Byron. Chunky Board Book series. HarperCollins.
Boats. 1994.
Planes. 1994.
Trains. 1994.

Bond, Michael. *Paddington at the Seashore.* HarperCollins, 1992.

Brown, Marc. Chunky Flap Book series. Random House.
Arthur Counts. 1998.
Arthur's Farm Tales. 1998.
D.W.'s Color Book. 1997.
Where Is My Frog? 1991.
Where's Arthur's Gerbil? 1997.
Where's My Sneaker? 1991.

Cowley, Rich. *Snap! Snap! Buzz Buzz.* Firefly Books, 1996.

Dunn, Phoebe. *Baby's Animal Friends.* Random House, 1988.
Farm Animals. Random House, 1984.

Freeman, Don. *Corduroy's Toys.* Viking, 1985.

Fujikawa, Gyo. *Good Night, Sleep Tight! Shhh . . .* Random House, 1990. (Chunky shape)

Hill, Eric. Spot Block Book series. Putnam.
Spot's Favorite Baby Animals. 1997.
Spot's Favorite Numbers. 1997.
Spot's Favorite Words. 1997.

Hirashima, Jean. *ABC.* Random House, 1994. (Chunky shape)

Schuster.
At the Shore. 1996.
Family Time. 1996.
Happy Days. 1996.
Let's Play. 1997.
My Best Friends. 1996.
Water Play. 1996.
Wheels Go Round. 1997.

Oxenbury, Helen. *Helen Oxenbury's Little Baby Books.* Candlewick Press, 1996.
Boxed set includes: *I Can; I Hear; I See; I Touch.*

Pienkowski, Jan. Nursery Board Book series. Simon & Schuster.
Colors. 1987.   *Sizes.* 1991.
Faces. 1991.   *Stop Go.* 1992.
Food. 1991.   *Time.* 1991.
Homes. 1990.   *Yes No.* 1992.

Ricklen, Neil. Super Chubby Book series. Simon & Schuster.
Baby Outside. 1996.   *Baby's Good Night.*
Baby's 123. 1990.   *Baby's Neighborhood.*
Baby's ABC. 1997.   *Baby's Playtime.* 1994.
Baby's Big & Little. 1996.   *Baby's Toys.* 1997.
Baby's Clothes. 1997.   *Baby's Zoo.* 1992.
Baby's Friends. 1997.   *Daddy and Me.* 1997.
Baby's Home. 1997.   *Mommy and Me.*
Baby's Good Morning. 1992.

Ross, Anna. *Knock Knock, Who's There?* Random House/Children's Television Workshop, 1994. (Chunky flap)

Ross, Katharine. *The Little Quiet Book.* Random House, 1989.

Santoro, Christopher. *Open the Barn Door.* Random House, 1993. (Chunky flap)

Scarry, Richard. *Richard Scarry's Lowly Worm Word Book.* Random House, 1981.
Richard Scarry's Cars and Trucks from A–Z. Random House, 1990. (Chunky shape)

Shappie, Trisha Lee. *Where Is Your Nose?* Scholastic, 1997.

Smollin, Michael. *In & Out, Up & Down.* Random House, Children's Television Network, 1982.
Ernie & Bert Can . . . Can You? Random House, Children's Television Network, 1982.

Snapshot Chubby Book series. Dorling Kindersley.
ABC. 1994.
Colors. 1994.
My Home. 1995.
My Toys. 1995.
Shapes. 1994.

My Friend Bear. 1998.

Bare Bear. Random House, 1984.

Running Bear. 1985.

Bang, Molly. *Ten, Nine, Eight.* First Tupelo Board Book edition. Tupelo Books, 1998.

Boynton, Sandra. Boynton Board Book series. Simon & Schuster.

But Not the Hippopotamus. 1995.

Blue Hat, Green Hat. 1995.

Doggies, A Counting and Barking Book. 1995.

Going to Bed Book. 1995.

Moo, Baa, La La La. 1995.

Opposites. 1995.

Hey! Wake Up! Workman Publishing, 2000.

Brett, Jan. *The Mitten: A Ukrainian Folktale.* Putnam, 1996. (Board book)

Brown, Margaret Wise. First Board Book editions. HarperCollins.

Child's Good Night Book. Pictures by Jean Charlot. 1996.

Goodnight Moon. Pictures by Clement Hurd. 1991.

Runaway Bunny. Pictures by Clement Hurd, 1991.

Carle, Eric. First Board Book editions. HarperCollins.

Do You Want to Be My Friend? 1995.

The Mixed-Up Chameleon. 1998.

The Secret Birthday Message. 1998.

The Very Quiet Cricket. Putnam, 1997.

Have You Seen My Cat? First Little Simon Board Book edition. Simon & Schuster, 1996.

The Very Hungry Caterpillar. First Board Book edition. Philomel Books, 1994.

Carle, Eric. Play-and-Read Books. Cartwheel Books.

Catch the Ball. 1998.

Let's Paint a Rainbow. 1998.

What's for Lunch? 1998.

Carlstrom, Nancy White. Illus. by Bruce Degen. Simon & Schuster. (Board book)

Bizz Buzz Chug-A-Chug: Jesse Bear's Sounds. 1997.

Hooray for Blue: Jesse Bear's Colors. 1997.

I Love You, Mama, Any Time of Year. Jesse Bear Board Book. 1997.

I Love You, Papa, In All Kinds of Weather. Jesse Bear Board Book. 1997.

Jesse Bear, What Will You Wear? 1996.

Choosing Colors. Photos by Sandra Lousada. Dutton Children's Books/Playskool, 1995. (Board book)

Cohen, Miriam. *Backpack Baby.* Star Bright Books, 1999.

Say Hi, Backpack Baby: A Backpack Baby Story. 2000.

Cousins, Lucy. Dutton Children's Books. (Board book)

Humpty Dumpty and Other Nursery Rhymes. 1996.

Book edition. Simon & Schuster, 1997.

Ehlert, Lois. *Color Farm.* First Board Book edition. HarperCollins, 1997.

Color Zoo. First Board Book edition. HarperCollins, 1997.

Eating the Alphabet. First Red Wagon Books. Harcourt Brace, 1996.

Fleming, Denise. *Count!* First Board Book edition. Henry Holt, 1997.

Mama Cat Has Three Kittens. 1998.

The Everything Book. 2000.

Hoban, Tana. *Black on White.* Greenwillow Books, 1993.

Red, Blue, Yellow Shoe. 1986.

What Is It? 1985.

White on Black. 1993.

Hooker, Yvonne. Illus. by Carlo A. Michelini. Poke and Look books. Grosset & Dunlap.

One Green Frog. 1989.

Wheels Go Round. 1989.

Hopp, Lisa. *Circus of Colors.* Illus. by Chiara Bordoni. Poke and Look book. Grosset & Dunlap, 1997.

Isadora, Rachel. *I Touch.* Greenwillow Books, 1991. (Board book)

Keats, Ezra Jack. *The Snowy Day.* Viking, 1996. (Board book)

Kirk, David. *Miss Spider's Tea Party: The Counting Book.* First Board Book edition. Callaway & Kirk/Scholastic Press, 1997.

Lewison, Wendy. *Nighty Night.* Illus. by Giulia Orecchia. Poke and Look book. Grosset & Dunlap, 1992.

Lundell, Margaretta. *Land of Colors.* Illus. by Nadia Pazzaglia. Poke and Look book. Grosset & Dunlap, 1989.

Lundell, Margo. *What Does Baby See?* Illus. by Roberta Pagnoni. Poke and Look book. Putnam & Grosset, 1990.

Martin, Bill. Illus. by Eric Carle. First Board Book editions. Henry Holt.

Brown Bear, Brown Bear, What Do You See? 1996.

Polar Bear, Polar Bear, What Do You Hear? 1997.

Martin, Bill, & Archambault, John. *Chicka Chicka ABC.* Illus. by Lois Ehlert. First Little Simon Board Book edition. Simon & Schuster, 1993.

Marzollo, Jean. *I Spy Little Book.* Illus. by Walter Wick. Scholastic, 1997. (Board book)

I Spy Little Animals. Photos by Walter Wick. 1998. (Board book)

Do You Know New? HarperCollins, 1997.

Mama, Mama. HarperFestival, 1999.

What's On My Head? 1998.

Miller, Virginia. *Be Gentle!* Candlewick Press, 1997.
 Eat Your Dinner! 1992.
 Go to Bed! 1993.
 In a Minute! 2000.
 On Your Potty! 1998.

Ogden, Betina, illus. *Busy Farmyard.* So Tall board book. Grosset & Dunlap, 1995.

Omerod, Jan. *101 Things to Do With a Baby.* Mulberry Books, 1993.

Opie, Iona Archibald. Illus. by Rosemary Wells. Mother Goose Board Book series. Candlewick Press.
 Pussycat, Pussycat and Other Rhymes. 1997.
 Humpty Dumpty and Other Rhymes. 1997.
 Little Boy Blue and Other Rhymes. 1997.
 Wee Willie Winkie and Other Rhymes. 1997.

Oxenbury, Helen. Baby Board Books. Wanderer Books.
 Dressing. 1981.
 Family. 1981.
 Friends. 1981.
 Playing. 1981.
 Working. 1981.

Pfister, Marcus. Board book. North-South Books.
 Hopper. 1998.
 Hopper Hunts for Spring. 1998.
 The Rainbow Fish. 1996.
 Rainbow Fish to the Rescue. 1998.

Pinkney, Andrea & Brian. *Pretty Brown Face.* Harcourt Brace, 1997.

Piper, Watty. *The Little Engine That Could.* Illus. by Christina Ong. Platt & Munk, 1991.

Potter, Beatrix. *The Tale of Peter Rabbit.* Illus. by Florence Graham. Pudgy Pal Board Book. Grosset & Dunlap, 1996.

Pragoff, Fiona. Fiona Pragoff Board Books. Simon & Schuster.
 Baby Days. 1995.
 Baby Plays. 1995.
 Baby Ways. 1994.
 It's Fun to Be One. 1994.
 It's Fun to Be Two. 1994.

Raffi. First Board Book editions. Crown Publishers.

Rey, H. A. & Margret. Board books. Houghton Mifflin, 1998.
 Curious George and the Bunny. 1998.
 Curious George's ABC's. 1998.
 Curious George's Are You Curious? 1998.
 Curious George's Opposites. 1998.

Rosen, Michael. *We're Going on a Bear Hunt.* Illus. by Helen Oxenbury. First Little Simon Board Book edition. Simon & Schuster, 1997.

Seuss, Dr. Bright and Early Board Book series. Random House.
 Dr. Seuss's ABC. 1996.
 The Foot Book. 1997.
 Mr. Brown Can Moo, Can You? 1996.
 The Shape of Me and Other Stuff. 1997.
 There's a Wocket in My Pocket. 1996.

Snapshot Board Book series. Dorling Kindersley.
 All about Baby by Stephen Shott. 1994.
 Baby and Friends by Paul Bricknell. 1994.
 Good Morning, Baby by Jo Foord, et al. 1994.
 Good Night, Baby by Mike Good & Stephen Shott. 1994.

Waddell, Martin. *Owl Babies.* Illus. by Patrick Benson. First Board Book edition. Candlewick Press, 1992.

Wells, Rosemary. *Max's Birthday.* Max Board Book. Dial Books for Young Readers, 1998.
 Old MacDonald. Bunny Reads Back Board Book. Scholastic, 1998.

Wilkes, Angela. *My First Word Board Book.* Dorling Kindersley, 1997.

Williams, Sue. *I Went Walking.* Illus. by Julie Vivas. First Red Wagon Books edition. Harcourt Brace, 1996.

Williams, Vera B. *More, More, More Said the Baby.* Tupelo Board Book edition. William Morrow, 1997.

Wood, Jakki. *Moo Moo, Brown Cow.* Illus. by Rog Bonner. First Red Wagon Board book. Harcourt Brace, 1996.

Ziefert, Harriet. Board Book. Dorling Kindersley.
 Food! 1996.
 Let's Get Dressed. Illus. by Susan Baum. 1997.
 My Clothes. 1996.

POP-UP BOOKS

Capucilli, Alyssa Satin. *Peekaboo Bunny: Friends in the Snow.* Scholastic, 1995.

Cousins, Lucy. *Maisy's ABC.* Candlewick Press, 1994.

Demarest, Chris L. *Honk!* Bell Books, 1998.

Doyle, Malachy. *Well, a Crocodile Can.* Millbrook Press, 2000.

Leslie, Amanda. *Flappy, Waggy, Wiggly.* Dutton, 1999.

Nagy, Krisztina (Illus.). *Fuzzy Bear's Bedtime.* Piggy Toes Press, 1999.

Nobles, Kristen. *Drive This Book.* Chronicle Books, 2001.
   Kiss This Book. Chronicle Books, 2001.

Rowe, Jeanette. *Whose Feet?* Little, Brown, 1998.

MOVEABLE BOOKS

Alexander, Harry. Mop Top Books series. Reader's Digest.
   Blue Rabbit. 2000.
   Red Dog. 2000.
   Yellow Bird. 2000.
   Green Cat. 2000.

Cousins, Lucy. *Maisy at the Farm.* Candlewick Press, 1998.

Davenport, Andrew. *Teletubbies: Po's Magic Watering Can.* Scholastic, 2000.

Davis, Billy (Illus.). *Tap the Tambourine!* Scholastic, 2000.

Dr. Seuss. *The Cat In The Hat's Great Big Flap Book.* Random House, 1999.

Maloney, Joan. *Teletubbies: The Boom-Boom Dance.* Scholastic, 2000.

Murphy, Chuck. *Slide 'n Seek Colors.* Simon & Schuster, 2001.

Regan, Dana. *Wheels on the Bus.* Scholastic, 1996.

Touch and Feel Farm. DK Publishing, 1998.

Touch and Feel Home. DK Publishing, 1998.

Watt, Fiona. *That's Not My Bunny.* Usborne, 2000.
   That's Not My Kitten. 2000.
   That's Not My Teddy. 1999.
   That's Not My Train. 2000.

Wells, Rosemary. *Goodnight, Max.* Penguin Putnam, 2000.

CLOTH BOOKS

Cousins, Lucy. *Flower in the Garden.* Candlewick Press, 1992.

Milne, A. A. *Hello, Eeyore.* Dutton Children's Books, 2000.
   Hello, Piget. 2000.
   Hello, Pooh. 1998.
   Hello, Tigger. 1998.

Ross, Anna. Furry Faces series. Random House.
   Big Bird. 1999.
   Cookie Monster. 1999.
   Elmo. 1999.
   Ernie. 1999.
   Grover. 1999.
   Oscar. 1999.

Warne, Frederick. *My Peter Rabbit Cloth Book.* Books, 1994.

BOARD BOOKS

Albee, Sarah. *Budgie and Pippa Count to Ten.* Simon & Schuster, 1996.
   Oreo Cookie Counting Book. 2000.

Alborough, Jed. *Hug.* Candlewick Press, 2000.

Awdry, Rev. W. *Thomas' Busy Day.* Random House, 2000.

Bailey, Debbie. *Hats.* Annick Press, 1991.

Boynton, Sandra. *Moo, Baa, La La.* Simon & Schuster, 1995.

Brown, Margaret Wise. *Goodnight Moon.* Harper & Row, 1947.

Carlstrom, Nancy White. *Jesse Bear's Tra-la Lub.* 1994.
   Jesse Bear's Tum-tum Tickle. 1994.

dePaola, Tomie. *Tomie's Little Mother Goose.* Putnam & Grosset, 1985.

Dadko, Mary Ann. *Barney's Color Surprise.* Barney Publishing, 1993.

Degen, Bruce. *Jamberry.* Harper & Row, 1983.

Eastman, P. D. *Go Dogs, Go.* Random House, 1961.

Endersby, Frank. *Baby Sitter.* Child's Play, 1986.

Freeman, Don. *Corduroy Goes to the Doctor.* Viking, 1987.
   Corduroy's Busy Street. Viking, 1987.
   Corduroy's Party. Viking, 1985.

Geddes, Anne. *1-2-3.* Especially Kids, 1995.
   Colors. 1995.
   Dress Ups. 1995.
   Faces. 1995.

George, Emma. *Hop and Play.* Joshua Morris Publishing, 1989.

Greenfield, Eloise. *Honey, I Love.* Crowell, 1978.
   Kia Tanisha. HarperCollins, 1997.

Hayward, Linda. *Mine!* Random House, 1988.

Hines, Anna. *What Can You Do in the Rain?* Greenwillow, 1999.
   What Can You Do in the Snow? 1999.
   What Can You Do in the Sun? 1999.
   What Can You Do in the Wind? 1999.

Papa, Papa. 2000.

McGrath, Barbara B. *M & M's Counting Board Book.* Charlesbridge, 1997.

Miller, Virginia. *Go to Bed.* Candlewick Press, 1993.
On Your Potty. 1994.

Opie, Iona. *Humpty Dumpty and Other Rhymes.* Candlewick Press, 1996.
Little Boy Blue. 1996.

Oxenbury, Helen. *Tom and Pippa.* Simon & Schuster, 1988.

Pandell, Karen. *Around the House.* DK Publishing, 1993.
In the Yard. DK Publishing, 1993.
I Love You, Sun, I Love You, Moon. G. P. Putnam's, 1994.

Pfister, Marcus. *Where Is My Friend?* NorthSouth Books, 1986.

Pinkney, Andrea & Brian. *Pretty Brown Face.* Harcourt Brace, 1997.

Tafuri, Nancy. *This Is the Farmer.* Greenwillow Books, 1994.

Tangvald, Christine & Rondi. *My Two Feet.* Chariot, 1990.
My Two Hands. 1990.

Waddell, Martin. *Owl Babies.* Candlewick Press, 1992.

Wellington, Monica. *Baby at Home.* Dutton Children's Books, 1997.
Baby Goes Shopping. 1997.
Bunny's Rainbow Day. 1999.

Wells, Rosemary. *Bear Went over the Mountain.* Scholastic, 1998.
BINGO. 1999.
Itsy Bitsy Spider. 1998.
Old MacDonald. 1998.
Max's Bath. Dial Books for Young Readers, 1985.

Williams, Sue. *I Went Walking.* Harcourt Brace, 1989.

Wolff, Ashley (Illus.). *Baby Beluga.* Crown, 1990.

Worth, Bonnie. *Bye-bye, Blankie.* Western Publishing, 1992.

VINYL BOOKS

Hoban, Tana. *Red, Blue, Yellow Shoe.* Greenwillow, 1994.

Warne, Frederick. *Benjamin Bunny.* Penguin Books, 1994.
Tom Kitten, Mittens, and Moppet. 1989.

Yablonsky, Buster. *Where Is Slippery Soap?* Nikelodeon, 2001.

SCRATCH AND SNIFF

DK Publishing.
Garden. 1999.
Food. 1999.
Party. 1999.

Carlstrom, Nancy White. *Jesse Bear, What Will You Wear?* Macmillan, 1986.

Cousins, Lucy. *Maisy* (series). Candlewick Press, 2001.

Crews, Donald. *Flying.* Greenwillow, 1986.

Davis, Katie. *Who Hoots?* Harcourt Brace, 2000.

Day, Alexandra. *Carl* (series). Farrar Straus Giroux, 1995.

Falwell, Cathryn. *We Have a Baby.* Clarion, 1993.

Florian, Douglas. *Vegetable Garden.* Voyager, 1991.

Ford, Miela. *Follow the Leader.* Greenwillow, 1996.
Little Elephant. 1994.

Fox, Mem. *Zoo Looking.* Mondo, 1996.

Frankel, Alona. *Once Upon a Potty* (His/hers versions). Barron's, 1984.

French, Vivian. *Not Again, Anna!* Levinson, 1998.
Oh No, Anna! Peachtree, 1997.

Gardiner, Lindsey. *Here Come Poppy and Max.* Little, Brown, 2000.

Geddes, Anne. *Down in the Garden (Alphabet Book).* Cedco, 1997.
Down in the Garden (Counting Book). 1997.

Ginsburg, Mirra. *Asleep, Asleep.* Greenwillow, 1992.

Hubbell, Patricia. *Pots and Pans.* Harper, 1998.
Bouncing Time. Harper, 2000.

Jay, Allison. *Picture This.* Dutton, 1999.

Krauss, Ruth. *Carrot Seed.* HarperTrophy, 1945.

LaCome, Julie. *I'm a Jolly Farmer.* Candlewick Press, 1994.

Lavis, Steve. *Cock-a-doodle-doo.* Lodestar Books, 1996.

Lewis, Kevin. *Chugga-chugga Choo-choo.* Hyperion, 1999.

Maccarone, Grace. *Cars! Cars! Cars!* Scholastic, 1995.
Oink, Moo! How Do You Do? Scholastic, 1995.

Mayer, M. *I was so mad.* A Golden Book, 1983.
Me Too! 1983.
When I Get Bigger. 1983.

Paul, Ann W. *Hello Toes! Hello Feet!* DK Ink, 1998.

Rau, Dana Meachen. *A Box Can Be Many Things.* Children's Press, 1997.

Reid, Rob. *Wave Goodbye.* Lee & Low, 1996.

Siddals, Mary McKenna. *I'll Play With You.* Clarion, 2000.

Sis, Peter. *Fire Truck.* Greenwillow, 1998.
Trucks, Trucks, Trucks. 1999.

Trapani, I. *I'm A Little Teapot.* Whispering Coyote Press, 1996.
The Itsy Bitsy Spider. 1993.

Whitman, Candace. *Now It Is Morning.* Farrar Straus Giroux, 1999.

Williams, Sue. *I Went Walking.* Harcourt Brace, 1989.

and Equipment for Children

Even though most materials and equipment appear safe, you will find that toddlers have an uncanny ability to find and remove parts. This may pose a threat. Therefore, to reduce safety hazards, you must constantly check and observe. When purchasing or choosing materials and equipment to use with toddlers, carefully determine if the items promote safety and development by using the following checklist.

SAFETY	Yes	No
A. Is it unbreakable?		
B. Is it durable?		
C. Is it washable?		
D. Is it too large to be swallowed?		
E. Is it free of removable parts?		
F. Is it free of sharp edges?		
G. Is it constructed from nontoxic materials?		
H. Is it free of pinching cracks?		
I. Is it suitable for the available space?		
PROMOTES DEVELOPMENT		
A. Is it developmentally appropriate?		
B. Does it challenge the child's development?		
C. Does it complement existing materials or equipment?		
D. Does it teach multiple skills?		
E. Does it involve the child?		
F. Is it nongender biased?		
G. Does it promote a multicultural perspective?		
H. Does it promote nonviolent play?		

Promoting Optimal Development

Materials and equipment play a major role in promoting a toddler's development, as well as provide enjoyment.

Materials and Equipment to Promote Development for Toddlers

animal, toy
baby lotion
balls
bells
blanket or mat
blocks for building, lightweight
books (black & white and picture
    books—cardboard, cloth, and/or
    vinyl)
carpet pieces
cars, large toy
cassettes or compact discs, a variety
    of music: jazz, lullabies, classical,
    etc.
couch or sturdy furniture
crayons, large
diaper-changing table
dishes, nonbreakable (e.g., cups,
    spoons, plates)
doll accessories: blanket, bed,
    clothes

dolls, multiethnic
doughs and clays
elastic bands
fill and dump toys
glider
high chair
household items (e.g., pots, pans,
    wooden spoons, metal or plastic
    bowls, laundry baskets)
infant seat
infant stroller
large beads to string
mirrors (unbreakable)
mobile
musical instruments, child-size
nesting cups
pacifier
pails and shovels
paintbrushes
pictures of infants
pillows

pop-up toys
props to accompany finger plays
puppets
puzzles with large pieces
push and pull toys
rattles, different sizes, shapes,
    weights, and textures
riding toys
rocking chair
rubber toys
squeeze toys
stacking rings
stroller
stuffed animals
sun catchers
tape or compact disc recorder
teething rings
towels
toy telephones
wheeled toys
wind chimes

in addition . . .
blocks
cardboard boxes
dramatic play items: pots, pans, dishes
dress-up clothes: hats, shoes,
    scarves, jewelry, purse
drum
hammer and peg toy

masks
nuts and bolts
pencils and washable felt-tip
    markers
ring toss game
sand toys: scoops, shovels, cans, sifters
simple puzzles
simple shape sorters

snap beads
transportation toys: cars, trucks,
    boats, trains, airplanes
tricycles
wagon
wheelbarrow
wheeled push toys

Thirteen to Thirty-Six Months

Movement activities, like music, are valuable for young children. Movement is an important tool for young children to express themselves. They can move to verbal directions or music. For example, you may ask the children to lumber along like an elephant or hop like a bunny. Remember children's responses to movement will vary depending on age.

Through movement activities children can:

♡ Learn vocabulary words such as fast, slow, soft, and loud

♡ Explore their bodies as they move

♡ Practice combining rhythm and movements

♡ Learn how movement is related to space

♡ Express their imaginations (Herr 2001, p. 140)

This appendix contains movement activities designed for young children. To introduce these activities, you should demonstrate the actions for the children, while simultaneously giving the directions.

LISTEN TO THE DRUM

Fast.
Slow.
Heavy.
Soft.
Big.
Small.

MOVING SHAPES

Try to move like something huge and heavy—
   an elephant.
Try to move like something small and heavy—
   a fat frog.
Try to move like something big and light—
   a beach ball.
Try to move like something small and light—
   a butterfly.

PRESENT PANTOMIME

You're going to get a present.
What is the shape of the box?
How big is the box? Feel the box.
Hold it. Unwrap the present.
Take it out. Now put it back.

OCCUPATION PANTOMIME

Show me how a clown acts.
Show me how a truck driver acts.
Show me how a baby acts.
Show me how a mama acts.
Show me how a daddy acts.
Show me how a bus driver acts.

PANTOMIME FEELINGS

Show me how you look when you are happy.
Show me how you feel when you are tired.
Show me how you feel when you get up in the
   morning.
Show me how you feel when you are sad.
Show me how you feel when you are mad.

TO BECOME AWARE OF SPACE

Place your leg in front of you.
Place your leg in back of you.
Lift your leg in front of you.
Reach up high to the ceiling.
Touch the floor.

TO BECOME AWARE OF TIME

Run very fast.
Walk very slowly.
Jump up and down.
Jump slowly.
Jump fast.
Sit down on the floor slowly.
Slowly curl up on the floor as small as possible.

Nursery Rhymes, and Chants

Finger plays, nursery rhymes, and chants help toddlers to develop social interaction skills, listening and auditory memory skills, expressive language skills, and concept formation. They also help toddlers become aware of their body parts and see themselves as persons who can do things.

Finger plays use a variety of actions and words together; some involve whole body actions. An example is the finger play "This Little Piggy," which is a favorite for infants. The younger the child, the shorter and simpler the rhyme and the body action need to be. For these children, larger body parts are more suitable. The young child will join you visually and participate in the actions before learning the words. Typically, after repeated exposure, the toddlers will gradually learn some of the words while others may learn the entire finger play. This appendix contains examples of finger plays, nursery rhymes, and chants that children may enjoy. Note that finger plays can be an important technique for teaching "Who am I?"; young children particularly enjoy these activities when their names are included.

ANIMALS

Can you hop like a rabbit?
   (*suit actions to words*)
Can you jump like a frog?
Can you walk like a duck?
Can you run like a dog?
Can you fly like a bird?
Can you swim like a fish?
And be still like a good child?
As still as this?

BODY TALK

When I smile, I tell you that I'm happy.
   (*point to the mouth*)
When I frown I tell you that I am sad.
   (*pull down corners of the mouth*)
When I raise my shoulders and tilt my head I tell you,
   "I don't know."
   (*raise shoulders, tilt head, raise hands, and shake head*)

BRUSHING TEETH

I move the toothbrush back and forth.
   (*pretend to brush teeth*)
I brush all of my teeth.
I swish the water to rinse them and then
   (*puff out cheeks to swish*)
I look at myself and smile.
   (*smile at one another*)

THE CHIMNEY

Here is the chimney,
   (*make hand into a fist with thumb inside*)
Here is the top.
   (*place other hand on top of fist*)

Open the lid.
   (*remove top hand*)
Out Santa will pop.
   (*pop up thumb*)

A CIRCLE

Around in a circle we will go.
Little tiny baby steps make us go very slow.
And then we'll take some great giant steps,
As big as they can be.
Then in a circle we'll stand quietly.

CIRCUS CLOWN

I'd like to be a circus clown
And make a funny face,
   (*make a funny face*)
And have all the people laugh at me
As I jump around the place.
   (*act silly and jump around*)

CLAP YOUR HANDS I

Clap your hands 1, 2, 3.
   (*suit actions to words*)
Clap your hands just like me.
Roll your hands 1, 2, 3.
Roll your hands just like me.

CLAP YOUR HANDS 2

Clap, clap, clap your hands,
As slowly as you can.
Clap, clap, clap your hands,
As fast as you can.

(*move arms faster*)
Tick, tock, tick, tock.
And the very tiny clocks make a sound
(*move still faster*)
Like tick, tick, tock, tock.
Tick, tock, tick, tock, tick, tock.

FIVE LITTLE PUMPKINS

(*hold up five fingers and bend them down one
    at a time as verse progresses*)
Five little pumpkins sitting on a gate;
The first one said, "My it's getting late."
The second one said, "There are witches in the air."
The third one said, "But we don't care."
The fourth one said, "Let's run, let's run."
The fifth one said, "It's Halloween fun."
"Wooooooo" went the wind,
    (*sway hand through the air*)
And out went the lights.
    (*loud clap*)
These five little pumpkins ran fast out of sight.
    (*place hands behind back*)

FRIENDS

I like my friends,
So when we are at play,
I try to be very kind
And nice in every way.

GOBBLE, GOBBLE

A turkey is a funny bird,
His head goes wobble, wobble.
    (*place hands together and move back and forth*)
And he knows just one word,
Gobble, gobble, gobble.

GRANDMA'S SPECTACLES

(*bring index finger and thumb together and place against face
    as if wearing glasses*)
These are Grandma's spectacles.
This is Grandma's hat.
    (*bring fingertips together in a peak over head*)
This is the way she folds her hands,
    (*clasp hands together*)
And lays them in her lap.
    (*lay hands in lap*)

Now let us count the balls we made:
    One,
    Two,
    Three
    (*repeat making the balls to reinforce the concepts by
    showing the increasing size*)

HICKORY, DICKORY, DOCK

Hickory, dickory, dock.
The mouse ran up the clock.
The clock struck one, the mouse ran down,
Hickory, dickory, dock.

I LOOKED INSIDE MY MIRROR

I looked inside my mirror
To see what I could see.
It looks like I am happy today,
Because that smiling face is me.

I LOVE MY FAMILY

Some families are large.
    (*spread arms out wide*)
Some families are small.
    (*bring arms close together*)
But I love my family
    (*cross arms over chest*)
Best of all!

JACK AND JILL

Jack and Jill went up a hill
To fetch a pail of water.
Jack fell down and broke his crown
And Jill fell tumbling after.

JACK-IN-THE-BOX

Jack-in-the-box
Sit so still
    (*squat or stoop down, placing hands over head as a cover*)
Won't you come out?
Yes, I will!
    (*open hands and jump up*)

And pulled out a plum
   (*point thumb up*)
And said, "What a good boy am I!"
   (*say out loud*)

LITTLE MISS MUFFET

Little Miss Muffet
Sat on a tuffet
Eating her curds and whey.
Along came a spider
And sat down beside her
And frightened Miss Muffet away!

RING AROUND THE ROSIE

(*teacher and children hold hands and walk around
   in a circle*)
Ring around the rosie,
A pocket full of posies,
Ashes, ashes,
We all fall down.
   (*everyone falls to the ground*)

THE MONKEY

The monkey claps, claps, claps his hands.
   (*clap hands*)
The monkey claps, claps his hands.
   (*clap hands*)
Monkey see, monkey do,
The monkey does the same as you.
   (*use pointer finger*)

The monkey pats his arm, pats his arm.
   (*pat arm*)
The monkey pats his arm, pats his arm.
   (*pat arm*)
Monkey see, monkey do,
The monkey does the same as you.
   (*use pointer finger*)

The monkey touches his head, touches his head.
   (*touch head*)
The monkey touches his head, touches his head.
   (*touch head*)
Monkey see, monkey do,
The monkey does the same as you.
   (*use pointer finger*)

The monkey gives a big smile, gives a big smile.
   (*smile big*)
The monkey gives a big smile, gives a big smile.
   (*smile big*)

Monkey see, monkey do,
The monkey does the same as you.
   (*use pointer finger*)

THE MUFFIN MAN

Oh, do you know the muffin man,
The muffin man, the muffin man?
Oh, do you know the muffin man
Who lives on Drury Lane?
Yes, I know the muffin man,
The muffin man, the muffin man.
Oh, yes, I know the muffin man
Who lives on Drury Lane.

THE MULBERRY BUSH

(*Since this is a lengthy finger play, begin with just a verse or
two and then gradually individually add the remaining verses
as the toddlers gain proficiency.*)

Here we go 'round the mulberry bush,
The mulberry bush, the mulberry bush.
Here we go 'round the mulberry bush,
So early in the morning.

This is the way we wash our clothes,
Wash our clothes, wash our clothes.
This is the way we wash our clothes,
So early Monday morning.

This is the way we iron our clothes,
Iron our clothes, iron our clothes.
This is the way we iron our clothes,
So early Tuesday morning.

This is the way we scrub our clothes,
Scrub our clothes, scrub our clothes.
This is the way we scrub our clothes,
So early Wednesday morning.

This is the way we mend our clothes,
Mend our clothes, mend our clothes.
This is the way we mend our clothes,
So early Thursday morning.

This is the way we sweep the house,
Sweep the house, sweep the house.
This is the way we sweep the house,
So early Friday morning.

This is the way we bake our bread,
Bake our bread, bake our bread.
This is the way we bake our bread,
So early Saturday morning.

activity can be substituted such as barbeque, play ball, mow the lawn, etc.)

MY PUPPY

I like to pet my puppy.
   (*pet puppy*)
He has such nice soft fur.
   (*pet puppy*)
And if I don't pull his tail
   (*pull tail*)
He won't say, "Grr!"
   (*make face*)

MY RABBIT

My rabbit has two big ears
   (*hold up index and middle fingers for ears*)
And a funny little nose.
   (*join the other fingers for a nose*)
He likes to nibble carrots
   (*separate thumb from other two fingers*)
And he hops wherever he goes.
   (*move whole hand jerkily*)

MY TOOTHBRUSH

I have a little toothbrush.
   (*use pointer finger*)
I hold it very tight.
   (*make hand into fist.*)
I brush my teeth each morning,
And then again at night.
   (*use pointer finger and pretend to brush*)

MY TURTLE

This is my turtle.
   (*make fist; extend thumb*)
He lives in a shell.
   (*hide thumb in fist*)
He likes his home very well.
He pokes his head out when he wants to eat.
   (*extend thumb*)
And pulls it back when he wants to sleep.
   (*hide thumb in fist*)

OLD KING COLE

Old King Cole was a merry old soul
   (*lift elbows up and down*)
And a merry old soul was he.
   (*nod head*)

ONE, TWO, BUCKLE MY SHOE

One, two, buckle my shoe.
   (*count on fingers as verse progresses*)
Three, four, shut the door.
   (*suit actions to words*)
Five, six, pick up sticks.
Seven, eight, lay them straight.
Nine, ten, a big tall hen.

OPEN, SHUT THEM

Open, shut them.
   (*suit actions to words*)
Open, shut them.
Open, shut them.
Give a little clap.
Open, shut them.
Open, shut them.
Open, shut them.
Put them in your lap.
Creep them, creep them
Right up to your chin.
Open up your little mouth,
But do not put them in.
Open, shut them.
Open, shut them.
Open, shut them.
To your shoulders fly,
Then like little birdies
Let them flutter to the sky.
Falling, falling almost to the ground,
Quickly pick them up again and turn
Them round and round.
Faster, faster, faster.
Slower, slower, slower.
   (*repeat first verse*)

PAT-A-CAKE

Pat-a-cake, pat-a-cake, baker's man.
Bake me a cake as fast as you can!
   (*clap hands together lightly*)
Roll it
   (*roll hands*)
And pat it
   (*touch hands together lightly*)
And mark it with a *B*
   (*write B in the air*)
And put it in the oven for baby and me.
   (*point to baby and yourself*)

Popcorn, popcorn
In a pot
What'll happen when you get hot?
Boom! Pop. Boom! Pop. Pop.
That's what happens when you get hot!

POPCORN CHANT 3

Popcorn, popcorn
In a dish
How many pieces do you wish?
1, 2, 3, 4
Eat those up and have some more!

RAINDROPS

Rain is falling down.
Rain is falling down.
    (*raise arm, flutter fingers to the ground, tapping the floor*)
Pitter-patter
Pitter-patter
Rain is falling down.

READY NOW, LET'S GO

I am a little kitty,
I have to tippy toe.
Come and do it with me.
Ready now, let's go.
    (*take tiny steps*)

I am a little rabbit.
I love to hop, hop, hop.
Come and do it with me.
It's fun we will never stop.
    (*hop around*)

I am a big bird.
I love to fly around using my wings.
Come and do it with me.
Ready now? Let's go.
    (*use arms as wings to fly*)

I am a great big elephant.
I take big steps so slow.
I'd love to have you join me.
Ready now? Let's go
    (*take slow, big steps*)

This is my right hand,
I'll raise it up high.
    (*raise the right hand up high*)
This is my left hand.
I'll touch the sky.
    (*raise the left hand up high*)
Right hand,
    (*show right palm*)
Left hand,
    (*show left palm*)
Roll them around
    (*roll hands over and over*)
Left hand,
    (*show palm*)
Right hand,
    (*show palm*)
Pound, pound, pound.
    (*hit fists together*)

SEE, SEE, SEE

See, see, see
    (*shade eyes with hands*)
Three birds are in a tree.
    (*hold up three fingers*)
One can chirp
    (*point to thumb*)
And one can sing
    (*point to index finger*)
One is just a tiny thing.
    (*point to middle finger, then rock baby bird in arms*
See, see, see
Three birds are in a tree.
    (*hold up three fingers*)

STAND UP TALL

Stand up tall
Hands in the air.
Now sit down
In your chair.
Clap your hands
And make a frown.
Smile and smile.
Hop like a clown.

"Tip me over, and pour me out."
    (bend to left)
I can change my handle
    (place left hand on hip and extend right hand out)
And my spout.
"Tip me over, and pour me out."
    (bend to the right)

TEDDY BEAR

Teddy bear, teddy bear, turn around.
Teddy bear, teddy bear, touch the ground.
Teddy bear, teddy bear, climb the stairs.
Teddy bear, teddy bear, jump into bed.
Teddy bear, teddy bear, turn out the lights.
Teddy bear, teddy bear, blow a kiss.
Teddy bear, teddy bear, say goodnight.
Goodnight.

TEN LITTLE DUCKS

Ten little ducks swimming in the lake.
    (move ten fingers as if swimming)
Quack! Quack!
    (snap fingers twice)
They give their heads a shake.
    (shake fingers)
Glunk! Glunk! Go go little frogs.
    (two claps of hands)
And away to their mothers,
The ten ducks run.
    (move hands in running motion from front to back)

TEN LITTLE FINGERS

I have ten little fingers and ten little toes.
    (children point to portions of body as they repeat words)
Two little arms and one little nose.
One little mouth and two little ears.
Two little eyes for smiles and tears.
One little head and two little feet.
One little chin, that makes _____ complete.

THIS LITTLE PIGGY

This little piggy went to market.
    (point to one finger at a time)
This little piggy stayed home.
This little piggy had roast beef.
This little piggy had none.
This little piggy cried, "Wee, wee, wee."
And ran all the way home.

Then we will run.
    (hold up three fingers while right hand runs away)

THREE LITTLE DUCKIES

Three little duckies
    (hold up three fingers)
Swimming in the lake.
    (make swimming motions)
The first ducky said,
    (hold up one finger)
"Watch the waves I make."
    (make wave motions)
The second ducky said,
    (hold up two fingers)
"Swimming is such fun."
    (smile)
The third ducky said,
    (hold up three fingers)
"I'd rather sit in the sun."
    (turn face to sun)
Then along came a motorboat.
With a Pop! Pop! Pop!
    (clap three times)
And three little duckies
Swam away from the spot.
    (put three fingers behind back)

THREE LITTLE MONKEYS

Three little monkeys jumping on the bed.
    (hold up three fingers)
One fell off and bumped his head.
Mama called the doctor and the doctor said,
No more monkeys jumping on the bed.
    (shake pointer finger as if scolding)

Two little monkeys jumping on the bed,
    (hold up two fingers)
One fell off and bumped his head.
Mama called the doctor and the doctor said,
No more monkeys jumping on the bed.
    (shake pointer finger as if scolding)

One little monkey jumping on the bed.
    (hold up one finger)
He fell off and bumped his head.
Mama called the doctor and the doctor said,
No more jumping on the bed.
    (shake pointer finger as if scolding)

(*put hands out as if on tree—shake*)
And down they came.
  (*hands above head and lower to ground*)
And ummmmm were they good!
  (*rub tummy*)

TWO LITTLE BLACKBIRDS

Two little blackbirds sitting on a hill.
  (*show two fingers*)
One named Jack.
  (*hold up one finger on right hand*)
One named Jill.
  (*hold up one finger on the left hand*)
Fly away Jack.
  (*move right hand behind back*)
Fly away Jill.
  (*move the left hand behind back*)
Come back Jack.
  (*return right hand*)
Come back Jill.
  (*return left hand*)
(Children's names can be substituted for Jack and Jill in
  this finger play.)

The other little kitten ran away.
  (*make running motion with other hand*)

ZOO ANIMALS

This is the way the elephant goes.
  (*clasp hands together, extend arms, move back and forth*
With a curly trunk instead of a nose.
The buffalo, all shaggy and fat.
Has two sharp horns in place of a hat.
  (*point to forehead*)
The hippo with his mouth so wide
Let's see what's inside.
  (*hands together and open wide and close them*)
The wiggly snake upon the ground
Crawls along without a sound.
  (*weave hands back and forth*)
But monkey see and monkey do is the
funniest animal in the zoo.
  (*place thumbs in ears and wiggle fingers*)

Music is a universal language and a natural form of expression for children of all ages. Toddlers need to have a wide variety of music experiences that are casual and spontaneous. They enjoy lullabies that are slow, soft, and soothing. In addition to lullabies, classical, folk and music from different ethnic and cultural groups should all be included. Children like songs about animals and familiar objects, which tell a story and contain frequent repetition. Choose simple songs with a strong melody that represent their age, abilities, and interests. Chances are children will more easily remember these songs. While singing, remember to convey enthusiasm.

Music is a valuable experience for young children. They enjoy listening to music while engaged in activities and napping. Music promotes the development of listening skills and builds vocabulary. It is a tool that provides an opportunity for learning new concepts such as up/down, fast/slow, heavy/light, and loud/soft. Music releases tension, stimulates the imagination, and promotes the development of auditory memory skills.

ALL ABOUT ME

Brushing Teeth
(Tune: "Mulberry Bush")
This is the way we brush our teeth,
Brush our teeth, brush our teeth.
This is the way we brush our teeth,
So early in the morning.

Good Morning
Good morning to you.
Good morning to you.
We're all in our places,
With bright shining faces,
Good morning to you.

ANIMALS

The Animals on the Farm
(Tune: "The Wheels on the Bus")
The cows on the farm go moo, moo, moo,
Moo, moo, moo, moo, moo, moo.
The cows on the farm go moo, moo, moo,
All day long.

The horses on the farm go nay, nay, nay,
Nay, nay, nay, nay, nay, nay.
The horses on the farm go nay, nay, nay,
All day long.

OTHER VERSES:
Pigs—oink
Sheep—baa
Chicken—cluck
Turkeys—gobble

The Ants Go Marching One by One
The ants go marching one by one.
Hurrah! Hurrah!
The ants go marching one by one.
Hurrah! Hurrah!
The ants go marching one by one.

The little one stops to suck her thumb
And they all go marching,
Down in the ground
To get out of the rain.
Boom Boom Boom

OTHER VERSES:
Two by two
The little one stops to tie his shoe
Three by three
The little one stops to scratch her knee
Four by four
The little one stops to shut the door
Five by five
The little one stops to wave goodbye.

Circus
(Tune: "Did You Ever See a Lassie")
Let's pretend that we are clowns, are clowns, are clowns.
Let's pretend that we are clowns.
We'll have so much fun.
We'll put on our makeup and make people laugh hard.
Let's pretend that we are clowns.
We'll have so much fun.

Let's pretend that we are elephants, are elephants, are
   elephants.
Let's pretend that we are elephants.
We'll have so much fun.
We'll sway back and forth and stand on just two legs.
Let's pretend that we are elephants.
We'll have so much fun.

Let's pretend that we are on a trapeze, a trapeze, a trapeze.
Let's pretend that we are on a trapeze.
We'll have so much fun.
We'll swing high and swoop low and make people
   shout "oh"!
Let's pretend that we are on a trapeze.
We'll have so much fun!

Find all the eggs and put them in a basket,
Find all the eggs and put them in a basket,
Early Easter morning.

Itsy Bitsy Spider
The itsy bitsy spider went up the water spout
Down came the rain and washed the spider out
Out came the sun and dried up all the rain
And the itsy bitsy spider went up the spout again.
(*This is also a popular finger play.*)

Kitty
(*Tune: "Bingo"*)
I have a cat. She's very shy.
But she comes when I call Kitty
K–I–T–T–Y
K–I–T–T–Y
K–I–T–T–Y
and Kitty is her name-o.

(*Variation: Let children think of other names.*)

Old MacDonald Had a Farm
Old MacDonald had a farm,
E-I-E-I-O.
And on his farm he had some cows,
E-I-E-I-O.
With a moo, moo here and a moo, moo there,
Here a moo, there a moo, everywhere a moo, moo.
Old MacDonald had a farm,
E-I-E-I-O.

OTHER VERSES:
Sheep—baa, baa
Pigs—oink, oink
Ducks—quack, quack
Chickens—chick, chick

Two Little Black Bears
(*Tune: "Two Little Blackbirds"*)
Two little black bears sitting on a hill
One named Jack, one named Jill.
Run away Jack
Run away Jill.
Come back Jack
Come back Jill.
Two little black bears sitting on a hill
One named Jack, one named Jill.

Cleanup Time 2
(*Tune: "Hot Cross Buns"*)
Cleanup time.
Cleanup time.
Put all of the toys away.
It's cleanup time.

Do You Know What Time It Is?
(*Tune: "The Muffin Man"*)
Oh, do you know what time it is,
What time it is, what time it is?
Oh, do you know what time it is?
It's almost cleanup time.
    (*Or, it's time to clean up.*)

A Helper I Will Be
(*Tune: "The Farmer in the Dell"*)
A helper I will be.
A helper I will be.
I'll pick up the toys and put them away.
A helper I will be.

It's Cleanup Time
(*Tune: "Looby Loo"*)
It's cleanup time at the preschool.
It's time for boys and girls
To stop what they are doing.
And put away their toys.

Oh, It's Cleanup Time
(*Tune: "Oh, My Darling Clementine"*)
Oh, it's cleanup time,
Oh, it's cleanup time,
Oh, it's cleanup time right now.
It's time to put the toys away,
It is cleanup time right now.

Passing Around
(*Tune: "Skip to My Loo"*)
Brad, take a napkin and pass them to Sara.
Sara, take a napkin and pass them to Tina.
Tina, take a napkin and pass them to Eric.
Passing around the napkins.

(*Fill in the appropriate child's name and substitute for "napkin" any object that needs to be passed at mealtime.*)

This Is the Way
(Tune: "Mulberry Bush")
This is the way we pick up our toys,
Pick up our toys, pick up our toys.
This is the way we pick up our toys,
At cleanup time each day.
(Substituting "before bedtime" opposed to "cleanup time"
could modify this song.)

Time to Clean up
(Tune: "Are You Sleeping?")
Time to clean up.
Time to clean up.
Everybody help.
Everybody help.
Put the toys away, put the toys away.
Then sit down. *(Or, then come here.)*
(Specific toys can be mentioned in place of "toys.")

We're Cleaning Up Our Room
(Tune: "The Farmer in the Dell")
We're cleaning up our room.
We're cleaning up our room.
We're putting all the toys away.
We're cleaning up our room.

FAVORITES

London Bridge
London Bridge is falling down,
Falling down, falling down.
London Bridge is falling down.
My fair lady.

Twinkle, Twinkle, Little Star
Twinkle, twinkle, little star,
How I wonder what you are!
Up above the world so high,
Like a diamond in the sky.
Twinkle, twinkle, little star,
How I wonder what you are!

Where Is Thumbkin?
Where is thumbkin?
Where is thumbkin?
Here I am,
Here I am.
How are you today, sir?
Very well, I thank you.
Fly away, fly away.

Feelings
(Tune: "Twinkle, Twinkle, Little Star")
I have feelings.
You do, too.
Let's all sing about a few.
I am happy. *(smile)*
I am sad. *(frown)*
I get scared. *(wrap arms around self)*
I get mad. *(sneer and wrinkle nose)*
I am proud of being me. *(hands on hips)*
That's a feeling, too, you see.
I have feelings. *(point to self)*
You do, too. *(point to someone else)*
We just sang about a few.

If You're Happy and You Know It
If you're happy and you know it
Clap your hands.
   (clap twice)
If you're happy and you know it
Clap your hands.
   (clap twice)
If you're happy and you know it
Then your face will surely show it.
If you're happy and you know it
Clap your hands.
   (clap twice)

If you're sad and you know it
Say boo-hoo.
   (rub your eyes)
If you're sad and you know it
Say boo-hoo.
   (rub your eyes)
If you're sad and you know it
Then your face will surely show it.
If you're sad and you know it
Say boo-hoo.
   (rub your eyes)

If you're mad and you know it
Wrinkle your nose.
   (wrinkle nose)
If you're mad and you know it
Wrinkle your nose.
   (wrinkle nose)
If you're mad and you know it
Then your face will surely show it.
If you're mad and you know it
Wrinkle your nose.
   (wrinkle nose)

Ding, ding, dong!
Ding, ding, dong!

Do You Know This Friend of Mine?
(Tune: "The Muffin Man")
Do you know this friend of mine,
This friend of mine,
This friend of mine?
Do you know this friend of mine?
Her name is _____.
Yes, we know this friend of yours,
This friend of yours,
This friend of yours.
Yes, we know this friend of yours.
Her name is _____.

The Muffin Man
Oh, do you know the muffin man,
The muffin man, the muffin man?
Oh, do you know the muffin man,
Who lives on Drury Lane?

Oh, yes we know the muffin man,
The muffin man, the muffin man.
Oh, yes we know the muffin man,
Who lives on Drury Lane.

Oh, how do you know the muffin man,
The muffin man, the muffin man?
Oh, how do you know the muffin man,
Who lives on Drury Lane.

Cause [Papaw] is the muffin man,
The muffin man, the muffin man.
[Pawpaw] is the muffin man,
Who lives on Drury Lane.

(Substitute names of other males who are important in the child's life, such as Daddy or Uncle Todd.)

OTHER VERSES:
He played two
He played knick knack on my shoe.
He played three
He played knick knack on a tree
He played four
He played knick knack at my door
He played five
He played knick knack on a hive.

TRANSPORTATION

Row, Row, Row, Your Boat
Row, row, row your boat.
Gently down the stream.
Merrily, merrily, merrily, merrily,
Life is but a dream.

The Wheels on the Bus
The wheels on the bus go round and round.
Round and round, round and round.
The wheels on the bus go round and round.
All around the town.

OTHER VERSES:
The wipers on the bus go swish, swish, swish.
The doors on the bus go open and shut.
The horn on the bus goes beep, beep, beep.
The driver on the bus says, "Move on back."
The people on the bus go up and down.

Using rhythm instruments is a method of teaching young children to express themselves. Rhythm instruments can be common household objects or purchased through school supply stores or catalogs. Examples include:

Commercially Purchased	Household Items
Drums	Pots
Jingle sticks	Pans
Cymbals	Lids
Rattles	Wooden spoons
Wrist bells	Aluminum pie pans
Shakers	Metal whisks
Maracas	Plastic bowls
Sandpaper blocks	

You can also improvise and construct these instruments—save cans, cardboard tubes that have plastic lids from nuts, chips, and coffee. These items can be used as drums. If you place noise-making objects inside the cans or tubes, they can be used as shakers. However, make sure that you secure the lid using a high-quality adhesive tape that children cannot remove.

Play dough and clay are satisfying materials for toddlers. Play dough is softer than clay and is usually preferred by the young toddler because it is pliable and easy to manipulate. When provided a handful of play dough, without encouragement, a child will begin to poke, push, roll, pinch, tear, squeeze, and pound it. Clay, on the other hand, is a firmer or stiffer medium, which requires more refined muscular development to successfully manipulate. As a result, clay typically is more appropriate for older toddlers and children.

Modeling materials such as play dough and clay are valuable tools for the young child. Play dough and play dough accessories provide young children with an opportunity to:

♡ explore materials using their senses
♡ represent their thoughts and ideas
♡ learn the physical nature of materials
♡ develop the ability to make choices
♡ learn to appreciate the value of tools in the human hands

♡ heighten perceptual powers
♡ develop small muscle coordination skills
♡ develop hand-eye coordination skills
♡ express their feelings, explore, and experiment

Colors can be added to play dough to increase interest. Food coloring is the preferred medium to add color to the dough because it will not rub off on a child's hands. Food coloring can be added directly to the liquids required in the recipe. Otherwise, colored tempera can be added to the flour. With this method, the dough requires kneading. A gallon-size, self-sealing plastic bag is a convenient way to mix and knead dough colored with tempera paint.

Give each child a piece of play dough the size of an orange or small grapefruit. Unless using Formica™, Corian™, or granite surface, cover the children's work area with a washable or disposable cover. Establish rules for playing with dough. Such rules might include the following: (1) dough should only be used at the table or other place you designate; (2) children should not be allowed to interfere with other children's use of dough; and (3) after using any modeling medium, children must wash their hands. While using play dough, toddlers need to be constantly supervised. Although nontoxic, play dough should not be consumed as it can upset a child's stomach.

Recipes for Doughs and Clays

Clay Dough

3 cups flour
3 cups salt
3 tablespoons alum

Combine ingredients and slowly add water, a little at a time. Mix well with spoon. As mixture thickens, continue mixing with your hands until it has the feel of clay. If it feels too dry, add more water. If it is too sticky, add equal parts of flour and salt.

Play Dough

2 cups flour
1 cup salt
1 cup hot water
2 tablespoons cooking oil
4 teaspoons cream of tartar
food coloring

Mix well. Knead until smooth. This dough may be kept in a plastic bag or covered container and used again. If it gets sticky, more flour may be added.

Favorite Play Dough

Combine and boil until dissolved:
2 cups water
½ cup salt
food coloring or tempera paint
Mix in while very hot:
2 tablespoons cooking oil
2 tablespoons alum
2 cups flour

Knead (approximately 5 minutes) until smooth. Store in covered airtight containers.

cornstarch, and water. Cook over a medium heat, while stirring constantly. When the mixture thickens and forms a ball, remove from the heat. Knead when cool and, if desired, add the food coloring. Note: If you are preparing the play dough for only one child, divide the recipe in half.

Cornstarch Play Dough

½ cup salt
¼ cup water
½ cup cornstarch
food coloring

Mix all ingredients thoroughly and cook over low heat, stirring constantly until the dough forms a ball. Add food coloring in desired color.

Laundry Modeling Dough

1½ cups laundry lint
1 cup warm water
⅓ cup flour
1 drop cinnamon or clove oil

Place lint and water in saucepan and stir. The lint will absorb most of the water. Add flour, stirring constantly. Add oil and cook over medium heat. When small peaks form, remove to a heatproof working surface and cool for ten minutes. (Note: This dough does not keep well, so use it immediately.)

Microwave Play Dough

2 cups flour
½ cup cornstarch
2 cups water
1 cup salt
1 tablespoon alum
1 tablespoon cooking oil
food coloring

Sand Dough

4 cups sand
3 cups flour
¼ cup cornstarch
¼ cup oil
1 cup water

In bowl, mix sand and flour together. Add cornstarch, oil, and water. If needed, add more water for desired texture.

Baker's Clay #1

1 cup cornstarch
2 cups baking soda
1½ cups cold water

Combine ingredients. Stir until smooth. Cook over medium heat, stirring constantly until mixture reaches the consistency of slightly dry mashed potatoes.

Turn out onto plate or bowl, covering with damp cloth. When cool enough to handle, knead thoroughly until smooth and pliable on cornstarch-covered surface.

Store in tightly closed plastic bag or covered container.

Baker's Clay #2

4 cups flour
1½ cups water
1 cup salt

Combine ingredients. Mix well. Knead 5 to 10 minutes. Roll out to ¼-inch thickness. Cut with decorative cookie cutters or with a knife. Make a hole at the top.

Bake at 250 degrees for 2 hours or until hard. When cool, paint with tempera paint and spray with clear varnish or paint with acrylic paint.

until easily manipulated (about cup).

Sawdust Dough

2 cups sawdust
3 cups flour
1 cup salt

Combine ingredients. Add water as needed. This dough becomes very hard and is not easily broken. It is good to use for making objects and figures that one desires to keep.

Cooked Clay Dough

1 cup flour
½ cup cornstarch
4 cups water
1 cup salt
3 or 4 pounds flour
coloring if desired

Stir slowly and be patient with this recipe. Blend the flour and cornstarch with cold water. Add salt to the water and boil. Pour the boiling salt and water solution into the flour and cornstarch paste and cook over hot water until clear. Add the flour and coloring to the cooked solution and knead. After the clay has been in use, if too moist, add flour; if dry, add water. Keep in covered container. Wrap dough with damp cloth or towel. This dough has a very nice texture and is very popular with all age groups. May be kept 2 or 3 weeks.

Play Dough

5 cups flour
2 cups salt
4 tablespoons cooking oil
add water to right consistency

Powdered tempera may be added in with flour or food coloring may be added to finished dough. This dough may be kept in plastic bag or covered container for approximately 2 to 4 weeks. It is better used as play dough rather than leaving objects to harden.

used for 2 to 3 days if stored in tight plastic bag.

Used Coffee Grounds

2 cups used coffee grounds
½ cup salt
1½ cups oatmeal

Combine ingredients and add enough water to moisten. Children like to roll, pack, and pat this mixture. It has a very different feel and look, but it's not good for finished products. It has a very nice texture.

be molded. It is very enjoyable for all age groups and is easy to work with. Also, the texture is very different from other materials ordinarily used for molding. It may be put up to dry, but articles are very slow to dry.

Fingerpaint Recipes

Liquid Starch Method

liquid starch (put in squeeze bottles)
dry tempera paint in shakers

Put about 1 tablespoon of liquid starch on the surface to be painted. Let the child shake the paint onto the starch. Mix and blend the paint. Note: If this paint becomes too thick, simply sprinkle a few drops of water onto the painting.

Soap Flake Method

Mix in a small bowl:
soap flakes
a small amount of water

Beat until stiff with an eggbeater. Use white soap on dark paper, or add food coloring to the soap and use it on light-colored paper. This gives a slight three-dimensional effect.

Uncooked Laundry Starch

A mixture of 1 cup laundry/liquid starch, 1 cup cold water, and 3 cups soap flakes will provide a quick fingerpaint.

Flour and Salt I

1 cup flour
1½ cups salt
¾ cup water
coloring

Combine flour and salt. Add water. This has a grainy quality, unlike the other fingerpaints, providing a different sensory experience. Some children enjoy the different touch sensation when 1½ cup salt is added to the other recipes.

Flour and Salt II

2 cups flour
2 teaspoons salt
3 cups cold water
2 cups hot water
food coloring

Add salt to flour, then pour in cold water gradually and beat mixture with eggbeater until it is smooth. Add hot water and boil until it becomes clear. Beat until smooth, then mix in coloring. Use ¼ cup food coloring to 8 to 9 ounces of paint for strong colors.

Instantized Flour, Uncooked Method

1 pint water (2 cups)
1½ cups instantized flour
    (the kind used to thicken gravy)

Put the water in the bowl and stir the flour into the water. Add color. Regular flour may be lumpy.

Cooked Starch Method

1 cup laundry starch dissolved in a
    small amount of cold water
5 cups boiling water added slowly
    to dissolve starch
1 tablespoon glycerine (optional)

Cook the mixture until it is thick and glossy. Add 1 cup mild soap flakes. Add color in separate containers. Cool before using.

Cornstarch Method

Gradually add 2 quarts water to 1 cup cornstarch. Cook until clear and add ½ cup soap flakes. A few drops of glycerine or oil of wintergreen may be added.

ironed.

Rainbow Stew

1 cup cornstarch
4 cups water
½ cup sugar
food coloring (if desired)

towels nearby or provide a large basin of water where children can rinse off.

Fingerpaint on a smooth table, oil cloth, or cafeteria tray. Some children prefer to start fingerpainting with shaving cream on a sheet of oil cloth.

colored.

Bubble Solutions

Bubble Solution #1

1 cup of water
2 tablespoons of liquid detergent
1 tablespoon glycerine
½ teaspoon sugar

Bubble Solution #2

⅔ cup liquid dish detergent
1 gallon of water
1 tablespoon glycerine (optional)

Allow solution to sit in an open container for at least a day before use.

Bubble Solution #3

3 cups water
2 cups Joy liquid detergent
½ cup Karo syrup

Source: Herr, J. (2000). *Creative resources for the early childhood classroom* (3rd ed.). Albany, NY: Delmar.

to Toddlers

The authors and Delmar Learning make every effort to ensure that all Internet resources are accurate at the time of printing. However, due to the fluid, time-sensitive nature of the Internet, we cannot guarantee that all URLs and Web site addresses will remain current for the duration of this edition.

The American Montessori Society Bulletin
American Montessori Society (AMS)
281 Park Avenue South, 6th Floor
New York, NY 10010-6102
(212) 358-1250; (212) 358-1256 FAX
www.amshq.org

Babybug
Cricket Magazine Group
PO Box 7437
Red Oak, IA 51591-2437
(800) 827-0227
www.babybugmag.com

The Black Child Advocate
National Black Child Development Institute (NBCDI)
1101 15th Street NW, Suite 900
Washington, DC 20005
(202) 833-2220; (202) 833-8222 FAX
www.nbcdi.org

Child and Youth Quarterly
Human Sciences Press
233 Spring Street, Floor 5
New York, NY 10013-1522
(212) 620-8000

Child Development and Child Development Abstracts and Bibliography
Society for Research in Child Development
University of Michigan
505 East Huron, Suite 301
Ann Arbor, MI 48104-1567
(734) 998-6578; (734) 998-6569 FAX
www.srcd.org

Child Health Alert
PO Box 610228
Newton Highlands, MA 02161
(781) 239-1762
ericps.ed.uiuc.edu/npin/nls/chalert.html

Childhood Education; Journal of Research in Early Childhood Education
Association for Childhood Education International (ACEI)
17904 Georgia Avenue; Suite 215
Olney, MD 20832
(301) 570-2111; (301) 570-2212 FAX
www.udel.edu/bateman/acei

Child Welfare
Child Welfare League of America (CWLA)
440 First Street NW, 3rd Floor
Washington, DC 20001-2085
(202) 638-2952; (202) 638-4004 FAX
www.cwla.org

Children Today
Superintendent of Documents
U.S. Government Printing Office
Washington, DC 20402
www.access.gpo.gov

Early Childhood Education Journal
Human Sciences Press
233 Spring Street, Floor 5
New York, NY 10013-1522
(212) 620-8000
www.wkap.nl/journalhome.htm/1082-3301

Developmental Psychology
American Psychological Association
750 First Street NE
Washington, DC 20002-4242
(202) 336-5500
www.apa.org

Dimensions of Early Childhood
Southern Association for Children Under Six
Box 56130 Brady Station
Little Rock, AR 72215
(800) 305-7322; (501) 227-5297 FAX

Earlychildhood.com
2 Lower Ragsdale, Suite 125
Monterey, CA 93940
(831) 333-5501; (800) 627-2829;
(831) 333-5510 FAX
www.earlychildhood.com

Early Childhood Research Quarterly
National Association for the Education of Young
  Children (NAEYC)
1509 16th Street NW
Washington, DC 20036-1426
(202) 232-8777; (202) 328-1846 FAX
www.naeyc.org

Educational Leadership
Association for Supervision and Curriculum
  Development (ASCD)
1703 North Beauregard Street
Alexandria, VA 22311-1714
(703) 578-9600; (800) 933-ASCD;
(703) 575-5400 FAX
www.ascd.org

Educational Researcher
American Educational Research Association
  (AERA)
1230 17th Street NW
Washington, DC 20036
(202) 223-9485; (202) 775-1824 FAX
www.aera.net

ERIC/EECE
University of Illinois
Children's Research Center
51 Gerty Drive
Champaign, IL 61820-7469
http://ericps.ed.uiuc.edu/eece

Exceptional Children
Council for Exceptional Children
1110 North Glebe Road, Suite 300
Arlington, VA 22201-5704
(703) 620-3660; (888) CEC-SPED;
(703) 264-9494 FAX
www.cec.sped.org

Scholastic, Inc.
555 Broadway
New York, NY 10012
www.scholastic.com/instructor

Journal of Family and Consumer Sciences
American Association of Family and Consumer
  Services (AAFCS)
1555 King Street
Alexandria, VA 22314
(703) 706-4600; (703) 706-4663 FAX
www.aafcs.org

Young Children
National Association for the Education of Young
  Children (NAEYC)
1509 16th Street NW
Washington, DC 20036-1426
(202) 232-8777; (202) 328-1846 FAX
www.naeyc.org

Other information may be obtained through various
professional organizations.

The following groups may be able to provide you with
other resources:

American Association for Gifted Children
Box 90270
Durham, NC 27708-0270
www.aagc.org

*American Association of Family and Consumer Services
(AAFCS)*
1555 King Street
Alexandria, VA 22314
(703) 706-4600; (703) 706-4663 FAX
www.aafcs.org

American Montessori Association (AMS)
281 Park Avenue South, 6th Floor
New York, NY 10010
(212) 358-1250; (212) 358-1256 FAX
www.amshq.org

*Association for Childhood Education International
(ACEI)*
17904 Georgia Avenue, Suite 215
Olney, MD 20832
(301) 570-2111; (800) 423-3563;
(301) 570-2212 FAX
www.udel.edu/bateman/acei

*Canadian Association for the Education of Young
Children (CAYC)*
   612 West 23rd Street
   Vancouver, BC V7M 2C3
   www.cayc.ca

Children's Defense Fund
   25 E Street NW
   Washington, DC 20001
   (202) 628-8787
   www.childrensdefense.org

Child Welfare League of America
   440 First Street NW, 3rd Floor
   Washington, DC 20001-2085
   (202) 638-2952; (202) 638-4004 FAX
   www.cwla.org

Council for Exceptional Children
   1110 North Glebe Road, Suite 300
   Arlington, VA 22201-5704
   (703) 620-3660; (888) CEC-SPED;
   (703) 264-9494 FAX
   www.cec.sped.org

International Reading Association
   800 Barksdale Road
   PO Box 8139
   Newark, DE 19714-8139
   (302) 731-1600; (302) 731-1057 FAX
   www.reading.org

   1707 L Street NW, Suite 550
   Washington, DC 20036
   (202) 785-4268
   www.nagc.org

National Black Child Development Institute (NBCDI)
   1101 15th Street NW, Suite 900
   Washington, DC 20005
   (202) 833-2220; (202) 833-8222 FAX
   www.nbcdi.org

National Committee to Prevent Child Abuse
   2950 Tennyson Street
   Denver, CO 80212
   (303) 433-2451; (303) 433-9701 FAX
   www.childabuse.org

National Education Association (NEA)
   1201 16th Street NW
   Washington, DC 20036
   (202) 833-4000
   www.nea.org

Society for Research in Child Development
   University of Michigan
   505 East Huron, Suite 301
   Ann Arbor, MI 48104-1567
   (734) 998-6578; (734) 998-6569 FAX
   www.srcd.org

Observer's Name: _____

Observation Date: _____

PHYSICAL DEVELOPMENT	OBSERVED	
Birth to Three Months	**Date**	**Comments**
Acts reflexively—sucking, stepping, rooting		
Swipes at objects in front of body, uncoordinated		
Holds head erect and steady when lying on stomach		
Lifts head and shoulders		
Rolls from side to back		
Follows moving objects with eyes		
Four to Six Months		
Holds cube in hand		
Reaches for objects with one hand		
Rolls from back to side		
Reaches for objects in front of body, coordinated		
Sits with support		
Transfers objects from hand to hand		
Grabs objects with either hand		
Sits in tripod position using arms for support		
Seven to Nine Months		
Sits independently		
Stepping reflex returns, so that child bounces when held on a surface in a standing position		
Leans over and reaches when in a sitting position		
Gets on hands and knees but may fall forward		
Crawls		
Pulls to standing position		
Claps hands together		
Stands with adult's assistance		
Learns pincer grasp, using thumb with forefinger to pick up objects		
Uses finger and thumb to pick up objects		
Brings objects together with banging noises		

The developmental milestones listed are based on universal patterns of when various traits emerge. Because each child is unique certain traits may develop at an earlier or later age.

Stands independently		
Walks independently		
Crawls up stairs or steps		
Voluntarily releases objects held in hands		
Has good balance when sitting; can shift positions without falling		
Takes off shoes and socks		
Thirteen to Eighteen Months		
Builds tower of two cubes		
Turns the pages of a cardboard book two or three at a time		
Scribbles vigorously		
Walks proficiently		
Walks while carrying or pulling a toy		
Walks up stairs with assistance		
Nineteen to Twenty-Four Months		
Walks up stairs independently, one step at a time		
Jumps in place		
Kicks a ball		
Runs in a modified fashion		
Shows a decided preference for one hand		
Completes a three-piece puzzle with knobs		
Builds a tower of six cubes		
Twenty-Five to Thirty-Six Months		
Maneuvers around obstacles in a pathway		
Runs in a more adult-like fashion; knees are slightly bent, arms move in the opposite direction		
Walks down stairs independently		
Marches to music		
Uses feet to propel wheeled riding toys		
Rides a tricycle		
Usually uses whole arm movements to paint or color		
Throws a ball forward, where intended		
Builds tower using eight or more blocks		
Imitates drawing circles and vertical and horizontal lines		
Turns pages in book one by one		
Fingers work together to scoop up small objects		
Strings large beads on a shoelace		

Additional Observations for Physical Development

The developmental milestones listed are based on universal patterns of when various traits emerge. Because each child is unique certain traits may develop at an earlier or later age.

Coos		
Laughs		
Smiles and coos to initiate and sustain interactions with caregiver		
Four to Six Months		
Babbles spontaneously		
Acquires sounds of native language in babble		
Canonical, systematic consonant-vowel pairings; babbling occurs		
Participates in interactive games initiated by adults		
Takes turns while interacting		
Seven to Nine Months		
Varies babble in loudness, pitch, and rhythm		
Adds *d, t, n,* and *w* to repertoire of babbling sounds		
Produces gestures to communicate often by pointing		
May say *mama* or *dada* but does not connect words with parents		
Ten to Twelve Months		
Uses preverbal gestures to influence the behavior of others		
Demonstrates word comprehension skills		
Waves good-bye		
Speaks recognizable first word		
Initiates familiar games with adults		
Thirteen to Eighteen Months		
Has expressive vocabulary of 10 to 20 words		
Engages in "jargon talk"		
Engages in telegraphic speech by combining two words together		
Experiences a burst of language development		
Comprehends approximately 50 words		
Nineteen to Twenty-Four Months		
Continues using telegraphic speech		
Able to combine three words		
Talks, 25 percent of words being understandable		
Refers to self by name		

The developmental milestones listed are based on universal patterns of when various traits emerge. Because each child is unique certain traits may develop at an earlier or later age.

Expressive language includes a vocabulary of approximately 250 words		
Twenty-Five to Thirty-Six Months		
Continues using telegraphic speech combining three or four words		
Speaks in complete sentences following word order of native language		
Displays effective conversational skills		
Refers to self as *me* or *I* rather than by name		
Talks about objects and events not immediately present		
Uses grammatical markers and some plurals		
Vocabulary increases rapidly, up to 300 words		
Enjoys being read to if allowed to participate by pointing, talking, and turning pages		

Additional Observations for Language and Communication Development

COGNITIVE DEVELOPMENT	OBSERVED	
Birth to Three Months	**Date**	**Comments**
Cries for assistance		
Acts reflexively		
Prefers to look at patterned objects, bull's-eye, horizontal stripes, and the human face		
Imitates adults' facial expressions		
Searches with eyes for sources of sounds		
Begins to recognize familiar people at a distance		
Discovers and repeats bodily actions such as sucking, swiping, and grasping		
Discovers hands and feet as extension of self		

The developmental milestones listed are based on universal patterns of when various traits emerge. Because each child is unique certain traits may develop at an earlier or later age.

Searches for a partially hidden object

Uses toys in a purposeful manner

Imitates simple actions

Explores toys using existing schemas such as sucking, banging, grasping, shaking, etc.

Seven to Nine Months

Enjoys looking at books with familiar objects

Distinguishes familiar from unfamiliar faces

Engages in goal-directed behavior

Anticipates events

Finds objects that are totally hidden

Imitates behaviors that are slightly different than those usually performed

Begins to show interest in filling and dumping containers

Ten to Twelve Months

Solves sensorimotor problems by deliberately using schemas, such as shaking a container to empty its contents

Points to body parts upon request

Drops toys intentionally and repeatedly looks in the direction of the fallen object

Waves good-bye

Shows evidence of stronger memory capabilities

Follows simple, one-step directions

Categorizes objects by appearance

Looks for objects hidden in a second location

Thirteen to Eighteen Months

Explores properties of objects by acting on them in novel ways

Solves problems through trial and error

Experiments with cause-and-effect relationships such as turning on televisions, banging on drums, etc.

Plays body identification games

Imitates novel behaviors of others

Identifies family members in photographs

The developmental milestones listed are based on universal patterns of when various traits emerge. Because each child is unique certain traits may develop at an earlier or later age.

Recognizes self in photographs and mirror		
Demonstrates deferred imitation		
Engages in functional play		
Finds objects that have been moved while out of sight		
Solves problems with internal representation		
Categorizes self and others by gender, race, hair color, etc.		
Twenty-Five to Thirty-Six Months		
Uses objects for purposes other than intended		
Uses private speech while working		
Classifies objects based on one dimension, such as toy cars versus blocks		
Follows two-step directions		
Concentrates or attends to self-selected activities for longer periods of time		
Points to and labels objects spontaneously, such as when reading a book		
Coordinates pretend play with other children		
Gains a nominal sense of numbers through counting and labeling objects in a set		
Begins developing concepts about opposites such as big and small, tall and short, in and out		
Begins eveloping concepts about time such as today, tomorrow, and yesterday		

Additional Observations for Cognitive Development

The developmental milestones listed are based on universal patterns of when various traits emerge. Because each child is unique certain traits may develop at an earlier or later age.

Finds comfort in the human face

Displays a social smile

Is quieted by a voice

Begins to differentiate self from caregiver

Four to Six Months

Seeks out adults for play by crying, cooing, or smiling

Responds with entire body to familiar face by looking at a person, smiling, kicking legs, and waving arms

Participates actively in interactions with others by vocalizing in response to adult speech

Smiles at familiar faces and stares solemnly at strangers

Distinguishes between familiar and nonfamiliar adults and surroundings

Seven to Nine Months

Becomes upset when separated from a favorite adult

Acts deliberately to maintain the presence of a favorite adult by clinging or crying

Uses adults as a base for exploration, typically

Looks to others who are exhibiting signs of distress

Enjoys observing and interacting briefly with other children

Likes to play and responds to games such as patty-cake and peekaboo

Engages in solitary play

Develops preferences for particular people and objects

Shows distress when in the presence of a stranger

Ten to Twelve Months

Shows a decided preference for one or two caregivers

Plays parallel to other children

Enjoys playing with siblings

Begins asserting self

Begins developing a sense of humor

Develops a sense of self-identity through the identification of body parts

Begins distinguishing boys from girls

The developmental milestones listed are based on universal patterns of when various traits emerge. Because each child is unique certain traits may develop at an earlier or later age.

being
Shares affection with people other than primary
   caregiver
Shows ownership of possessions
Begins developing a view of self as autonomous when
   completing tasks independently		

Nineteen to Twenty-Four Months		
Shows enthusiasm for company of others Views the world only from own, egocentric perspective Plays contentedly alone or near adults Engages in functional play Defends possessions Recognizes self in photographs or mirrors Refers to self with pronouns such as *I* or *me* Categorizes people by using salient characteristics such as race or hair color Shows less fear of strangers		
Twenty-five to Thirty-Six Months		

Observes others to see how they do things
Engages primarily in solitary or parallel play
Sometimes offers toys to other children
Begins to play cooperatively with other children
Engages in sociodramatic play
Wants to do things independently
Asserts independence by using "no" a lot
Develops a rudimentary awareness that others have
   wants or feelings that may be different than
   their own
Makes demands of or "bosses" parents, guardians, and
   caregivers
Uses physical aggression less and uses words to solve
   problems
Engages in gender stereotypical behavior		

Additional Observations for Social Development

The developmental milestones listed are based on universal patterns of when various traits emerge. Because each child is unique certain traits may develop at an earlier or later age.

Feels and expresses enjoyment
Shares a social smile
Reads and distinguishes adults' facial expressions
Begins to self-regulate emotional expressions
Laughs aloud
Quiets self by using techniques such as sucking a
    thumb or pacifier

Four to Six Months

Expresses delight
Responds to the emotions of caregivers
Begins to distinguish familiar from unfamiliar people
Shows a preference for being held by a familiar person
Begins to assist with holding a bottle
Expresses happiness selectively by laughing and smiling
    more with familiar people

Seven to Nine Months

Responds to social events by using the face, gaze, voice,
    and posture to form coherent emotional patterns
Expresses fear and anger more often
Begins to regulate emotions through moving into or out
    of experiences
Begins to detect the meaning of others' emotional
    expressions
Looks to others for clues on how to react
Shows fear of strangers

Ten to Twelve Months

Continues to exhibit delight, happiness, discomfort,
    anger, and sadness
Expresses anger when goals are blocked
Expresses anger at the source of frustration
Begins to show compliance to caregivers' requests
Often objects to having playtime stopped
Begins eating with a spoon
Assists in dressing and undressing
Acts in loving, caring ways toward dolls or stuffed
    animals, typically
Feeds self a complete meal when served finger foods
Claps when successfully completing a task

The developmental milestones listed are based on universal patterns of when various traits emerge. Because each child is unique certain traits may develop at an earlier or later age.

Begins to understand complicated patterns of behavior

Demonstrates the ability to communicate needs

May say "no" to something they want

May lose emotional control and have temper tantrums

Shows self-conscious emotions such as shame, guilt, and shyness

Becomes frustrated easily

Nineteen to Twenty-Four Months

Expresses affection to others spontaneously

Acts to comfort others in distress

Shows the emotions of pride and embarrassment

Uses emotion words spontaneously in conversations or play

Begins to show sympathy to another child or adult

Becomes easily hurt by criticism

Experiences a temper tantrum when goals are blocked, on occasion

Associates facial expressions with simple emotional labels

Twenty-Five to Thirty-Six Months

Experiences increase in number of fears

Begins to understand the consequences of basic emotions

Learns skills for coping with strong emotions

Seeks to communicate more feelings with specific words

Shows signs of empathy and caring

Loses control of emotions and throws temper tantrums

Able to recover from temper tantrums

Enjoys helping with chores such as cleaning up toys or carrying grocery bags

Begins to show signs of readiness for toileting

Desires that routines be carried out exactly as has been done in the past

Additional Observations for Emotional Development

The developmental milestones listed are based on universal patterns of when various traits emerge. Because each child is unique certain traits may develop at an earlier or later age.

Child's name:_____

Date of birth:_____

Location:_____

Date and time:_____

Observer's name:_____

Behavioral Description of Observations:	Interpretations of/Reflections on Observations:

Date and time: _____March 2, 2xxx_____ 2:00–2:25 p.m._____

Observer's name: _Jane U._____

Behavioral Description of Observations:	Interpretations of/Reflections on Observations:
Christina is playing with a toy truck. She says, "Katy, can I keep it?" She repeats this two times until a teacher responds, "No, the toys are for all the children to use at school." She drops the truck on the floor and walks over to the shelf. She picks up a guitar and plays it while walking around the room looking at the other children. The teacher says, "It's snack time. Wash your hands, Christina." Christina says to the boy beside her, "It's snack time." She walks to the snack table and sits down.	Working on ownership issues. Social development: Helping classmate to follow routine of classroom.
Christina sits in a hunched position between a boy and a girl. She says, "Look, bananas" in an excited voice while reaching for the plate. She grabs the plate and takes two bananas. The teacher says, "Start with one banana. If you eat the first one, you can have one more." Christina peels the banana using her thumb and forefinger on her right hand. She puts the entire banana in her mouth and grabs for a second banana. The teacher says, "Chew up your banana. I don't want you to choke. Thank you for sitting while you are chewing." Christina smiles and takes a second banana and peels it in the same manner as before. She takes a large bite of the banana, eating half of it at once. She grabs her glass of milk with both hands and takes a large gulp. She burps loudly. The teacher says, "Excuse you." Christina leaves the table and dumps the uneaten part of the banana in the waste can. She uses a rag (the teacher gave her) to wash each finger individually and then wipes her face.	She didn't wash her hands, and the teacher didn't catch it! Okay with this limit. Continues eating snack. Good fine motor skills to peel own banana. She seems very hungry—when did she last eat? Receptive to positive reinforcement by teacher, seemed pleased with own behavior. In the process of learning manners. She didn't repeat the statement, though. Good self-help skills.
She walks in a stiff legged motion to another area of the classroom.	Always on the move!!

A panel is a two-dimensional display to communicate with others the learning that occurred during an activity. Panels present the learning of a group of children; thus, different children and their work must be featured. For ease of reading, you should neatly handwrite or type your message. Then, adhere all sections mentioned in the following list on a foam board, poster board, or trifold board.

A panel should contain the following information:

♡ Title of the activity
♡ A record of the children's *actual* words while engaging with the materials or interacting with peers
♡ Artifacts to document representations of the children's thinking—drawings paintings, writings, and/or graphs—or photographs of the children's work on sculptures, creative drama/movements, or roles during dramatic play
♡ A narrative that highlights and explains what learning and interactions occurred

To fulfill the goal of communicating with others, the panel will need to be displayed in a prominent location. Invite others to look at and converse about the children's work. Include the children as part of the audience by reviewing their work as a way to promote language, cognitive, and social development. Also, build on the experience during future activities.

For additional resources on making panels, see:

Gandini, L., & Pope Edwards, C. (Eds.). (2001). *The Italian approach to infant/toddler care.* New York: Teachers College Press.
Helm, J. H., Beneke, S., & Steinheimer, K. (1998). *Windows on learning: Documenting young children's work.* New York: Teachers College Press.
Pope Edwards, C., Gandini, L., & Forman, G. (Eds.). (1993). *The hundred languages of children.* Norwood, NJ: Ablex.

Name: _____ Date: _____

Developmental area: _____

Child's developmental goals:

Materials:

Preparation:

Nurturing strategies:

Variations:

Home to Center

Toddler's name:_____ Parent's name: _____

Day/date: _____ Time of arrival: _____ Time of departure: _____

Child picked up by: _____

FILLED IN BY PARENT:

Toddler seems:
- [ ] Normal, typical
- [ ] Bit fussy
- [ ] Not acting like usual

Toddler slept:
- [ ] Soundly
- [ ] Woke up several times
- [ ] Did not sleep well

Toddler ate:
- [ ] Meal before coming _____
- [ ] Snack before coming _____
- [ ] Nothing

Toddler changed/used toilet: [ ] Bowel movement   Time _____

                                       [ ] Wet   Time _____

SPECIAL INSTRUCTIONS FOR TODAY:

_____

_____

_____

_____

Parent's signature: _____

Caregiver's signature: _____

Read toddler's daily communication: Home to center _____

INTERACTIONS/ACTIVITIES: *(Description of adult interaction, developmental tasks, and activities that sustained child's interest)*

_____

_____

_____

Breakfast:

[ ]   Ate well   [ ]   Ate a little bit   [ ]   Not hungry today   _____

Lunch:

[ ]   Ate well   [ ]   Ate a little bit   [ ]   Not hungry today   _____

Nap time:

[ ]   Slept   [ ]   Quietly rested   _____

Toileting:

[ ]   Diapers only   [ ]   Sat on toilet   [ ]   Used toilet

[ ] Bowel movement Time _____   [ ] Wet Time _____

NOTES TO PARENTS:

_____

_____

_____

Caregiver's signature: _____

Parent's signature: _____

We need: [ ] Diapers/underpants   [ ] Change of clothing

        [ ] Blankets   [ ] Other: _____

*Adapted with permission from New Horizon Child Care, Inc.

13 to 24 Months

Sorting Shapes, Show Me, and Many Other Activities for Toddlers

Judy Herr, Ph.D., University of Wisconsin-Stout
Terri Swim, Ph.D., University of Akron

Responding in a warm, loving, and responsive manner to a crying infant or playing patty cake with a young toddler both exemplify ways that caregivers and families promote healthy brain development. Recent research on brain development emphasizes the importance of environment and relationships during the child's first three years of life.

Creative Resources Infant and Toddler Series is an exciting series of resources divided by age and classroom criteria. This series explores child development at the critical stages of life that occur in all domains including physical, cognitive, language and communication, social and emotional. To support and enhance the child's development in all these areas, this unique series includes specially designed activities for infants and toddlers. This series will help you create a strong foundation for the thinking and learning progressions of the children in your care.

The ultimate goal of this book is to assist in promoting healthy development of our youngest children. Thus it should be part of all parents' and caregivers' libraries.

"I would certainly recommend this book to teachers, directors, and child care providers. The Appendix is wonderful as well." — *Jody Martin, Curriculum Coordinator, Aurora, CO*

"The authors clearly understand the subtle differences in working with newborns, young infants, mobile infants, waddlers and toddlers. This text is desperately needed in the field." — *Marie Brand, Head Start Trainer, New Paltz, NY*

"I think directors as well as teachers will find this resource easy to understand and access." — *Jody Martin, Curriculum Coordinator, Aurora, CO*

"The richness and depth is not found in other books...and, most importantly, the clear and careful consideration that is obvious throughout each activity that how you are with children is not as important as what you are doing with them." — *Irene Cook, Taft College, Taft, CA*

Also Available in the Creative Resources Infant and Toddler Series:

Rattle Time, Face to Face, and Many Other Activities for Infants: Birth to 6 Months
ISBN: 1-4018-1832-3

Making Sounds, Making Music, and Many Other Activities for Infants: 7 to 12 Months
ISBN: 1-4018-1839-0

Rhyming Books, Marble Painting, and Many Other Activities for Toddlers: 25 to 36 Months
ISBN: 1-4018-1841-2

Developmental Milestones, Checklists, Lesson Plans and many other features are also available on-line at academic.cengage.com

DELMAR
CENGAGE Learning

For your lifelong learning solutions, visit **delmar.cengage.com**
Visit our corporate website at **www.cengage.com**

ISBN-13: 978-1-401-81834-0
ISBN-10: 1-401-81834-X

90000

9 781401 818340